Evidence-based Policy and Practice in Mental Health Social Work

Other titles in this series

To order, please contact our distributor: BEBC Distribution, Albion Close, Parkstone, Poole, BH12 3LL. Telephone: 0845 230 9000, email: **learningmatters@bebc.co.uk.**

You can also find more information on each of these titles and our other learning resources at **www.learningmatters.co.uk**

Evidence-based Policy and Practice in Mental Health Social Work

MARTIN WEBBER

Series Editor: Keith Brown

LearningMatters

First published in 2008 by Learning Matters Ltd

British Library Cataloguing in Publication Data

A CIP record for this book is available from the British Library.

ISBN: 978 1 84445 149 4

Cover and text design by Code 5 Design Associates Ltd
Project Management by Swales and Willis
Typeset by Swales & Willis Ltd, Exeter, Devon
Printed and bound in Great Britain by TJ International, Padstow, Cornwall

Learning Matters Ltd
33 Southernhay East
Exeter EX1 1 NX
Tel: 01392 215560
info@learningmatters.co.uk
www.learningmatters.co.uk

FSC
Mixed Sources
Product group from well-managed
forests and other controlled sources
Cert no. SGS-COC-2482
www.fsc.org
© 1996 Forest Stewardship Council

Contents

List of Figures

List of Tables

Foreword to the Post-Qualifying Social Work Practice series

All the texts in the Post-Qualifying Social Work Practice series have been written by people with a passion for excellence in social work practice. They are primarily written for social workers who are undertaking post-qualifying social work awards, but will also be useful to any social worker who wants to consider up-to-date practice issues.

The books in this series are also of value to social work students as they are written to inform, inspire and develop social work practice.

Keith Brown
Series Editor
Centre for Post-Qualifying Social Work, Bournemouth

About the author

Martin Webber is a qualified social worker and has worked as an Approved Social Worker in a community mental health team in the Royal borough of Kingston-upon-Thames.

Since September 2006 he has been Programme Leader of the MSc in Mental Health Social Work with Children and Adults at the Institute of Psychiatry, King's College, London, a post-qualifying social work programme accredited by the General Social Care Council at the advanced level. The programme is for experienced social workers who wish to acquire research training and become advanced practitioners. He also teaches on other programmes in the Institute of Psychiatry and at Bournemouth University and the University of Manchester.

His research interests are in social inclusion, social capital and mental health social work. He has published papers in national and international peer-reviewed journals and contributed to two edited books: *Social Capital and Health* (2007) and *Social Perspectives in Mental Health* (2005).

Acknowledgements

This book is a substantially updated and re-written version of an earlier publication on evidence-based practice written for Bournemouth University's post-qualifying mental health social work courses. My thanks go to Keith Brown (Bournemouth University) for his helpful suggestions and encouragement during the long re-write.

Chapters 6 to 11 were developed from course materials of the research methods and critical appraisal module of the MSc in Mental Health Social Work in Children and Adults at the Institute of Psychiatry. These were written alongside the development of an e-learning version of this module, a project funded by a grant from the Skills for Care Innovation Fund.

The case studies in Chapter 12 are drawn from the work of two graduates of the MSc in Mental Health Social Work in Children and Adults – Leda Velosa and Tony West. I am very grateful for their permission to include these.

I would also like to thank my colleague Alan Rushton (King's College London), for his comments about various aspects of this book and my PhD supervisors Peter Huxley (University of Wales, Swansea) and Tirril Harris (King's College London) for their patience while I have completed it.

Finally, I am most grateful to Andrea, Caitlin and Freya for their patience while I have been locked away in the study. Thank you.

Martin Webber
March 2008

Preface

This book provides an authoritative and accessible guide to the evidence base that underpins contemporary policy and practice for mental health social workers in the UK. It critically engages with the notion of evidence-based practice in mental health social work and provides a guide to becoming an evidence-based practitioner. In doing so, it provides an accessible guide to appraising quantitative and qualitative research relevant to mental health social work practice.

This book is designed to accompany post-qualifying courses in mental health social work. Chapters 1 to 5 are relevant for practitioners studying post-qualifying courses up to Higher Specialist Level and Chapters 6 to 12 are written for practitioners working at the Advanced Level in the post-qualifying framework.

This book is also relevant for all social work students, practitioners and managers with an interest in evidence-based practice. It will also be of interest to other mental health professionals, particularly those taking on the approved mental health professional role in England and Wales.

The first chapter reviews contemporary evidence-based practise in social work and the nature of 'evidence'. It explores different methods used in mental health research that will be explored in more depth later in the book. It also provides a critical evaluation of some of the criticisms of the evidence-based practice paradigm with reference to the epistemology of social work research.

Chapter 2 provides a historical review of social work practice in mental health services from the asylum to the community. It demonstrates that mental health social work in statutory settings is a synergy between legal process and professional practice with practitioners negotiating between competing roles.

A further dimension is added in Chapter 3 – the contemporary service context in which mental health social workers practice. Mental health policy since the 1990s fundamentally influences mental health social work practice today. The policy context for mental health social work practice is reviewed in Chapter 3 and the empirical evidence supporting it (or otherwise) is reviewed in Chapter 4. Examples of studies that have been influential to policy-makers are discussed, with particular reference to assertive outreach, early intervention in psychosis and crisis resolution and home treatment teams.

Chapter 5 provides an introduction to becoming an evidence-based practitioner. It outlines the processes of defining a practice question and searching for relevant evidence. The process of appraising research evidence is outlined in Chapters 6 to 11.

Chapters 6 to 9 introduce four quantitative methods that are used in research relevant to mental health social work. Chapter 11 gives guidance on the critical appraisal of qualitative studies. Each of these chapters reviews a method, gives relevant examples and presents guidelines for its critical appraisal. Additionally, critical appraisal questions and a multiple choice self-test at the end of each chapter give readers the opportunity to test their knowledge and practice their critical appraisal skills.

Sandwiched between the quantitative and qualitative chapters is Chapter 10, an introduction to statistical techniques that are commonly found in papers reporting quantitative research. Elements of this chapter are frequently referred to in Chapters 6 to 9. It is a useful source of guidance to understanding the statistics that are presented in the papers suggested for reading and should be bookmarked!

Finally, Chapter 12 presents the concept of 'advanced practitioners', who are well-placed to disseminate research findings to influence policy and practice in mental health social work. Case studies of advanced practitioners are presented to illustrate how they can provide leadership in developing practice on the basis of research evidence.

Chapter 1

Epistemology and evidence-based practice in mental health social work

Introduction

Mental health social workers typically work within multidisciplinary settings alongside colleagues from a variety of health disciplines. In statutory settings, mental health social workers work in community mental health teams, early intervention teams, assertive outreach teams, crisis resolution and home treatment teams and a range of specialist services. Many of these services are the products of evidence-based mental health policy (Department of Health, 1999c; Thornicroft, 2000). As these services increasingly impinge on social work practice, it is important for social workers to have the skills and confidence to engage with the research evidence on which they are based.

In these services social workers typically work alongside psychiatrists, psychologists, community psychiatric nurses, occupational therapists, education and employment workers and other social care workers. Increasingly social workers are called upon to justify their practice to their health colleagues whose training is founded on empirical research evidence from within a scientific paradigm. As social work practice is traditionally derived from theoretical schema rather than empirical research, this can lead to a number of misunderstandings. In the worst case, the profession is perceived as lacking in credibility as it struggles to articulate its evidence base.

This presents a serious challenge for mental health social work, which already faces the battle of convincing sceptical health managers of the strengths of the profession. Social workers undoubtedly make a unique contribution to these teams and Approved Social Workers (ASWs) have been particularly respected for their specialist knowledge and application of mental health law (Gilbert, 2003). However, their contribution to the mental health evidence base is meagre in contrast to the prolific research activity of psychiatrists and allied health professionals (Huxley, 2001; McCrae *et al.*, 2003).

To equip social work practitioners with the skills to understand and evaluate the evidence on which their practice is based, the notion of evidence-based practice may be a useful concept to consider. Although it has its origins in medicine, the concept can help practitioners to consider the best available empirical research evidence when they are making important decisions in their day-to-day work. To gain influence on mental health policy and its own professional future, social work needs to develop its evidence base and the confidence to assert its contribution to mental health services (McCrae *et al.*, 2004).

This chapter will review contemporary evidence-based practice in social work and the nature of 'evidence'. We will outline different methods used in mental health research that will be explored in more depth later in this book. We will then critically evaluate some of the criticisms of the evidence-based practice paradigm with reference to the epistemology of social work research.

A brief history of evidence-based practice in social work

Contemporary interest in evidence based practice in social work can be traced to an article written by Geraldine MacDonald and colleagues in the early 1990s (Macdonald *et al.*, 1992). In contrast to earlier reviews that focused solely on experimental studies (e.g. Reid and Hanrahan, 1980), MacDonald and her colleagues looked at the results from experimental studies, quasi-experimental studies, pre-experimental and client-opinion studies of the effectiveness of social work. They found that three-quarters of reviewed papers produced positive results, evidence to bolster the profession which they felt at that time was rather 'beleaguered' (p.640).

However, this review acknowledged that the evidence on the effectiveness of social work practice was limited to research on therapeutic work which did not reflect the full complexity of social work roles. Discrete interventions such as behavioural therapy or family therapy can be more easily subjected to methodologically rigorous studies such as randomised controlled trials than complex social work interventions that involve a range of tasks including advocacy, liaison, co-ordination, making referrals and management of resources, for example. This early indication that effectiveness research can be biased towards the easily-researchable is a theme we will return to later.

In 1996 the Department of Health invested in the establishment of the Centre for Evidence-Based Social Services (CEBSS) at the University of Exeter. Headed by Professor Brian Sheldon, a leading exponent of evidence-based practice, this development saw a renewed focus on the research evidence that underpins social work practice. The Centre worked in partnership with 15 local social services departments to develop evidence-based practice. Similar academic centres for evidence-based practice in health and social care were established at universities in Salford, Oxford, Nottingham and York.

At the same time Department of Health policy was placing a stronger emphasis upon evidence. For example, the *Framework for the Assessment of Children in Need and their Families* (Department of Health, 2000a) and the *National Service Framework for Mental Health* (Department of Health, 1999c), both placed a strong emphasis on research evidence to inform practice and service models.

Definition of evidence-based practice

What exactly do we mean by the phrase 'evidence-based practice'? Sheldon and colleagues adapted a definition of evidence-based medicine (Sackett *et al.*, 1996) and derived the following, which has remained as the core definition of evidence-based practice in social work ever since:

> *Evidence-based social care is the conscientious, explicit and judicious use of current best evidence in making decisions regarding the welfare of those in need of social services. (Sheldon and Chilvers, 2000: 5, adapted from Sackett et al., 1996)*

This adaptation embodies a conceptual transfer from medicine to social care. Some see this as the colonising of social care practice by medicine, whose traditions, values and origins are different and, possibly, at odds with each other. However, others argue that the concept validates social care interventions through the production of good evidence of effectiveness. These perspectives will be discussed below. Meanwhile, let's consider the three key elements of the definition that its authors highlight.

Key elements of evidence-based practice

Firstly, a *conscientious* practitioner is one who uses interventions with good evidence of their effectiveness. This may sound obvious, but social workers are not immune from making mistakes. Professional competence is crucial to the future of social work and is scrutinised through the process of registration with the General Social Care Council. By using the most effective interventions and having an up-to-date understanding of personal and social problems, social workers are more likely to be able to provide an effective service to the people they work with.

It is good practice for social workers to be as *explicit* as possible with the people they work with about what they are doing and why they are doing it. It is important to review available options with service users, informed by a thorough assessment of their needs and an understanding of research on relevant effective interventions.

Finally, *judicious* practice is based on the exercise of sound, prudent and sensitive judgement. It requires practitioners not to be influenced by outside pressures. Social workers operate under the potential spotlight of media infamy and professional disgrace if a tragedy were to unfold as a result of a decision they made. For example, if a social worker working as an Approved Mental Health Professional decided on the best-available evidence not to compulsorily admit someone to hospital, although they had the necessary medical recommendations to do so, and this person went on to commit a homicide, their professional career would be all but over. It has even been suggested that the risk-averse society in which we live could have been responsible for the increasing numbers of people admitted to hospital under the Mental Health Act 1983 during the 1990s (Rogers and Pilgrim, 2003). An imperative of evidence-based practice is to remain judicious in the face of these external pressures.

Evidence-based practice is about considered rather than reflexive action. Or, in other words, it requires practitioners to consider evidence before making decisions, rather than acting first and reflecting after the event. This involves a critical appraisal of research findings to inform judgements about possible courses of action. However, it also requires supervisors to assist practitioners and discuss case-specific pieces of evidence in supervision with them.

Definition of evidence

What exactly do we mean by 'evidence'? According to the Cambridge Advanced Learner's Dictionary, 'evidence' is 'one or more reasons for believing that something is or is not true' (Cambridge Dictionaries, 2007). This definition is rather vague so let's explore it a little further.

Imagine that you are sitting on a jury of a murder trial. A number of witnesses will take the stand to give evidence. They might include the defendant, witnesses of the incident, character witnesses, police, paramedics, forensic scientists, pathologists or expert witnesses, for example.

Jury members are asked to assess the reliability of the evidence given by each witness to assist them in deciding on the defendant's guilt or innocence. It is likely that they will consider evidence given by witnesses of the incident or character witnesses to be of varying quality and reliability. People who witnessed the incident may have had a limited view of it or may have forgotten some details about it by the time of the trial. Also character witnesses often present biased evidence in favour of the person's character that they are defending. Their evidence often encounters fierce cross-examination from opposing barristers.

On the other hand, the evidence provided by forensic scientists or pathologists is often considered to be consistently valid and reliable. It often holds up under cross-examination and can hold the key to the jury making a decisive verdict. Their evidence is often held in high regard as it is seen to be objective, scientific and independent (although there have been, of course, cases where it has been found to be flawed).

Scientific paradigm

In the same way, evidence in health and social care that is largely considered to be consistently valid and reliable is based on scientific principles. The scientific paradigm has been conveniently summarised by Bolton (2002) and comprises the following elements:

- Objectivity of observation, based in sense-experience – this is the opposite of subjective, esoteric, un-replicable knowledge based in intuition.

- Experiment – knowledge is not only based on observation of reality, but in the process of intervention and observation. The idea of an experiment is a question that we test out.

- Causality – the aim of the experiment is to determine a causal process, to find explanations of events and to make predictions.

- Generality – causality is vital to the establishment of general laws of nature.

Randomised controlled trials

The application of scientific principles to evaluations of health and social care interventions is most clearly exemplified in the methodology of the randomised controlled trial (RCT). This is widely used in medicine in the evaluation of drug treatments and in psychology in the evaluation of talking or behavioural therapies, for example. It is now increasingly being applied to social care interventions, but not without its attendant problems.

The RCT is widely viewed as the 'gold standard' method of intervention evaluation. It involves the random allocation of a study population to a new intervention, known as the 'case group', or to a benign or placebo intervention, known as the 'control group'. The random allocation controls the influence of any other associated factors and is perhaps the most important element of this methodology. Accurate measurements of the outcomes of interest are taken using standardised measures before and after the intervention. The effect of the intervention is calculated using a statistical comparison between the two groups, which need to be sufficiently large to detect this accurately.

The UK 700 study is an example of an RCT (Burns *et al.*, 1999). Seven hundred and eight people with a diagnosis of a psychotic illness from four UK centres were randomly allocated to standard case management (caseload 30–35 per case manager) or intensive case management (10–15 per case manager). Clinical symptoms and social functioning were measured before randomisation, and one and two years after the start of the intervention. Tom Burns and colleagues found that there was no significant decline in overall hospital use among those receiving intensive case management, nor were there any significant gains in clinical or social functioning.

Hierarchy of evidence

As the RCT is considered to give a reliable result of the effectiveness of health and social care interventions it is pivotal in the hierarchy of evidence. The Bandolier classification of evidence is a good example of such a hierarchy and was used in the *National Service Framework for Mental Health* (Department of Health, 1999c). It classifies evidence on a typology from 1 to 5:

Type 1:   Good systematic review

Type 2:   Good randomised controlled trial

Type 3:   Good intervention study (no randomisation)

Type 4:   Well-designed observation study

Type 5:   Expert opinion

Systematic reviews

A systematic review is a combination of a number of RCTs of a particular intervention to produce a single effect size for a particular outcome. It is considered to be the best form of evidence of the effectiveness of an intervention and ideally would involve a large number of well-conducted RCTs, with large samples and little bias. The Cochrane Collaboration is the largest group producing high quality systematic reviews of, primarily, health interventions. Although it contains some reviews of social care interventions, these will increasingly be conducted by its new sister organisation, the Campbell Collaboration.

An example of a systematic review is the Cochrane review of assertive community treatment (Marshall and Lockwood, 1998). This brought together a number of RCTs of assertive community treatment (ACT). It found that people allocated to ACT were more likely to stay in contact with services than people receiving standard community care and were less likely to be admitted to hospital. It also concluded that ACT was more effective at improving accommodation status, employment and satisfaction with services for people with severe mental health problems than standard community care. Although many of the trials reviewed here were conducted in the US, where the nature of both assertive outreach and community care is different from the UK, this systematic review has been very influential in the development of the *National Service Framework for Mental Health* (Department of Health, 1999c) because of its methodological strengths.

Quasi-experimental studies

As we have already provided an example of an RCT (Burns *et al.*, 1999) we will move on to discuss type 3 in the Bandolier classification. This type is an intervention study where there was no randomisation into the case or control groups. They are sometimes referred to as quasi-experimental studies and, if designed well, can produce some reliable evidence. The PRiSM psychosis study in south London (Thornicroft *et al.*, 1998) is one example of this type of evidence. Here, two differently organised community mental health teams were studied. One provided a more intensive service with separate teams for acute care and for rehabilitation and the other was a single generic team. Epidemiologically representative samples of people with a psychotic diagnosis were followed up over two years in the two teams. The study found little or no evidence in favour of one over the other across a range of outcomes including hospital admissions and mental health.

Observation studies

The well-designed observation study in type 4 does not refer to the qualitative method of participant observation. Instead, it denotes studies that take careful measurements of groups of people in situations when it is more difficult to allocate them to different interventions. Methods used which fall within this category include case-control and cohort studies. A good example of a longitudinal cohort study is one conducted in north London of 670 long stay patients of a psychiatric hospital discharged into the community between 1985 and 1993 (Trieman *et al.*, 1999). Trieman and colleagues followed this cohort up five years after their discharge and found that replacing a psychiatric hospital with full residential facilities in the community worked well for the majority of long stay patients. Crime and homelessness presented few problems for this group, dispelling initial fears.

Expert opinion

Finally, if there is no support for an intervention from one of the above types of evidence, the opinion of experts is sought. This might be from academics who have researched in the field, practitioners with hands-on experience or service users or carers receiving the intervention. Methods used to gather this data are frequently qualitative in nature, involving focus groups or in-depth interviews. Much of the research in the social science tradition falls within this category. Diana Rose's (1998a) work collating the views of service users on mental health services is a good example of this. Research of this kind is often of great value to social workers and the most controversial aspect of the Bandolier classification is the location of this form of evidence at the bottom.

Evidence-based practice in social work

What do social workers make of the notion of evidence-based practice and the scientific method of evaluating practice? In the late 1990s, the Centre for Evidence-Based Social Services conducted a large cross-sectional survey of practitioners' attitudes towards evidence based practice (Sheldon and Chilvers, 2000; Sheldon and Macdonald, 1999). This provided a baseline for much of its subsequent activities and gave us a snapshot of social services workers' attitudes towards it.

This survey found that workers generally supported the idea of evidence-based practice, but they were not aware of the available research evidence. Understanding of research terminology amongst respondents was generally low. Although practitioners considered it important to keep up to date with research findings, there were organisational barriers to achieving this. Training courses contained few references to research and it was agreed that it was unusual to be asked 'where is the evidence for this?' in social care. Other studies (e.g. Booth *et al.*, 2003; Mullen and Bacon, 2004) have since found similar results.

Reflecting on these results, Sheldon and his colleagues highlighted several obstacles to implementing evidence-based practice. Firstly, there is generally a lack of emphasis upon empirical evidence in social work. This is partly because the tradition of what constitutes evidence in social work emphasises understanding and subjective meaning and interventions based on theoretical schema, rather than the use of highly developed bodies of empirical knowledge. More social workers would have heard of Freud or Bowlby, than Cochrane, for example.

Statutory social work practice, in particular, is constrained by statutory and policy requirements. Decision-making at a practice level is partly determined by the legal framework in which it takes place. Although this does depend often on the production of 'evidence' to support the legal case, this is individual behavioural evidence and rarely evidence from empirical research. For example, during mental health act assessments, Approved Mental Health Professionals are required to present evidence that the criteria for compulsory admission are met (or are not met, as may be the case), but this evidence is quite different from that found within the covers of peer-reviewed journals.

Further, social work suffers from a relative lack of expertise in the scientific paradigm. It is usually only on advanced level post-qualifying training courses that practitioners have the opportunity to acquire knowledge and skills in this approach. Research competence is not a core requirement of the social work degree. The increased emphasis it places on practice competence further undermines attempts to integrate research training into qualifying social work courses, diminishing the likelihood that these skills can be readily obtained.

When qualified, a practitioner's involvement in research is often limited to providing information or completing forms. In many cases the feedback of results is minimal or non-existent. Where they do exist, they rarely involve a systematic consideration of practice or policy implications.

In general, there is far less funding for social care research as opposed to health-care research. There are far more health professionals involved in the research process largely because there are more fellowships in health. Opportunities for practitioner research are limited. Charities such as the Social Worker's Educational Trust, who provide modest grants for practitioner research, are notable exceptions.

The organisational culture within social work settings is frequently not conducive to undertaking research. There is a virtually exclusive focus on casework and very limited opportunities for reflection on research evidence in social work forums or journal clubs, for example. This is reflected in the limited range of journals that were read by practitioners in Sheldon's survey in south-west England. Most practitioners only read *Community Care*, which contains more descriptive work than material from empirical trials. Very few get the time to read empirical research findings and when they do they find that they are often not presented in a digestible form.

What can be done about this situation? Peter Huxley (2002) made the following suggestions about evidence-based practice in mental health social work and social care:

Firstly, the amount of low quality evidence that is currently disseminated needs to be reduced. This would increase a focus on methodologically rigorous research and to help ensure that interventions are supported by the best quality evidence available.

This process could be assisted by the development of a kite-mark system for the standards of social evidence. Using such a system, practitioners would be able to more readily judge for themselves the quality of the research that they are reading without necessarily having to undertake specific critical appraisal skills training. Allied to this is the development of more easily accessible sources of kite-marked practice-based evidence. Currently the database which is freely available to social work practitioners is Social Care Online, but this includes peer-reviewed journal papers alongside magazine articles, making it difficult for most readers to ascertain the quality of its material.

Also, it would be important to teach critical appraisal skills training and evidence-based practice on qualifying courses, a development which is yet to occur.

In terms of mental health social work, it is important to ensure that the mental health content of social work education is consistent with the *National Service Framework* (Department of Health, 1999c).

Further, as he has argued elsewhere (Huxley, 2001), there needs to be support for an increase in the infrastructure that will allow social care staff to participate in the generation and consumption of high-quality evidence. Increased funding for social care research and post-basic education to develop staff capable of conducting high quality research will go some way to assisting with this. In terms of mental health, Peter Huxley has had some success with his call for social science fellowships (Huxley, 2001), but there is a long way to go.

Although there hasn't been a replication study of Sheldon's large survey of attitudes towards evidence-based practice, a recent qualitative study suggests that little has changed since the late 1990s (McCrae *et al.*, 2005).

Critique of evidence-based practice

Considering that the notion of evidence-based practice does not fit squarely with the experience of many social workers, it is not surprising that some have not entirely warmed to the idea. Notable amongst these is Stephen Webb, who wrote a paper in the *British Journal of Social Work* in 2001 critiquing the idea of evidence-based practice in social work (Webb, 2001). His strongly worded critique prompted a response from Brian Sheldon in a later issue of the journal (Sheldon, 2001).

Webb argued that evidence-based practice impedes professional judgement:

> *Evidence-based practice entraps professional practice within an instrumental framework which regiments, systematises and manages social work within a technocratic framework of routinized operations. (Webb, 2001: 71)*

Webb's discussion of the rationality implied in the notion of evidence-based practice inferred that social workers were limited to practising in a circumscribed fashion using only a limited number of interventions with proven effectiveness. He implies that the exercise of professional judgement is limited as decisions are made by the best available research evidence rather than professional experience. On the contrary, even within an evidence-based practice framework, professional judgement is still required in the decision-making process.

Research evidence is one facet of a social worker's decision-making process. A large proportion of social work practice is constrained by local or institutional policies, particularly within statutory agencies, and this can influence the decision-making process in any given instance to a greater or lesser degree. Social workers still need to exercise their professional judgement to make the best decision in the interests of service users and carers. They need to consider the values and preferences of the client, the best available research evidence and work within relevant policies. This requires the exercise of sound professional judgement which has an important place in the implementation of evidence-based practice.

Positivism and its critiques

Scepticism of the scientific method presents a barrier to some people accepting the evidence-based practice paradigm in social work. In particular, the neutrality and objectivity of science has been questioned. For example, Stephen Webb (2001) referred to the Frankfurt School of Critical Theory which argued that there is no certain foundation for empirical knowledge and that positivistic methodologies are linked to ideological foundations in wider society. Further, he cited Polanyi (1967) who stressed the way in which beliefs and assumptions are tacitly involved in all scientific judgements. In many cases, he argued, scientists are unable to make these explicit which make their claim to objectivity suspect. The philosopher Karl Popper is a key critique of positivism. He argued that when we report on scientific observations, we use language that goes beyond the limited data received through our senses and draws on theoretical assumptions (Popper, 1959).

The rejoinder to these criticisms is that if the science is sound, it doesn't necessarily matter that theoretical assumptions are applied. For example, Kendler (1991) argued that:

> The crucial question is not whether the scientist's behaviour is free of preconceptions, but whether his or her scientific observations can be detached from those inferences . . . Regardless of an observer's value judgements, theoretical preconceptions, social beliefs, or any other predisposition, consensual agreement will be guaranteed if a minimal commitment to natural science methodology is maintained. (Kendler, 1991: 140)

Popper and falsificationism

Karl Popper's scientific method is widely respected as a credible alternative to crude positivism. Popper argued that any number of scientific experiments which produce positive results cannot confirm a scientific theory. However, a single experiment which produces a negative result can refute it. The mission of science, therefore, is to disprove theories. Hypotheses that cannot be disproved are held to be robust and a true state of nature (Popper, 1959). Popper's scientific method has been termed 'falsificationism'.

As well as providing a philosophy of science, Popper's ideas are important for evidence-based social work practice. There is a danger that social workers may use 'everyday reasoning' to make their decisions. This means that they may be likely to notice a biased range of confirming evidence and make decisions on the basis of common sense (Moscovici and Hewstone, 1983). Popper's scientific method is significantly different from everyday reasoning because it systematically exposes beliefs to severe testing. Social workers need to be more critical and aware of evidence that runs counter to the theoretical assumptions on which they are basing their decision and actions (Munro, 2002).

There is some evidence to suggest that social workers are able to think and work in this way. A study of social workers (Osmo and Rosen, 2002) found that they tend to use confirmatory search strategies when finding information about cases, that is, information to support their hypothesis about what the problem is. But, when asked to justify their use of information, they adopted unbiased strategies that were more open to contradictory information, overriding the more closed, biased strategies. This suggests that building into the decision-making process the requirement to provide a rationale may encourage a critical approach to decision making, a conclusion that other studies have suggested as well.

Evidence 'biased' practice

A history of scepticism towards the scientific method has contributed towards a lack of development in the evidence base for social work in contrast to medicine and psychology. However, this is not the only reason for the lack of robust evidence for social work and social care interventions.

The evidence-base is biased towards the easily measurable and social work interventions are rarely amenable to randomised controlled trials. In mental health services psychological and pharmacological interventions are by far the most prevalent forms of evidence-based treatments. Bio-medical treatments and cognitive behavioural therapy are much more amenable to the randomised controlled trial methodology than complex social work interventions. Clinical guidelines are skewed towards psychological therapies and drug treatments for this very reason. In the National Institute for Clinical Excellence guidelines for the treatment of depression (National Collaborating Centre for Mental Health, 2004), for example, only one social intervention – befriending – was referred to as being potentially effective as there has been a trial which reported its beneficial effect (Harris *et al.*, 1999).

There are also some inherent difficulties with the scientific methods used in health and social care research. For example, randomised controlled trials have been criticised because the participants are not necessarily representative of the population from which they are drawn (Slade and Priebe, 2001). This would mean that the results may not be generalisable beyond the group who took part in the study.

Critique of hierarchy of evidence

A fundamental critique of the hierarchical approach to evidence is the denigration of social science research methods such as ethnography or discourse analysis, which are demoted to the bottom of the evidential hierarchy. These methods are valuable for exploring processes and interventions which are not amenable to the randomised controlled trial methodology. The most obvious example of this is the statutory work of a mental health social worker. For example, Alan Quirk and his colleagues (2000) conducted a major ethnographic study of mental health act assessments and drew some important conclusions about the valuable social role the Approved Social Worker played.

The hierarchy of evidence is also challenged from within medicine. Miller and Jones-Harris (2005) argued that research evidence should be valued according to its inherent strengths rather than valuing quantitative research over qualitative research. They state, for example, that qualitative research such as phenomenological, ethnographic or grounded theory studies are best for answering questions about beliefs, attitudes or personal experiences, whereas quantitative research such as randomised controlled trials are better for answering questions about the effectiveness of interventions.

Making a similar point, though with their tongues firmly in their cheeks, Smith and Pell (2003) conducted a systematic review of randomised controlled trials of the use of parachutes in reducing the risk of injury after gravitational challenge. Not surprisingly, they were unable to identify any randomised trials of parachutes, but concluded that their safety can be determined by observation studies which show only a very small likelihood of injury or mortality. They concluded confidently:

> we feel assured that those who advocate evidence based medicine and criticise use of interventions that lack an evidence base will not hesitate to demonstrate their commitment by volunteering for a double blind, randomised, placebo controlled, crossover trial [of the parachute]. (Smith and Pell, 2003: 1460)

The Social Care Institute for Excellence has taken such critiques on board and has developed an alternative typology of evidence. Their typology is based on source of knowledge, rather than a hierarchy, and it places equal value on organisational, practitioner, policy community, academic, and user and carer research (Pawson et al., 2003).

Rationale for this book

The rationale for this book is to enhance practitioners' confidence in the evidence that underpins policy and practice in mental health social work. As much of the research which has influenced mental health policy is largely quantitative in nature – and as quantitative methods are rarely taught on qualifying social work programmes, or indeed many post-qualifying social work programmes – this book will focus mainly upon these. We will explore in later chapters research methods drawn from epidemiology – cross-sectional studies, randomised controlled trials, cohort studies and case-control studies. To enable advanced social work practitioners to challenge the dominance of medicine and psychology in mental health services, we need to equip ourselves with the skills and confidence to critically appraise research conducted within their paradigms. Additionally, if social work and social care interventions are to receive the endorsement of influential bodies such as the National Institute for Clinical Excellence, we need to provide high-quality evidence of their effectiveness. However, we are not 'throwing the baby out with the bath water' and have included a chapter on critically appraising qualitative research, as we recognise its value to evidence-based social work practice.

Critical realism

Finally, it is not possible to assume neutrality in the epistemological debate in a book such as this. Although my focus on empirical research gives this the appearance of having a positivist bias, I argue that through the process of critical appraisal, and my experience as a social work academic, a critical realist stance is a more accurate reflection of my philosophical position on knowledge. Critical realism recognises both objective observations (science) and subjective perceptions (human experience) and understands knowledge as a negotiation between the two. A relevant contemporary example of this can be found in the work of Anne Rogers and David Pilgrim in their works on inequality and mental health (Rogers and Pilgrim, 2003) and sociology of mental health (Pilgrim and Rogers, 2005). Their books are highly recommended reading for mental health social workers, as they provide the essential context for contemporary practice. Also their work provides the context for the next three chapters, which are a critical introduction to mental health policy and the role of social workers within mental health services.

BOX **1.1**

Glossary of 'isms' in contemporary epistemology

This brief glossary provides an easy reference for some of the terms used in this chapter.

Positivism

Knowledge of the world is obtained through applying the scientific method to experiences (observations) perceived through the natural senses. Relationships are logically construed to make connections among observable phenomena. The key tenets are that the world exists independently of human observers; and the world is composed of a single set of phenomena and relations among them, which are knowable by observation (objectivity).

Scientism

Only knowledge obtained through the scientific method is valid.

Empiricism

The validity of statements of fact can be assessed only against empirical observations. Propositions that assume non-observable phenomena are valueless.

Falsificationism

Science evolves by the successive rejection of falsified theories. When experimental observation makes a theory untenable, or falsifies it, a new theory is found with greater explanatory power. This theory can account for the previously unexplained phenomena and, as a result, provide greater opportunity for its own falsification.

Social constructivism

Knowledge is not purely objective, but is at least partly socially constructed (subjectivity).

Relativism

An extreme form of subjectivity or constructivism, asserting that there is no external objective basis for evaluating one proposition as more valid or warranted than any other proposition.

(Critical) Realism

Lies between positivism and constructivism. The world exists independently of human observers, but we cannot comprehend it in an objective manner but only through our personal and social biases and experiences. Nevertheless, the reality of the world constrains our perceptions and understandings of it.

Chapter 2

Contemporary mental health social work: a synergy of professional practice and legal process

Introduction

Mental health social work in statutory agencies is largely defined by a fusion of generic social work practice and legal process. On the one hand mental health social workers engage with social systems and apply theoretical and empirical knowledge to understand, intervene and promote change in the lives of individuals. On the other hand, those approved under mental health law in the UK also have the power to apply legal processes to ensure the best possible outcomes for the people they work with.

This chapter will trace the history of the statutory functions of mental health social workers in the UK in the context of a long process of deinstitutionalisation. In doing so, it will also review the political, economic and social context of the changes in mental health policy over the past century that has influenced the development of contemporary community mental health services. It will also trace the development of the professional identity of mental health social workers to place their statutory functions in the wider context of their role within mental health services.

Relieving officers

> In this district when we have a case to be certified we inform the relieving officer of the fact and the matter then passes out of our hands. The Poor-law medical officer is called in and he signs the necessary papers and pockets the fee. We believe that in many districts the relieving officer requests the attending practitioner to sign the certificate and arranges the interview with the magistrate ... (Fairplay & Co, 1902: 960)

An anonymous correspondent, using the pseudonym 'Fairplay & Co', wrote to *The Lancet* in 1902 to raise the issue of corruption in the process of certifying a 'lunatic'. In passing, s/he refers to the role of the relieving officer which appears surprisingly contemporary:

- The relieving officer is the person who is contacted when someone needs 'certifying'.

- The relieving officer contacts the medical officer and arranges for him/her to sign the paperwork.

- The medical officer takes the fee and leaves.

- The relieving officer completes the process of commitment by arranging the interview with the magistrate.

Relieving officers were Poor Law officials responsible for the distribution of 'outdoor relief' to the poor in the nineteenth century. Outdoor relief can be compared to contemporary community care in the sense that it was provided to people in their own homes rather than in institutions, such as workhouses or asylums. Relieving officers were required to see applicants for relief to assess their health, their ability to work, their family background and the means available to them. He (relieving officers were usually men) would provide those eligible, or 'worthy' of relief, sums of money each week. If the need for relief was urgent, the relieving officer would take the destitute person to a workhouse or provide food to them in their home (Rolph et al., 2003a).

Relieving officers were authorised to convey poor people with mental health problems – 'pauper lunatics' – to an asylum. Under The Care and Treatment of Lunatics Act 1845 a Poor Law union medical officer was required to notify the relieving officer within three days of discovering a pauper lunatic. The relieving officer then had three days in which to obtain a medical certificate and bring the individual before a justice (a magistrate). Under the law, the justice had no option but to commit the pauper lunatic to a county asylum or a licensed madhouse. However, the following extract from the *Daily News* in 1851 suggests that as the final arbiter in the process of certification, the justice retained some discretion in this matter:

> *Mr Warrington, relieving officer of the Poplar union, came before Mr Ingham, with a young woman named Barlow, for the purpose of obtaining the magistrate's signature to a certificate that she was a pauper lunatic, preparatory to her removal to the county asylum. The surgeon who had certified as to the pauper's lunacy, was asked by the magistrate the grounds of his opinion, and he said the nurse in the workhouse had informed him the unfortunate young woman was in the practice of leaving her father's house in the night time, and running about the streets in a state of nudity, that she had been guilty of other obscenities, and that she was decidedly* non compos mentis. *He did not of his own knowledge know anything of the facts. From the interview he had with the pauper he should conclude she was insane.*

> *Mr Ingham put some questions to the young woman, which she answered calmly and rationally, and said it was not true that she had acted in the manner stated.*

> *Mr Ingham said his signature to the certificate was required to consign a fellow-creature to a lunatic asylum, and he did not think he should be justified on doing so on the evidence of the surgeon … He refused to sign the certificate, and recommended that the young woman should be taken back to the workhouse, and when there is more satisfactory evidence of her insanity he would sign the necessary papers. (Staff reporter, 1851)*

At this time in the mid-nineteenth century relieving officers were of a higher status than medical officers, though the emerging profession of psychiatry was beginning to assert itself as the asylums grew in number and size. Relieving officers had some, albeit limited, discretion available to them when they were asked to visit a pauper lunatic. They could either order a workhouse admission, asylum admission or grant outdoor relief. If the pauper lunatic was suicidal or dangerous, the relieving officer was legally obliged to initiate the proceeding for certification in an asylum. In situations when this wasn't the case, the relieving officer had some more discretion.

The Victorian asylums contained the most unwell, unmanageable or dangerous members of society. However, they were not restricted to this group of people – only about half of the people admitted before 1865 fell into this category (Smith, 2006) and there is also evidence of a high turnover of patients (Ray, 1981). For example, 36 per cent of patients in the Northampton General Lunatic Asylum left it within a year between 1846 and 1875 (Smith, 2006). Also, 49 per cent of the patients admitted to the Buckinghamshire Asylum were discharged and three-quarters of these were in there for less than a year (Wright, 1999). Therefore, the role of the relieving officer in overseeing the process of certification may have involved some expedient use of the asylum.

The asylum was both a custodial institution for those at risk of harming themselves or other people and a place of safety for the 'deserving' pauper lunatic. It is possible that the relieving officers used asylums as a temporary respite for members of the latter group, mediating between the needs of destitute families and their legal obligations. For example, asylum populations grew during the agricultural depression of the 1860s, possibly reflecting a response of relieving officers to poverty and malnourishment (Howkins, 1985).

Asylums cost three times as much as a workhouse or outdoor relief for a pauper lunatic (Wright, 1999), so they were not the first choice for a relieving officer if the pauper lunatic posed no risk. However, there is some evidence to suggest that asylums were a more attractive alternative (Smith, 2006). For example, committal to an asylum did not involve the institutionalisation of the whole family, as admission to a workhouse might have done; there is some evidence that the diet was more substantial; medical treatment was available in asylums; and the physical surroundings there were probably better than in the workhouse. Therefore, it is likely that the relieving officer used his discretion to arrange certification for those who posed no risk in order to provide respite for families whose emotional and financial resources were drained.

Following the 1890 Lunacy Act relieving officers were responsible for the after-care of the people they had admitted to the asylum. With limited resources at their disposed, they oversaw an elementary form of community care (Westmoreland, 1964).

Duly authorised officers

The Mental Treatment Act 1930 created the post of duly authorised officer, which effectively replaced the relieving officer, a process which was completed with the birth of the National Health Service in 1946. Duly authorised officers were asked to visit people with mental health problems to assess their needs for treatment under two different legislations.

Firstly, they had to decide if the individual was suitable for admission to hospital voluntarily or for temporary treatment (up to six months initially, renewable once for a total period of 12 months in all) under the Mental Treatment Act 1930. The duly authorised officer made applications for temporary treatment with two medical recommendations (with obvious similarities to contemporary practice in England and Wales, for example).

Secondly, they had to decide if the individual needed treatment urgently. They were authorised under s.20 Mental Treatment Act 1930 to remove the person to hospital for up to three days if they posed a risk to themselves or others. This period of time allowed them to take proceedings under the Lunacy Act 1890.

Thirdly, the duly authorised officer had a similar role under the Lunacy Act 1890 to that of the relieving officer. They had to contact a magistrate who would take proceedings to certify the individual, if medical evidence supported this. The duly authorised officer then took the individual to hospital within seven days.

Mental welfare officers

Duly authorised officers were mainly mental welfare officers who worked for local authorities. There was no properly recognised training for mental welfare officers, although many local authorities provided courses. Whilst mental welfare officers appeared largely very proficient in their roles, they lacked the authority that professional status may have brought. Doctors, for example, sometimes found it difficult to accept their decisions when they were performing their statutory functions:

> *Quite often the authorised officer will not issue an order when a doctor wants a patient admitted. Reasonably enough he may hesitate to take this responsibility if he cannot satisfy himself as to the patient's unsoundness of mind ... Even if their name is changed to mental-health officers and some of them attend a few psychiatric lectures (Dr. Macmillan, Nov. 24) the fact remains that the man called in to decide the fate of a patient with acute mental illness is usually an untrained layman who is not administratively responsible to the hospital where he takes the patient. (Asher, 1956: 1266)*

Mental welfare officers delivered community care to people with mental health problems with very few resources at their disposal. Rolph and colleagues' (2003b) oral history of mental welfare officers in East Anglia described a group in Lowestoft in the 1950s who lobbied local firms for extra resources to supplement those supplied by the local authority. They were able to rent cheap buildings and obtain loans to provide housing to people when they left hospital. They also set up a home help service to provide additional care to people in their own homes.

Mental welfare officers worked increasingly closely with psychiatrists and often attended out-patient clinics, albeit in a frequently subservient role. Russell Reeve described his experience of this in Cambridgeshire in the 1950s:

> *We would refer people to the outpatients, the psychiatrist would ask us to sit in with him. We would give a summary in front of the patient on why they were there and*

> *what we were finding and areas of anxiety and the psychiatrist would then talk to them, summarise, prescribe one way or the other ... And more than often, he would say 'Well I will see the patient again in three weeks' or something like that ... so that would work quite well ... so that was a good way of helping somebody to stay at home. (Rolph et al., 2003b: 348)*

Pargiter and Hodgson (1959) described the benefits of this early multi-disciplinary working in an article in *The Lancet*. They described how mental welfare officers, who worked with older adults with mental health problems, attended outpatient clinics to improve communication and ensure continuity of care:

> *In this way, the M.W.O. is in at the beginning of the case; and if, for instance, a social report is needed, he knows exactly what is wanted. He also knows the treatment prescribed and often can arrange for adequate supervision, perhaps by explaining the treatment to relatives or neighbours. His presence at the first interview paves the way for his acceptance as a friend and counsellor by patient and relatives. When home visits are necessary, he is accepted into the home instead of being kept on the doorstep explaining his presence, or being treated with fear and suspicion as the official who takes people from their family circle into a mental hospital. (Pargiter and Hodgson, 1959: 728)*

They also describe how the statutory functions of the mental welfare officer did not necessarily impede their 'social work'.

> *The M.W.O. is accepted as a friend and confidante by many patients-even those whom he has had to remove to hospital under a legal order. When these patients return to the outpatient clinic for follow-up they often laugh with him about their disturbed behaviour. Patients soon get to know that they will get help and sympathy from him, and this is a most useful form of psychiatric first-aid. (Pargiter and Hodgson, 1959: 728)*

The Mental Health Act 1959 removed judicial controls prior to compulsory admission stating that applications were to be made by mental welfare officers or an individual's nearest relative. This enhanced their authority as a counter-weight to psychiatric opinion. Even before this, though, they exercised their independent judgement and refused admission where they did not believe it to be justified. In London, for example, doctors referred 20 per cent more people for admission than were actually admitted by mental welfare officers (Miles *et al.*, 1961).

As with mental health social workers performing statutory roles today, mental welfare officers' decisions were not always well received. Neville Porter described a GP's annoyance at his refusal to admit one of his patients in the 1960s:

> *When I visited, we talked about her problems for some time. She made it clear she did not want to go to hospital. I decided that the medical evidence could not be substantiated and that she was 'compos mentis' at the time of my visit. I told her that she could stay at home and that I would be visiting fairly often during the next few days. That evening I spoke to her GP who became extremely angry, insisting I had no right to reject his medical diagnosis ... but she managed to keep on an even keel for over a year after that. (Rolph et al., 2003b: 351–2)*

Mental welfare officers and duly authorised officers were predominantly men (Rolph *et al.*, 2002), continuing a gender division within mental health social work that can be traced back to the nineteenth-century Poor Law relieving officers. Rolph and colleagues' (2003b) oral history of mental welfare officers included the following perspective of a trainee mental welfare officer in Birmingham in 1968:

> *Work with mentally ill people was really a sectioning service … It was very strongly oriented in working mentally ill people towards compulsory admissions and there was little in the way of prevention, little in the way of after-care … the predominantly male MWOs saw their job as controlling and catching 'mad' people … they didn't see their task as curative, rehabilitative or therapeutic care. The general view was that a lot of it was man's work. (Rolph et al., 2003b: 355)*

Although this view contradicts the idea that mental welfare officers saw their role as helping to avoid the need for hospital admissions and supporting community care, it does suggest the existence of a widespread perception that the role was gender-specific. Women, meanwhile, were developing the profession of 'psychiatric social work' which was more professional but less well paid.

Psychiatric social workers

Psychiatric social work has its origins in nineteenth-century philanthropy as typified by the Charity Organisation Society (COS). The COS aimed to help families facing destitution and to organise other voluntary organisations to make best use of resources. Their work was characterised by a process of thorough investigation, a forerunner of case work in contemporary social work.

Helen Bosanquet (1860–1925) was highly influential in the COS in the UK and in early social work training at the London School of Economics. She argued that charitable visiting should be grounded in formal training for objective casework and that social workers needed training in history, social structure and economics as well as professional skills. In addition to these influences, the first training course for psychiatric social workers at the London School of Economics was heavily influenced by psychiatry and psychoanalysis. Early psychiatric social workers worked either in child guidance clinics or mental hospitals.

Forerunners of contemporary child and adolescent mental health teams, child guidance clinics in the early twentieth century comprised psychiatrists, psychologists and psychiatric social workers. The role of the social worker was to investigate the family's background and the social context of the child. However, rather than 'merely' providing relief, they focused on individual adjustment and personality to promote change in the lives of 'troublesome' children. As women, the early psychiatric social workers were an asset to these teams:

> *As women of 'sentiment' their presence gave legitimacy and public recognition to the whole undertaking of child guidance at a time when neither psychiatry nor psychology could provide such an acceptance grounded in science. Assigning to the social worker the role of intermediary between the clinic and the agency clients made the clinic's public face a familiar one. Speaking the same language, working on the same turf,*

> *usually of the same gender, social workers from the clinic could convey new psychiatric recommendations in a familiar discourse. Both psychiatry and psychology needed the female social workers and the feminine values they represented in 1920. (Jones, 1999: 82–3)*

Psychiatric social workers who worked with adults were based in psychiatric hospitals such as the Maudsley Hospital in south London. They worked closely with psychiatrists and were involved in the after-care of discharged patients. Their psychodynamic training separated them ideologically from mental welfare officers, who were also much more numerous. Also, it was commonly perceived as being undesirable for psychiatric social workers to undertake the statutory functions of duly authorised officers. The following extract from Allen Daley's statement about mental health social work in 1949 has a surprisingly contemporary feel to it. Negotiating statutory roles and therapeutic relationships in mental health social work has a long history!

> *It is doubtful whether psychiatric social workers would be willing to undertake the work and it is certain that many would consider that if they came to be associated with the duty of securing the compulsory removal of the mentally sick (which is the essential function of the authorised officer) it would seriously interfere with their primary function of assisting patients to solve their family relationship and other social problems. It may be that this final act of taking away the patient's liberty ought not to involve one who is so vitally and intimately concerned with the treatment of the patient, but should be the duty of someone with a more independent and impartial approach to the problem. There should, of course, be the closest liaison between the duly authorised officer and the psychiatric social worker. (Daley, 1949: 148)*

The Seebohm Report (1968) and the creation of unified local authority social services departments in 1971 brought together mental welfare officers and psychiatric social workers. However, the increase in generalist social work at this time led to a loss of specialist mental health skills and deterioration in the professional relationship between psychiatrists and social workers. This was exacerbated by a concentration on child care within social services (Sheppard, 1991a). However, the creation of the Approved Social Worker role in the 1983 Mental Health Act provided renewed impetus to mental health social work.

Approved Social Workers

Approved Social Workers (ASWs) had extended powers and greater professional autonomy to exercise an independent opinion than duly authorised officers under the 1959 Mental Health Act (Cohen, 1990). Their role was to conduct a social assessment of the individual's circumstances and investigate the possibility of using other services to avoid the need for a hospital admission. However, as there was little additional investment in alternative services to hospital in the early 1980s, ASWs had few options except to admit people who met the criteria for detention.

The largest study of the early implementation of the Mental Health Act 1983 (Barnes *et al.*, 1990) found that only 10 per cent of people referred to an ASW for assessment for admission under sections 2, 3 or 4 were provided with an alternative to hospital care. The most frequent alternative services provided were support from a social worker, GP, mental health professional or from within the individual's own social network. Residential alternatives to hospital were used very infrequently. ASWs suggested that over a quarter of all hospital admissions could have been prevented if suitable alternative resources had been available. A later study similarly found a low level of incidents that resulted in the provision of 'alternative care', suggesting the continued absence of alternative community provision for people experiencing mental health crises (Hatfield *et al.*, 1992). Outcomes of mental health act assessments today remain dependent upon the existence of realistic alternatives to in-patient care (Quirk *et al.*, 2003).

ASWs played an important role in bringing the social perspective into mental health act assessments (Huxley and Kerfoot, 1993; Sheppard, 1991b). They performed a variety of roles and were respected for managing highly complex situations. A qualitative study of mental health act assessments observed that:

> ASWs have multiple perceived roles during MHA assessments, including 'applicant', 'social worker', 'care manager', 'advocate', 'hate figure', 'therapist', 'bureaucrat', '(social) policeman-executioner', 'ongoing contingency manager' and 'impresario (stage manager)'. There can sometimes be tensions between these roles. (Quirk et al., 2000: 7)

In the context of limited realistic alternatives to hospital for people with acute mental health problems and a risk-averse culture in mental health services following a series of high profile tragedies (e.g. Blom-Cooper *et al.*, 1995; Ritchie *et al.*, 1994), the number of compulsory admissions increased significantly in the 1990s (Audini and Lelliott, 2002; Hotopf *et al.*, 2000; Lelliott and Audini, 2003). Positive risk taking and the creation of innovative care plans to keep people out of hospital have become less frequent and ASWs have argued that their power and independence is somewhat illusory. In the opinion of one ASW:

> When I first started I felt very powerful and once argued against the two doctors. Not anymore, as it's really hard as you have to come up with a care plan, and put yourself on the line. (Quirk et al., 2000: 46)

As the number of compulsory detentions rose, there was a corresponding decrease in the number of practicing ASWs in England and Wales (Huxley *et al.*, 2005b). The lengthy review of the Mental Health Act 1983 led to uncertainty about the future of their role. It is therefore unsurprising to find high levels of stress and burnout in the ASW workforce prior to the enactment of the Mental Health Act 2007 (Evans *et al.*, 2006; Huxley *et al.*, 2005a). In the midst of this uncertainty, ASWs remained committed to their role and derived satisfaction from helping people during acute mental health crises. For example:

> If anything my role as an ASW gives me the most satisfaction despite being the most difficult and potentially risky aspect of my job. I feel this is because I am using my personal skills and my own judgement to effect change for others. This is often unwelcome change as it involves compulsory admission but this can lead to longer term improvement in the client's life and health. I take some satisfaction from that knowledge. (Huxley et al., 2005a: 1073)

The Mental Health Act 2007 opened up the ASW role to other mental health professionals. At the time of publication of this book, ASWs were undergoing conversion training to take on the new Approved Mental Health Professional (AMHP) role from October 2008. While the AMHP role was perceived to be a threat to the social perspective which social workers brought to mental health act assessments, the Mental Health Act 2007 also created the role of Approved Clinician. Supplanting the role of Responsible Medical Officer, the Approved Clinician role is open to mental health professionals other than psychiatrists. This provides experienced social workers with the opportunity to lead the professionals involved in an individual's care, building upon their expertise as Social Supervisors under the 1983 Mental Health Act.

Deinstitutionalisation of mental health care

During the quarter of a century in which social workers undertook the ASW role, they witnessed the culmination of a long process of deinstitutionalisation of mental health care in the UK. The number of psychiatric inpatient beds declined from about 150,000 in 1955 in England (Rogers and Pilgrim, 1996) to about 30,000 in 2005 (Winterton, 2007). Similar moves from institutional to community care has occurred elsewhere in Europe and the US (Goodwin, 1997). An ASW's responsibility to consider the least restrictive alternative for people assessed under the Mental Health Act was an integral component of this over-arching mental health policy.

A number of factors have contributed towards the move away from institutional care of people with mental health problems. Firstly, with institutional care becoming increasingly expensive, governments were prompted to seek less costly alternatives (Scull, 1977). The economic argument was particularly important from the 1970s onwards, when consecutive administrations sought to reduce the fiscal burden of welfare (Busfield, 1986). It can best be illustrated in the run-down of long-stay hospitals which was initially accompanied by little or no investment in alternative community services.

Secondly, there was the moral argument that institutional care was more akin to custody than humane treatment. Goffman's (1961) critique of institutional mental health care and a series of lawsuits in the 1960s and 1970s in the US (Brown, 1985) revealed the failure of the state to provide anything more than custodial care. These arguments influenced the review of the 1959 Mental Health Act, but when the principle of the least restrictive alternative found its way into the 1983 Mental Health Act (section 13(2)), it was a significantly diluted version of the vision of civil libertarians (Barnes *et al.*, 1990). Medical treatment in hospital was assumed inviolable and neither ASWs nor patients were particularly empowered to question it.

Thirdly, the pharmacological revolution argument (Busfield, 1986) suggested that successful use of major tranquillisers made community care possible. This argument is problematic for a number of reasons: the decline in the number of psychiatric beds started before the introduction of these drugs; the hospital closure programme affected a large number of people who did not take them; the rate of hospital closure did not accelerate after the introduction of these drugs; and the effectiveness of the drugs themselves was questionable (Rogers and Pilgrim, 1996).

Finally, there has been a shift in the psychiatric discourse towards 'mental health' and psychological interventions which are better suited to community rather than institutional care (Rogers and Pilgrim, 1996). This found its apotheosis in the *National Service Framework* which we explore in more detail in Chapter 3.

Some argue that we are witnessing a process of re-institutionalisation with an increase in the number of forensic and prison beds across Europe to match the decline in the number of psychiatric beds (Priebe *et al.*, 2005). This argument is slightly dented by the inclusion of supported housing in the reckoning which, whilst on one extreme can be very institutional in nature, includes many projects that are small in size and have strong connections with the local community. However, if de-institutionalisation was a complete success there would be no need for a specific social inclusion policy for people with mental health problems (Office of the Deputy Prime Minister, 2004; Social Exclusion Unit, 2004).

Contemporary mental health social work

The role of a social worker in contemporary mental health services goes far beyond their statutory duties. Social work brings to the multidisciplinary environment a unique focus on the broader personal and social concerns which present alongside mental health problems. Social workers look beyond individual psychopathology to the broader issues of individual and family welfare, relationships, identity, housing and valued social roles:

> *The domain of social work in mental health is that of the social context and social consequences of mental illness. The purpose of practice is to restore individual, family, and community wellbeing, to promote the development of each individual's power and control over their lives, and to promote principles of social justice. Social work practice occurs at the interface between the individual and the environment: social work activity begins with the individual, and extends to the contexts of family, social networks, community, and the broader society. (Bland and Renouf, 2001: 238)*

In the UK, social workers practise in a variety of multidisciplinary contexts which increasingly define their work. In adult services, for example, social workers practise in early intervention teams, assertive outreach teams, crisis resolution and home treatment teams, and community mental health teams alongside a range of other professionals. These teams are largely creations of contemporary mental health policy which, in contrast to mental health law, largely seeks to provide care and support to people with mental health problems in their own home. In order to fully understand contemporary mental health social work practice we will now explore the policy which defines it and the empirical evidence on which it is based.

Chapter 3

Mental health policy in the UK: beyond the national service framework

Introduction

Since the 1990s there has been a renewed focus on mental health policy in the UK. This has had far-reaching implications for mental health social work. In the short term it provoked uncertainty and anxiety amongst practitioners about the future role of social work in mental health services, reflected in the high levels of stress and burnout in the profession in the mid-2000s (Evans *et al.*, 2006). However, it is too early to tell what the longer term implications of the reforms will be.

This chapter explores the landscape of mental health services since the publication of the *National service framework for mental health* (Department of Health, 1999c). It identifies the key roles for social work in contemporary mental health services and highlights policies in which practitioners are well-placed to adopt professional leadership over. It also provides a conceptual framework for understanding the various policy initiatives which set them in their broader context.

Mental health and social services reform

The New Labour Government came to power in the UK in 1997 promising widespread reform of the National Health Service (NHS). It presented a long-term vision for health and social care, underpinned by sustained investment in services.

It set out its vision for the reform of mental health services in *Modernising mental health services: Safe, sound and supportive* (Department of Health, 1998a). This claimed that community care had failed because it left some people vulnerable and others a threat to themselves or others. In particular, it pointed to a group of isolated people with severe mental health problems who did not engage with services, carers who were overburdened by their responsibilities and chronic underfunding of services. It was an overtly political document attempting to demonstrate the failures of the previous administration. However, it did announce the establishment of the National Institute for Clinical Excellence and a National Service Framework for adult mental health, suggesting that mental health policy was to become increasingly evidence-based.

At the same time, the new Government set out its case for reform of social services

(Department of Health, 1998b). It aimed to promote independence and direct payments for adults, and to improve the quality of care for vulnerable children. It also emphasised the importance of partnership working with the NHS in the provision of support to people with mental health problems.

National service framework for mental health

The *National service framework for mental health* (NSF) (Department of Health, 1999c) aimed to improve the quality and consistency of mental health services in the UK through the setting of national standards. The NSF was developed through a largely rational model of policy making. An external reference group, consisting of academics, psychiatrists, GPs, service users, social workers and mental health voluntary sector organisations examined and validated the evidence prior to the Department of Health developing the policy. Each of the seven standards was based on evidence as far as possible. We will explore the evidence-base for the policy in Chapter 4, but first we will examine its implications for mental health social workers.

Standard 1: mental health promotion

BOX 3.1

Health and social services should:

- *promote mental health for all, working with individuals and communities*

- *combat discrimination against individuals and groups with mental health problems, and promote their social inclusion.*

The NSF put social inclusion and mental health promotion at the forefront of mental health policy. Combating stigma and discrimination is a core social work value so this policy objective effectively validated good social work practice and provided opportunities for practitioners to offer professional leadership.

While there were aspects of Standard 1 that were beyond the social work role – such as public health, for example – it did refer to the deleterious effect of long term unemployment on mental health. Mental health social workers are well placed to take a local lead on supported employment, vocational training or befriending schemes, for example.

Social inclusion policy

Social inclusion has subsequently become a key policy goal and the social inclusion programme of the National Institute for Mental Health in England has led the implementation of the recommendations of the Social Exclusion Unit's report on people with mental health problems (Office of the Deputy Prime Minister, 2004; Social Exclusion Unit, 2004). It challenged mental health services to adopt recovery as an intervention goal.

One of the wide-ranging influences of social inclusion policy has been a transformation of day services. These have moved from traditional provision within mental health or social services towards providing a range of opportunities for supported employment, occupation and mainstream social contact. This change has provoked anxiety amongst many long-term users of day services, particularly as they appreciated the safe environment and sense of 'asylum' they provided (Bates, 2007).

The Mainstream project in Liverpool was cited as a good example within the policy:

Imagine is a voluntary sector organisation that runs the Mainstream project. Mainstream supports people with mental health problems to access wider opportunities rather than just mental health services. Each staff member ('bridge builder') is responsible for making links with a particular sector and supporting clients in these areas. Sectors include education and training; employment; visual and performing arts; sports and leisure; volunteering; and faith, spirituality and cultural communities. Clients define their own support needs and aspirations, and the client and bridge builder identify possible opportunities to meet these in mainstream settings. Bridge builders offer dedicated, tailored support to clients as they develop the confidence to use mainstream services and further develop social networks. (Office of the Deputy Prime Minister, 2004, factsheet 3: p. 2)

Mental health social workers can equally adopt the role of bridge builder for their clients promoting their social inclusion and enhancing their access to social capital (Webber, 2005). Social workers can seek out appropriate resources within mainstream provision, develop relationships with service providers and act as a broker to enhance opportunities for social engagement and inclusion in the wider community.

Standards 2 and 3: primary care and access to services

BOX **3.2**

Any service user who contacts their primary health care team with a common mental health problem should:

- *have their mental health needs identified and assessed;*

- *be offered effective treatments, including referral to specialist services for further assessment, treatment and care if they require it.*

Any individual with a common mental health problem should:

- *be able to make contact round the clock with the local services necessary to meet their needs and receive adequate care;*

- *be able to use NHS Direct, as it develops, for first-level advice and referral on to specialist helplines or to local services.ion.*

These standards have less immediate relevance for mental health social work. However, access to social work assessments is inferred in the policy and made explicit in the case of social work involvement in court diversion schemes and mental health act assessments. Also, close liaison with primary care is important to ensure efficient referral to secondary services.

Standards 4 and 5: effective services for people with severe mental illness

---

BOX 3·3

All mental health service users on CPA should:

- *receive care which optimises engagement, anticipates or prevents a crisis, and reduces risk;*

- *have a copy of a written care plan which:*

  - *includes the action to be taken in a crisis by the service user, their carer, and their care co-ordinator;*

  - *advises their GP how they should respond if the service user needs additional help;*

  - *is regularly reviewed by their care co-ordinator;*

  - *enables them to access services 24 hours a day, 365 days a year.*

Each service user who is assessed as requiring a period of care away from their home should have:

- *timely access to an appropriate hospital bed or alternative bed or place, which is:*

  - *in the least restrictive environment consistent with the need to protect them and the public;*

  - *as close to home as possible.*

a copy of a written after care plan agreed on discharge which sets out the care and rehabilitation to be provided, identifies the care co-ordinator, and specifies the action to be taken in a crisis.

These standards should be very familiar to all social workers working in adult mental health services. They reinforce good practice under the Care Programme Approach (Department of Health, 1999b). However, a recent audit (Commission for Healthcare Audit and Inspection, 2007) identified that improvements can still be made. For example, it found that:

- many people who used services were not fully involved in decisions about their own care;

- too few people were offered or received a written copy of their care plan;

- services users were not always aware of who their care co-ordinator was;

- not enough care reviews were taking place;

- people needed help with employment.

(Commission for Healthcare Audit and Inspection, 2007)

Components of effective care plans may include housing; social support; access to education, training and employment; income; and carer support. As social workers are skilled in holistic assessments and working within the recovery paradigm, they can offer professional leadership over the care planning process for these important aspects of people's lives.

Social workers often work with the people with the most complex needs in community mental health care. Case complexity has increased since the introduction of the NSF for mental health (Huxley *et al.*, 2008), suggesting that the targeting of resources towards those with the most severe mental health problems has been successful.

Assertive outreach

The NSF addressed the problem of non-engagement with mental health services with a review of the effectiveness of specialist services (see Chapter 4 for a discussion of this evidence). It recommended assertive outreach or assertive community treatment as an appropriate method of providing services to people who do not engage with treatment plans on discharge from hospital. Assertive outreach workers hold smaller caseloads than other mental health professionals in community mental health teams and visit their clients at home more frequently. They help their clients to maintain their tenancies, secure an adequate income, sustain daily living skills and adhere to treatment plans to help them to maintain their mental health and develop their independence. Social workers are key members of assertive outreach teams as they have expertise in working flexibly to assess and meet needs to people within their own homes.

Assertive outreach teams in the UK are based on the US assertive community treatment (ACT) model developed by Arnold Marx, Leonard Stein and Mary Ann Test in the early 1970s. The ACT model was developed from good social work practice, as the following recollection of a meeting in 1970 by one of its founders Mary Ann Test illustrates:

We directed the discussion toward what kinds of interventions might be more helpful to our patients. Eventually one of the paraprofessionals commented, 'You know, the patients that Barb Lontz works with intensively don't come back. Maybe we should all go out and do what Barb does.' Barb Lontz was an innovative and spirited social worker on the ward that, among other things, helped clients with discharge planning. Indeed, when time allowed her, Barb did far more than plan discharge. She drove patients to their new residence in the community and then spent countless hours and days providing them with 'hands on' support and assistance to help them live in the community. Barb helped clients move in and get sheets on the bed and a telephone installed; she taught clients how to use the local laundromat by doing laundry with them again and again. She instructed them to ride the bus to the mental health center to get medications by going side by side with them as many times as was needed. She worked next to her clients at the sheltered workshop until they felt comfortable. Barb telephoned clients often to problem solve and provide emotional support; she gave clients and their family and/or landperson her home telephone number to call evenings or weekends if a crisis arose. If there was an emergency, she drove out and intervened. As we listed the clients with whom Barb had worked intensively and continuously in this fashion, it was indeed apparent that almost none of them had come back to the hospital! ... Finally, the room filled with excitement when a staff member proclaimed, 'We ought to close B-2 down and all go out into the community like Barb and help our clients out there, where they really need support and where it will do the most good!' (Test, 1998: 5)

The ACT model is based on the following principles:

- The ACT team is the primary provider of services with minimal referrals to other providers. Roles of team members are interchangeable to ensure that services are not disrupted by staff absence or turnover.

- Services are provided within community settings such as a person's own home or neighbourhood.

- Treatment and intervention plans are developed with the client, based on individual strengths and needs.

- ACT team members are pro-active with their clients, assisting them to engage in treatment and live independently.

- ACT services are intended to be long-term due to the severe impairments often associated with serious and persistent mental health problems.

- The ACT team encourages all clients to participate in employment and provides vocational rehabilitation services.

- The ACT team also coordinates and provides substance misuse services.

- ACT team members provide psycho-education to clients and their families to ensure collaboration in the treatment process.

- With the active involvement of the client, ACT staff work to include the client's natural support systems in treatment. This often involves work around improving family relationships in order to reduce conflicts and increase the individual's autonomy.

- ACT team members help clients to become less socially isolated and more integrated into the community by encouraging participation in community activities and membership in organisations of their choice.

- The ACT team provides health education, access and coordination of health care services.

Fidelity to the ACT model in assertive outreach teams in the UK has been difficult to achieve. In London, for example, there is evidence of only moderate fidelity to the model

(Wright *et al.*, 2003). Areas of practice which did not adhere to the ACT model were a lack of expertise and service provision in substance misuse care; lack of consultant psychiatrist and vocational specialist inputs; less frequent contact with clients; lack of a role for service users in the team; less responsibility for 24 hour crises.

Crisis resolution and home treatment

The NSF outlined the importance of 24 hour access to services to ensure a rapid response and early intervention in the event of mental health crises. It suggested that hospital admission is not always appropriate or even possible because of 100 per cent bed occupancy – a problem which still persists (Desai and Kinton, 2006). To avoid hospital admissions wherever possible, specialist teams were advocated as an effective means of providing support and treatment at home. On this basis the *NHS plan* (Department of Health, 2000b) announced the establishment of 335 crisis resolution and home treatment teams accessible to all people in contact with the specialist mental health services.

The *Mental health policy implementation guide* (Department of Health, 2001a) set out the rationale for crisis resolution and home treatment teams. They should be able to:

- act as a 'gatekeeper' to mental health services, rapidly assessing individuals with acute mental health problems and referring them to the most appropriate service;

- for individuals with acute, severe mental health problems for whom home treatment would be appropriate, provide immediate multi-disciplinary, community based treatment 24 hours a day, 7 days a week;

- ensure that individuals experiencing acute, severe mental health difficulties are treated in the least restrictive environment as close to home as clinically possible;

- remain involved with the client until the crisis has resolved and the service user is linked into on-going care;

- if hospitalisation is necessary, be actively involved in discharge planning and provide intensive care at home to enable early discharge;

- reduce service users' vulnerability to crisis and maximise their resilience.

(Department of Health, 2001a: 11–12)

The model is based on successful experiences of crisis assessment and treatment teams in Australia (Carroll *et al.*, 2001). John Hoult is largely credited with implementing the model in the UK after moving from Sydney to Birmingham in the early 1990s (Johnson, 2007).

Social workers are integral members of crisis resolution and home treatment teams. However, as the teams are largely based on medical models of treatment, are primarily composed of nurses relocated from in-patient wards and require working unsocial hours – which can be difficult for social workers with families – there have been difficulties recruiting social workers to some teams (Furminger and Webber, in press). When they function effectively, they appear to provide a less restrictive alternative to hospital admission. However, approved social workers have found that they struggled to negotiate informal admissions because of fewer beds being available and had to use the Mental Health Act 1983 to gain access to hospital for their clients (Furminger and Webber, in press), contrary to the Code of Practice (Department of Health and Welsh Office, 1999).

Early intervention in psychosis

The NSF referred to the importance of early assessment and intervention for young people with a first episode of psychosis, drawing on evidence that this improves outcomes (Birchwood *et al.*, 1997). The *NHS plan* (Department of Health, 2000b) aimed to achieve early intervention for all young people with psychosis to reduce the period without treatment by setting up specialist teams. Early intervention services were established in order to:

- reduce the stigma associated with psychosis and improve professional and lay awareness of the symptoms of psychosis and the need for early assessment;

- reduce the length of time young people remain undiagnosed and untreated;

- develop meaningful engagement, provide evidence-based interventions and promote recovery during the early phase of illness;

- increase stability in the lives of service users, facilitate development and provide opportunities for personal fulfilment;

- provide a user centred service i.e. a seamless service available for those from age 14 to 35 that effectively integrates child, adolescent and adult mental health services and works in partnership with primary care, education, social services, youth and other services;

- at the end of the treatment period, ensure that the care is transferred thoughtfully and effectively.

(Department of Health, 2001a: 43–4)

A snapshot of early intervention in psychosis services in 2005 illustrated that there was some way to go towards consistent national provision at that point, but this is steadily improving (Pinfold *et al.*, 2007). These teams are multi-disciplinary and there is strong agreement from expert clinicians that social workers should be involved (Marshall and Rathbone, 2004). There are a number of distinct roles for social work within these teams.

Firstly, there is evidence to suggest that families and carers play a crucial role in helping people with a first episode of psychosis to access services (Singh and Grange, 2006). Social workers have expertise in working with families and complex social systems where there may be competing interests. Some young people may not want to access services because of the stigma associated with them, so social workers have an important role in working sensitively with them and their immediate social network to provide care, support and treatment.

Secondly, the lack of engagement with mental health services of some young people with early psychosis requires workers to adopt an assertive style of working. As discussed above the practice of assertive outreach originates in good social work practice and social workers can advise on its sensitive implementation with this group of vulnerable people.

Thirdly, social workers' experience of supporting people to work towards recovery makes a vital contribution to early intervention services. These new teams aim to promote recovery through the maintenance of an individual's education, training or employment where appropriate. They also seek to minimise the disruption that episodes of psychosis could bring to an individual's social network. These are the natural territory of social workers who can, and do, make an important contribution to early intervention services.

Standard 6: caring about carers

Standard 6 reinforces government policy (Department of Health, 1999a) about assessing and meeting the needs of carers of people with mental health problems. Carers must have care plans in addition to those of service users and these should be reviewed at least annually. Carers' plans should include:

- information about the mental health needs of the person for whom they are caring, including information about medication and any side-effects which can be predicted, and services available to support them;

- action to meet defined contingencies;

- information on what to do and who to contact in a crisis;

- what will be provided to meet their own mental and physical health needs, and how it will be provided;

- action needed to secure advice on income, housing, educational and employment matters;

- arrangements for short term breaks;

- arrangements for social support, including access to carers' support groups;

- information about appeals or complaints procedures.

(Department of Health, 1999c: 72)

Working with carers evokes a number of conflicting ethical imperatives. On the one hand some people with mental health problems may not want information about them shared with family members or carers. On the other hand, family members or carers may be concerned about the individual's mental health and ask the care co-ordinator for information about their care. Clinical judgement must remain at the heart of decision-making in this area (Slade *et al.*, 2007). Social workers are well-attuned to these kinds of complexities and can offer advice and leadership within teams on these issues.

Standard 7: preventing suicide

> **BOX 3.5**
>
> *Local health and social care communities should prevent suicides by:*
>
> - *promoting mental health for all, working with individuals and communities (Standard 1);*
> - *delivering high quality primary mental health care (Standard 2);*
> - *ensuring that anyone with a mental health problem can contact local services via the primary care team, a helpline or an A&E department (Standard 3);*
> - *ensuring that individuals with severe and enduring mental illness have a care plan which meets their specific needs, including access to services round the clock (Standard 4);*
> - *providing safe hospital accommodation for individuals who need it (Standard 5);*
> - *enabling individuals caring for someone with severe mental illness to receive the support which they need to continue to care (Standard 6);*
>
> *and in addition:*
>
> - *support local prison staff in preventing suicides among prisoners;*
> - *ensure that staff are competent to assess the risk of suicide among individuals at greatest risk;*
> - *develop local systems for suicide audit to learn lessons and take any necessary action.*

Suicide prevention was a key government priority (Department of Health, 1999d) and the NSF re-stated this as the final standard. Suicide rates have been falling since the late 1990s, but there remain considerable inequalities. For example:

- men are three times more likely than women to commit suicide, with younger men being a particularly high risk group;

- there are large regional variations in the UK with Scotland having the highest suicide rates;

- suicide rates in the most deprived areas are twice as high than the least deprived areas;

- certain occupational groups such as doctors, nurses, pharmacists, vets and farmers are at higher risk, partly because of ease of access to the means of suicide.

(Brock *et al.*, 2006)

Suicide prevention was made a priority for mental health services because more than one in ten people with severe mental health problems kill themselves (Department of Health, 1999c). Also, a national inquiry into suicides in the late 1990s found that one in four people who committed suicide were in contact with mental health services in the year before their death (Appleby, 1999).

Suicide rates peak in the weeks and months immediately following discharge from psychiatric wards for people with severe mental health problems (Qin and Nordentoft, 2005). Those with unmet needs (as defined by services) are at a particularly high risk of suicide, particularly those who are socially isolated (Tidemalm et al., 2005). As a result of this, the Department of Health required mental health services to contact every person discharged within a week after they left hospital. While discharge planning and the provision of seamless care from hospital to the community is the responsibility of mental health services as a whole, social workers can play an important role in this by helping to ensure that an individual's social circumstances in the community are conducive to recovery as much as possible. In particular, they can seek to establish supportive networks which can alert services in the event of future risk of suicide.

Progress towards policy goals

Early progress towards meeting the standards of the NSF for mental health appeared promising (Appleby, 2004). In particular, assertive outreach, early intervention and crisis resolution and home treatment teams have been established across the country in the wave of new investment in services. However, a financial crisis in the NHS in 2005–6 curtailed this investment and service innovations had to be at zero cost. Mental health services without crisis resolution and home treatment teams, for example, closed in-patient wards and transferred nursing staff, with little experience of working in the community, to these new services.

Social inclusion has now become a key policy objective (Appleby, 2007a, b). Although the role of mental health social workers is not made explicit in policy documents, possibly because they constitute quite a small component of the mental health workforce as a whole, they have a key role to play in providing professional leadership of the social inclusion agenda. The challenge for practitioners is to identify opportunities for influencing policy and practice within their teams and services to effect lasting change in the culture and orientation of mental health services from a medical to a social model which the social inclusion policy implies.

Reform of the Mental Health Act 1983

Alongside the introduction and implementation of the NSF for mental health there has been a slow process of reform of the 1983 Mental Health Act. An expert committee (Richardson, 1999) was commissioned to consider which changes were required and a systematic review of research related to the Mental Health Act was undertaken (Wall et al., 1999).

The review of the 1983 Mental Health Act was the most fundamental one of its kind since the Percy Commission prior to the 1959 Act. It reflected on 40 years of change and development of community mental health services. In particular there has been the . . .

> . . . *development of new drug treatments, a growing understanding of the role of other therapeutic approaches, and recognition of the important part that social care plays in treatment and support of people with mental disorder. Many patients, for whom long spells of inpatient treatment in hospital would once have been the only option, now get appropriate care at home or in other non-institutional settings. (Department of Health and Home Office, 1999: Chapter 2)*

The review thus aimed to break the automatic link between compulsory care and detention in hospital and proposed compulsory treatment in the community. Following a sequence of consultations a white paper (Department of Health and Home Office, 2000) was published followed by two draft bills (Department of Health, 2002, 2004a). Consistent dissent from an alliance of mental health service users and professionals stalled the progress of reform and a final bill was eventually published in 2006 which eventually received royal assent in 2007.

The main changes made to existing mental health law in the Mental Health Act 2007 are:

- introduction of supervised treatment in the community for people who have received compulsory care in hospital;
- broadening of the range of professionals involved in the key roles in the Mental Health Act as discussed in Chapter 2;
- introduction of a maximum period prior to referral to a mental health review tribunal;
- introduction of a single definition of mental disorder;
- introduction of a new requirement that suitable treatment must be available for people subject to compulsory orders;
- amending the provisions for nearest relatives to bring them into line with human rights legislation;
- abolishing finite restriction orders.

Both the Mental Health Act 2007 and Mental Capacity Act 2005 are fundamentally important policies for mental health social workers. However, as these have been expertly appraised for social workers elsewhere (Brown, 2006; Brown and Barber, 2008) they will not be examined in detail in this volume.

Typology of mental health policy

It can be quite difficult to conceptualise, or understand the importance of, the vast array of mental health policy that has been produced since the late 1990s. To assist mental health social workers to navigate their way through this mass of documentation, we have produced a simple and crude typology which can provide an over-arching framework (Figure 3.1). There are three layers in this policy framework.

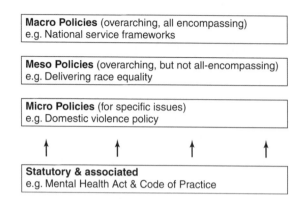

Figure 3.1 *Typology of mental health policies*

Firstly, the *macro policies* are overarching and all encompassing. They affect all mental health services, require significant service reconfigurations and contain key government targets. The NSF for mental health (Department of Health, 1999c) and the social inclusion policy (Social Exclusion Unit, 2004) are two good examples of these. The Department of Health has subsequently published national service frameworks for children (Department of Health, 2004b) and older people (Department of Health, 2001b) which also fall into this category.

Secondly, *meso policies* apply to all mental health services but are targeted towards specific sectors of the population who use them. The initiative to improve mental health services for black and minority ethnic communities in England (Department of Health, 2005) is a good example of this type of policy. The vision for *Delivering Race Equality* is that by 2010 there will be:

- less fear of mental health services among BME communities and service users;
- increased satisfaction with services;
- a reduction in the rate of admission of people from BME communities to psychiatric inpatient units;
- a reduction in the disproportionate rates of compulsory detention of BME service users in inpatient units;
- fewer violent incidents that are secondary to inadequate treatment of mental illness;
- a reduction in the use of seclusion in BME groups;
- the prevention of deaths in mental health services following physical intervention;
- more BME service users reaching self-reported states of recovery;
- a reduction in the ethnic disparities found in prison populations;

- a more balanced range of effective therapies, such as peer support services and psychotherapeutic and counselling treatments, as well as pharmacological interventions that are culturally appropriate and effective;

- a more active role for BME communities and BME service users in the training of professionals, in the development of mental health policy, and in the planning and provision of services; and

- a workforce and organisation capable of delivering appropriate and responsive mental health services to BME communities.

(Department of Health, 2005: 4–5)

Thirdly, *micro policies* address important specific issues. An example of this is the programme of work tackling the mental health effects of domestic and sexual violence and abuse (Itzen, 2006). This cross-government programme aims to ensure that services and professionals in all sectors and settings are equipped to identify and provide effective interventions for those whose mental and physical health has been affected by domestic and sexual violence and abuse. Social workers have a key role to play in this.

Finally, underpinning mental health policy are statutes such as the Mental Health Act or Mental Capacity Act and their associated code of practices. These have far reaching implications for mental health social work and provide a foundation for practice.

Statutes frequently have different concerns from other mental health policies. Their evidence-base is usually weaker, although they wield tremendous power and influence over mental health services. In the following chapter we will review the evidence base for contemporary mental health policy and contrast the Mental Health Act 2007 with the *National Service Framework for mental health* to illustrate these differences.

Chapter 4

Evidence-based or risk averse? The empirical foundations of contemporary mental health policy and practice

Introduction

The *National service framework for mental health* (NSF) (Department of Health, 1999c) heralded the dawning of an era of evidence-based mental health policy. It was explicitly based upon research evidence and the new configuration of mental health services was determined by interventions with proven effectiveness. However, an exploration of the evidence which was drawn upon to develop the policy reveals that its description as an evidence-based policy needs to be treated with a little caution.

This chapter critically reviews the research evidence that underpins the key aspects of the NSF which have affected mental health social work practice. It also presents insights from subsequent research and other studies relevant for contemporary mental health social work. Finally it reviews the evidence surrounding two aspects of the Mental Health Act 2007 to highlight how a political agenda of public safety can override empirical research evidence.

National service framework for mental health

The NSF used the bandolier classification of evidence (see Chapter 1) to illustrate how robust the research evidence was that underpinned the seven standards. After each citation in the document a roman numeral from I to V was used to identify the type of evidence that was being referred to. This helped the reader to see at a glance how many systematic reviews, randomised controlled trials and so on were referred to within the policy.

Graham Thornicroft (who led the expert group which compiled the research evidence for the Department of Health) later illustrated that the evidence base for the policy was not comprehensive and that more research was required (Thornicroft *et al.*, 2002). A review of Department of Health funded research that related to the seven NSF standards revealed gaps in the evidence base (Table 4.1).

Table 4.1 Department of Health funded studies (1992–2000) in relation to NSF standards (Table 1 in Thornicroft et al., 2002, p. 365)

National Service Framework Standard	Evidence type by Bandolier classification					
	I	II	III	IV	V	Total
1 – Mental health promotion	–	1	1	1	3	6
2,3 – Primary care and access to services	2	7	6	7	6	28
4,5 – Effective services for people with severe mental health problems	2	11	6	29	6	54
6 – Caring for carers	–	–	–	1	–	1
7 – Preventing suicide	–	3	1	4	–	8
Total	4	22	14	42	15	97

Table 4.1 shows that the majority (42/97) of the Department of Health funded studies were observational studies (type IV) whereas only about a quarter (26/97) were either systematic reviews or randomised controlled trials, which are considered to be the most robust forms of evidence in the bandolier classification. This indicates a lack of high quality studies being funded by the Department of Health during this period.

Table 4.1 also shows that the evidence base for standards one, six and seven is relatively poor. This has improved slightly since 2000. For example a systematic review of family interventions for people with schizophrenia (Pharoah *et al.*, 2003) provided useful evidence for standard six. In contrast, there has been substantially more government-funded research in primary care and access to services (standards two and three) and in secondary mental health services (standards four and five). However, the UK evidence about key aspects of the NSF for mental health services is not convincing and we turn to this now.

Community mental health teams

Most mental health social workers in statutory settings are employed in community mental health teams (CMHTs) that bring together health and social care professionals within an integrated management structure. These teams form the bedrock of community mental health care but have been surprisingly under-evaluated. For example, the Cochrane systematic review of CMHTs (Malone *et al.*, 2007) included only three randomised controlled trials, all conducted in the UK. The only consistent difference it found in comparison with non-team standard care was lower hospital admission rates for people in receipt of CMHT care. Many of the presumed benefits of CMHTs such as lower cost, improved social functioning, greater user and carer satisfaction have not been found in randomised controlled trials.

Case management has long been the modus operandi of CMHTs, but this too has not fared too well in randomised controlled trials. The Cochrane review of case management for people with severe mental health problems (Marshall *et al.*, 1998) found that it increased the numbers of people maintaining contact with services but almost doubled the numbers admitted to hospital in comparison to standard community care. The authors questioned the extent to which UK community care is evidence-based:

> *In the UK the statutory introduction of case management has been doubly unfortunate. First, health and social services have been forced to practise a dubious intervention whose main effect is likely to be an increase in demand for hospital beds . . . Second, the obligatory nature of the Care Programme Approach has fossilised community care in an ineffective mode whilst impeding attempts to develop superior alternatives. (Marshall et al., 1998: 8)*

The US model of assertive community treatment (ACT), however, appears much more effective.

Assertive outreach

As described in Chapter 3, assertive outreach services in the UK are based upon ACT. The Cochrane review of randomised controlled trials of ACT, which showed its effectiveness in reducing hospital admissions and time spent in hospital, and increasing engagement with services in contrast to community care (Marshall and Lockwood, 1998), was highly influential in the development of assertive outreach in the UK. However, the majority of studies included in this review were conducted in the US.

UK studies have provided less convincing evidence. The largest trial of intensive case management (the UK 700 study) found no significant decline in overall hospital use among those who received intensive case management or any significant gains in clinical or social functioning (Burns et al., 1999). A more recent trial (Killaspy et al., 2006) found similar findings and concluded that community mental health teams were as effective as ACT teams, but ACT may be better at engaging people and may lead to greater satisfaction with services.

The social outcomes of UK assertive outreach teams are also equivocal. The UK 700 study found that standard community mental health team care improved the quality of life of people with psychosis to the same extent as intensive case management (Huxley et al., 2001). The social functioning of the participants in the REACT trial in London also did not differ between the intervention or control group (Killaspy et al., 2006). Similar findings were found in an observation study of assertive outreach users in north Birmingham (Commander et al., 2005).

The relative ineffectiveness of assertive outreach in the UK can be explained in part by the findings of a recent systematic review (Burns et al., 2007). This found that assertive outreach works best in trials in which participants make more use of hospital. In areas which have lower hospital admission rates, possibly as a result of better community care, assertive outreach should therefore be a lower priority. The review also highlighted that trials with less fidelity to the ACT model had poorer outcomes (Burns et al., 2007).

Crisis resolution and home treatment

Systematic reviews of trials of crisis resolution and home treatment (CRHT) teams have not produced definitive results. The Cochrane review of crisis intervention teams found that it may help to avoid repeat hospital admissions and it appears more satisfactory than in-patient care (Joy *et al.*, 1998). A later systematic review of home treatment (Burns *et al.*, 2001) found similar results. Home treatment was successful at reducing length of hospital stays in comparison to in-patient services. However, when home treatment was compared to usual community services, there was no difference.

The introduction of CRHT teams in the UK has led to a reduction in the rate of inpatient admissions (Glover *et al.*, 2006). This finding corresponded with the results of a randomised controlled trial of a crisis resolution team in north London which reduced hospital admissions at the time of a crisis in comparison to community mental health team care (Johnson *et al.*, 2005b). However, CRHT teams do not appear to reduce compulsory admissions. Two observational studies found that the use of section 2 of the Mental Health Act 1983 (assessment orders) increased after the introduction of CRHT teams whilst the use of section 3 (treatment orders) decreased over time (Dunn, 2001; Furminger and Webber, in press). Social workers report that by assessing people for home treatment prior to a mental health act assessment, CRHT teams may increase the likelihood of a compulsory admission because the individual's mental health has deteriorated further and an informal admission can be difficult to negotiate following a reduction in the number of beds (Furminger and Webber, in press).

More research is needed on which interventions within CRHT teams produce the best outcomes, and a wider range of outcomes need to be studied. This includes work on social networks and social interventions that mental health social workers could take a lead on (Johnson, 2007). Users of CRHT services appear to value a number of aspects of the intervention and highlight the importance of therapeutic relationships with the professionals (Hopkins and Niemiec, 2007), an area of expertise for social workers.

Early intervention in psychosis

Proponents of early intervention in psychosis have argued that by engaging people in treatment at a very early point, or even when they are in the prodromal phase, they would be less likely to develop schizophrenia and would achieve better outcomes more generally. Two systematic reviews have indicated that people with shorter untreated periods of psychosis have better outcomes (Marshall *et al.*, 2005; Perkins *et al.*, 2005). However, a Cochrane review of trials of early interventions in psychosis was unable to draw any definitive conclusions about its effectiveness (Marshall and Rathbone, 2004).

The idea of early intervention in psychosis is not new, but the rigorous evaluation of specialist early intervention in psychosis services is still in its infancy (Singh and Fisher, 2007). Two randomised controlled trials of early intervention in psychosis services have shown promising results. The Lambeth Early Onset service in London has provided some evidence that early intervention can reduce and maintain engagement over longer periods of time than community mental health team care (Craig *et al.*, 2004). Eighteen months later, those receiving support from this service were more likely to regain or establish new social relationships, spend longer in vocational activity, have better social functioning, have a better quality of life and be more satisfied with their service than the comparison group, but there was no improvement in their psychotic symptoms (Garety *et al.*, 2006). A trial in Denmark produced similar results (Petersen *et al.*, 2005). Other trials, however, have found that early intervention teams are no more effective than community mental health teams (e.g. Kuipers *et al.*, 2004).

There is some evidence to suggest that working closely with young people and focusing on their needs helps in a number of life domains such as education, employment, housing, income, leisure, religion and social relationships. For example, the Antenna Outreach Team in Haringey, London, provides a culturally sensitive service to young people from the African and Caribbean communities and helps to engage them in a range of community services (Greatley and Ford, 2002). As there are fewer opportunities for social workers in these teams, it is perhaps not unsurprising that the social outcomes of these services have not received a higher profile in the research conducted to date.

Mental health social work

There have been no recent randomised controlled trials of the effectiveness of social work practice in community mental health services. However, older trials have indicated that social work is at least as effective as psychological or pharmacological approaches to mental health problems.

A trial of a home-based social work family intervention for children who deliberately poisoned themselves in the late 1990s found that the intervention reduced suicidal ideation in the children without major depression at no extra cost to mental health services (Byford *et al.*, 1999; Harrington *et al.*, 1998). Although the trial did not show the efficacy of the intervention for children with severe depression, it does indicate that social workers can provide effective services within child and adolescent mental health settings. Further, a trial of task-centred social work with adults who had deliberately self-poisoned themselves found that it did not reduce the risk of future self-poisoning, but it did help people with their social problems and they were more satisfied with it than standard care (Gibbons *et al.*, 1978).

Two trials of social work with people with depression in primary care found that it was just as effective as GP care in terms of clinical and social outcomes (Corney and Clare, 1983; Scott and Freeman, 1992). In one trial the social work intervention cost twice as much as GP care but it was the most positively evaluated by the patients (Scott and Freeman, 1992). In the other trial social work was most effective for women with both major difficulties with their partner and enduring depression (Corney and Clare, 1983).

Our evidence about mental health social work comes largely from a range of diverse research designs including cross-sectional studies and qualitative research (Gould, 2006). A full discussion of this evidence-base is beyond the scope of this book and readers are encouraged to search and evaluate evidence for themselves, following the guidance set out in the following chapters. However, to illustrate the variety of methods used we present here a summary of some of the recent findings grouped by research design. Cross-sectional surveys are relatively common in mental health social work practice. For example, a recent national survey of mental health social workers in the UK (Evans *et al.*, 2006) found that practitioners reported high levels of stress and emotional exhaustion and low levels of job satisfaction. Feeling under valued at work, excessive job demands, limited latitude in decision-making, and unhappiness about the place of mental health social work in modern services contributed to the poor job satisfaction and most aspects of burnout. These results could be explained in part by the fact that social workers work with those who have the most complex needs in community mental health teams (Huxley *et al.*, 2008).

Approved social workers (ASWs) in England and Wales were experienced practitioners, but their numbers were in decline in the years leading up to the new Mental Health Act (Huxley *et al.*, 2005b). They were also more burnt out than mental health social workers without statutory responsibilities (Evans *et al.*, 2005). In Northern Ireland, they were similarly highly qualified and experienced. One survey found that two-thirds of ASWs there did not make compulsory detentions when requested to, highlighting the independent perspective they brought to their statutory work (Manktelow *et al.*, 2002).

Qualitative studies draw out many useful and relevant insights for social work practice. For example, a study of mental health social work academics and managers identified three types of social workers – genericists, eclecticists and traditionalists – as a means of understanding contemporary practice in community mental health teams (McCrae *et al.*, 2004). Also, the positive role of conjoint social work assessments in multi-disciplinary mental health teams has been noted (Mitchell and Patience, 2002).

A series of qualitative studies on mental health social work in Australia provide a useful insight into practice. A focus group study testing Fook *et al.*'s (2000) theory of social work expertise in mental health social work found that it was characterised by the qualities of belief, optimism and caring (Ryan *et al.*, 2004).

An observational study (Ryan *et al.*, 2005) found evidence that mental health social work practice can be summarised by the following themes:

- the knowledge;

- a lot of hard grind;

- we are here for the clients;

- the complicated and the difficult;

- the stone in the shoe;

- going ten rounds with the system;

- the importance of supervision;

- the emotive content of the work.

Use of the Mental Health Act

Studies about the use of the Mental Health Act 1983 have provided a wealth of data which has informed ASW practice and will provide the empirical basis for Approved

Mental Health Professional practice. Above all, studies have consistently indicated that people who were assessed under the Mental Health Act 1983 were predominantly socially disadvantaged and rates of detention were highest in areas of social deprivation (Bindman *et al.*, 2002; Hatfield, in press). Those who had low social support were particularly at risk of being admitted under an emergency compulsory order (Webber and Huxley, 2004).

People of African and Caribbean origin were over four times more likely to be detained than those of white British origin (Bhui *et al.*, 2003; Harrison, 2002; Morgan *et al.*, 2005). Women aged over 65 were more likely to be detained than men in this age group, whereas the converse was true for younger men (Audini and Lelliott, 2002). People aged over 65 were more likely to be detained because of self-neglect and their risk of suicide was lower than younger people (McPherson and Jones, 2003). Detention rates increased in the 1990s, particularly for young men, but have since levelled off (Lelliott and Audini, 2003; Wall *et al.*, 1999). Both older and younger people with a full understanding of their rights were more likely to appeal against their detention (Rimmer *et al.*, 2002).

Studies investigating guardianship (s.7) and supervised discharge (s.25a) under the 1983 Mental Health Act provide useful insights which inform the development of supervised community treatment under the 2007 Mental Health Act. For example, one study found that people on supervised discharge orders were more likely to be non-compliant with treatment plans and have problems of substance misuse, whereas those on guardianship orders were more disabled and impaired (Hatfield *et al.*, 2001). A higher proportion of people of African Caribbean origin were subject to supervised discharge (Hatfield *et al.*, 2001). The majority of people subject to supervised discharge were compliant with their orders (Hatfield *et al.*, 2004; Pinfold *et al.*, 2001), but mental health professionals rated guardianship more highly than supervised discharge (Pinfold *et al.*, 2002). Service users appeared to simultaneously resist and accept the orders (Canvin *et al.*, 2005).

The role of the nearest relative has been an important one in mental health law (Rapaport and Manthorpe, in press). However, there is evidence to suggest that they have been generally under-informed of their rights (Marriott *et al.*, 2001). In spite of this, one study found that people discharged by their relative had no worse clinical outcomes than those who were not (Shaw *et al.*, 2003).

Only one intervention that has been evaluated in a randomised controlled trial has been found to reduce the risk of compulsory detention. Unlike advance directives (Papageorgiou *et al.*, 2002), joint crisis plans have reduced the likelihood of a compulsory detention under the Mental Health Act 1983 (Henderson *et al.*, 2004).

Social interventions

The evidence base for social interventions that are at the disposal of mental health social workers is patchy and incomplete. On the one hand there are well-evaluated interventions which social workers can deliver or refer people to. For example, volunteer befriending helps people to recover from depression (Harris *et al.*, 1999). Supportive social networks appear to reduce the risk of depression and promote recovery. Fresh-start events such as gaining employment after a long period of unemployment are also important for recovery (Harris, 2001).

For people with psychosis, family interventions which reduce expressed emotion within households appear to reduce the likelihood of relapse or hospital admission (Pharoah *et al.*, 2003). Additionally, there is evidence that paid employment may encourage recovery and promote social inclusion (Leff and Warner, 2006; Warner, 2000). Supported employment appears to be the most effective way of helping people with severe mental health problems to gain, and stay in, competitive employment (Crowther *et al.*, 2001).

On the other hand, some commonly used social interventions have a much weaker evidence base. For example, a Cochrane review of supported housing for people with mental health problems was unable to draw any conclusions because of the lack of randomised controlled trials conducted (Chilvers *et al.*, 2006). Most of the studies of housing support are small local evaluations of services, often without control groups, although there are some exceptions in the international literature (e.g. Brunt and Hansson, 2004; Nelson *et al.*, 2007; Siegel *et al.*, 2006).

Uses and misuses of evidence

Evidence provided by empirical research can be used, abused or ignored by policy makers. Contradictory messages from research make particularly uncomfortable reading. For example, there is evidence to suggest that day service users have larger social networks than day hospital users (Catty *et al.*, 2005). However, the drive towards social inclusion has meant the closure of many traditional day services which may mean the loss of these valuable social contacts, potentially leading to social isolation for those previously dependent upon these services.

Also, standard seven of the NSF implies that improving mental health services can prevent suicide. While this may be true for those in contact with services, three out of four people who committed suicide were not in contact with mental health services in the previous year (Appleby, 1999). In fact, there is evidence that suggests that suicide rates are not linked to the effectiveness of mental health services (Gunnell and Frankel, 1994; Lewis and Sloggett, 1998). Also, people with severe mental health problems say that their own social networks are just as helpful as mental health services when they feel suicidal (Eagles *et al.*, 2003).

The reform of the Mental Health Act 1983 provides a useful illustration of the tensions between research evidence and political imperatives. Two contentious reforms – broadening of the ASW role to other mental health professionals and supervised community treatment orders – illustrate this effectively.

Approved mental health professionals

The expert committee who reviewed the Mental Health Act 1983 reported that more research was needed to evaluate the proposal to expand the ASW role to encompass other mental health professionals (Richardson, 1999). Subsequent research found that ASWs effectively manage complex assessments involving a number of competing demands, inter-changeable roles and challenging dynamics (Quirk et al., 2000; Quirk et al., 2003). In their day to day work mental health social workers manage the most complex cases in community mental health teams (Huxley et al., 2008), explaining their ability to perform the demanding tasks of an ASW. Evidence from the homicide inquiries in the 1990s also indicated that ASWs made a valuable and unique contribution to mental health services (Stanley and Manthorpe, 2001).

It is possible that the declining number of ASWs (Huxley et al., 2005b) may be used as an argument for opening the role to other mental health professionals. However, this decline could be reversed by addressing some of the reasons for stress and burnout in mental health social work as mentioned above, saving the burden that will be imposed on other sectors of the mental health workforce (NHS Confederation, 2003). The Mental Health Alliance, Social Perspectives Network and other campaigning groups have highlighted the potential loss of a social perspective in mental health assessments if the role was performed by a community psychiatric nurse or occupational therapist, echoing consultation responses (Department of Health, 2000c). However, despite a spirited campaign to keep the ASW role and the lack of international evidence about other mental health professionals taking it on, the Approved Mental Health Professional role remained intact in the 2007 Mental Health Act.

Supervised community treatment

Compulsory community treatment is a feature of mental health law in many jurisdictions throughout the world such as Australia, New Zealand, Canada and the United States. It was introduced in Scotland in the Mental Health (Care and Treatment) (Scotland) Act 2003. In contrast to south of the border, the Scottish Executive followed the advice of its expert group and a wide consultation and kept the focus of its mental health law on care and treatment.

In England and Wales the Mental Health Act 2007 has been widely criticised as focusing more on public safety than the care and treatment of people with mental health problems (Crichton and Darjee, 2007) and as lacking in principles (Thornicroft and Szmukler, 2005). The proposals to introduce compulsory community treatment were criticised as being a knee-jerk response to high profile homicides committed by people with mental health problems. However, unlike other jurisdictions, supervised community treatment can only be used as a hospital discharge option for someone already receiving compulsory treatment. This made it broadly equivalent to supervised discharge under the 1983 Mental Health Act, albeit with additional safeguards. This policy change has been made in light of evidence that the majority of people who were subject to supervised discharge were compliant with their orders (Hatfield et al., 2004; Pinfold et al., 2001). Also, and more significantly, a comprehensive analysis of 72 empirical studies of community treatment orders across the world found that there was no robust evidence for either their positive or negative effects (Churchill, 2007).

Compulsory community treatment challenges the value base of mental health social work (Campbell et al., 2006) and has been introduced in the absence of good evidence for its effectiveness. As highlighted throughout this chapter it is not uncommon for policies to be introduced on the basis of ambiguous evidence. Although there are gaps in the evidence base for mental health policies and mental health social work interventions, it is important for practitioners not to have gaps in their knowledge base so that their practice is fully informed by the latest research findings. In the next chapter we will begin the journey towards becoming an evidence-based practitioner.

Chapter 5

Becoming an evidence-based practitioner: steps towards evidence-based practice in mental health social work

Introduction

The development of contemporary mental health services in the UK is increasingly influenced by empirical research. As we have seen in Chapter 4 the implementation of the *National Service Framework for mental health* (Department of Health, 1999c) has prompted the commissioning of services with research evidence of their effectiveness. Although this evidence-base does not provide unequivocal evidence of how services should be organised in order to provide the best outcomes for people who use them, it is growing in both size and influence. This leads some practitioners to conclude that:

> I work in an evidence-based service; therefore I am already an evidence-based practitioner. (Mental health social worker, London)

This view fundamentally misunderstands the process and skills involved in becoming an evidence-based practitioner. As we have explored in Chapter 1, the concept of evidence-based practice relates to a professional's expertise in drawing upon empirical research in their decision-making. Mental health social workers need to look beyond the service or structure they are working in for answers to questions about best practice.

There are four steps practitioners need to take in order to become more evidence-based in their practice:

1 Produce a practice question.

2 Undertake a search for evidence.

3 Critically appraise the research evidence.

4 Implement the evidence in practice.

This chapter will explore the first two steps in this process – defining a practice question and undertaking a search for evidence. The third step – critical appraisal – involves more detailed consideration and is the subject of Chapters 6 to 11. The final step in the process to becoming an evidence-based practitioner – implementing research evidence in practice – is considered in Chapter 12.

Identifying gaps in knowledge

Consideration of gaps in your knowledge base may be necessary to help you define a practice question. How you become aware of these gaps is very much a personal process. You may already be aware of them or have a good idea about an area of practice that you are keen to find the evidence for. You may find it useful to discuss this with a supervisor or colleague. Activity 5.1 may stimulate some thoughts for you.

ACTIVITY **5.1**

Gaps in knowledge
Read the following case scenario and then answer the questions below:

You are an Approved Mental Health Professional assessing Martin Curtis for admission to hospital under the Mental Health Act. He is 35 years old and of white British ethnicity. He has been a persistent drug user since his mid-teens and was diagnosed as suffering from schizophrenia in his early 20s for which he is reluctant to take prescribed medication. He has limited contact with his family who live far away and has few stabilising influences in the community. He is currently hearing voices that are telling him to harm himself and he is refusing to accept anti-psychotic medication or a hospital admission voluntarily.

Curtis' lifestyle is chaotic and disorganised. He has moved home regularly, is normally in debt and is often seen begging in the local shopping centre. He has recently been evicted from sheltered housing because of his drug-taking and occasional aggressive outbursts that have led to police involvement. He has been arrested for criminal damage and assault three times and is on a probation order for a number of shoplifting offences. A community mental health team knows him, but there has been limited input because of his reluctance to carry out any recommendations. Curtis has also indicated his intention 'to get as far away from mental health services as possible'. His nocturnal lifestyle has resulted in the involvement of agencies outside the normal day care services, resulting in poor information exchange and care co-ordination.

1 What alternative services or interventions would you consider when assessing Curtis?

2 What is the evidence for the effectiveness of the interventions you are proposing?

3 If you are unsure about the evidence-base for these interventions, would you like to investigate them further?

Writing a practice question

The starting point in the process of evidence-based practice is the definition of a problem or practice issue that you are interested in investigating further. There are a variety of techniques for doing this, but an iterative process will help to ensure that your question is as clearly defined as possible. This is particularly important if you are planning to conduct some additional original research on the topic.

1 Identify problem or practice issue

The cycle of evidence-based practice is often initiated by curiosity about a particular problem or issue that has arisen from practice. Mental health social workers frequently have topics that they are passionate about or are curious to investigate further. The process of identifying a topic may therefore be quite straightforward. However, if you are planning to investigate the topic in some detail, and spend considerable time doing so, it is worth considering a topic which will maintain your interest over an extended period of time.

2 Discuss your ideas with your colleagues

The next step is to discuss your initial thoughts with your immediate colleagues who may have some experience of the same practice issue. Investigate their perceptions of the problem to see if they share your concerns about the topic. They will be able to help you to decide whether this practice issue is worth investigating and may be able to point you towards evidence about it. Also, it will be useful to stimulate their interest in the topic and to discuss how your investigation may benefit their practice, if you are likely to need their assistance at all.

3 Commit your initial thoughts to paper

Write down your initial thoughts about the practice issue you are interested in investigating. The process of elaborating this will assist you to see whether or not you can define the topic succinctly enough for a literature search.

4 Draft your question

From your initial thoughts about the problem, write your practice question. What exactly is the problem that you are interested in investigating further?

Practice questions could be either general or specific. General questions are often about particular issues, but with no specific extra frame of reference to potentially refine a search. For example: what are the outcomes for people with mental health problems and complex social needs in community mental health care? In contrast, a more specific question might be: how effective are social workers in improving the quality of life of people with mental health problems and complex social needs in comparison with community psychiatric nurses?

5 Evaluate your question against the SMART criteria

If you are moving beyond a literature search and are planning to undertake a piece of practitioner research, you may consider developing a more precise research question. This can then be evaluated against the SMART criteria to test whether or not it is rigorous enough to withstand scrutiny.

The SMART criteria for setting objectives are attributed to Peter Drucker (1954). He wrote a seminal management text in the 1950s and the acronym – SMART – has been since developed to embody some of the key ideas about setting objectives that he proposed. Each letter within the acronym refers to a particular aspect of an objective and can equally be applied to research questions.

S = Specific

Firstly, the research question needs to be as specific and precise as possible. Don't use 'woolly' or imprecise language that can be interpreted in a number of different ways. If necessary, give brief definitions for concepts that could be interpreted in more than one way. The research question needs to be concrete, detailed, focused (but not too narrow) and well defined.

For example, if we were undertaking a longitudinal study to investigate the role of social support in recovery from depression, we may start with the question: to what extent does social support help people to recover from depression?

M = Measurable

Secondly, as well as being clearly defined, the concepts within your research question need to be operationalised. That is, you need to state how you will measure each of the concepts that you will be evaluating. This is important because the same concept could be measured in a number of different ways and for different purposes.

For quantitative studies, it is important to use an established research instrument which measures the concept with known validity and reliability in the population you will be researching (see Chapter 6). For qualitative studies, concepts will not be measured in the same way, but it will still be important to state how you will explore or measure ideas (see Chapter 10).

Following our example about social support and depression, we may like to add in a little more detail to explain how we will be measuring our concepts. For example, to what extent does social support (as measured by the Close Persons Questionnaire (Stansfeld and Marmot, 1992)) help people to recover from depression (as measured by the Hospital Anxiety and Depression Scale (Zigmond and Snaith, 1983))?

A = Achievable

Arguably, this is the most important criterion against which to evaluate your research question. You will need to ensure that the research question can be answered in a project that is achievable within the time and resources that you have available. While it is very tempting to attempt something ambitious that will have widespread implications for social work practice, it is best to be realistic. Write a research question which is more limited in scope, but one which you are confident in answering. You will quickly become disheartened if you find in the middle of the project that you don't have the time to complete it. It is best to do a modest project well than attempt an ambitious project and not complete it.

One way of ensuring that your research project is achievable is keeping it local and collecting data from within your agency or local area. For example: To what extent does social support (as measured by the Close Persons Questionnaire (Stansfeld and Marmot, 1992)) help people to recover from depression (as measured by the Hospital Anxiety and Depression Scale (Zigmond and Snaith, 1983)) in one London borough?

R = Relevant

Ensure that your research question is as relevant to your practice, agency or working environment as possible. This will help to motivate you and maintain your interest at difficult times in the research process. If you have a clear focus on the outcome of the research for your practice and agency, it will serve as a reminder why you started out with it in the first place.

Doing a project of direct relevance to your practice will also help to secure the interest and co-operation of your manager or other colleagues that you may need at some point. This is particularly relevant if you are asking for resources from within your agency or the co-operation of staff in completing questionnaires, for example.

The research project also needs to be relevant to a current research priority or need. If it is obscure and has no wider relevance it can be difficult to secure funding, should this be required.

Following our example through, if your agency is particularly interested in informal support provided by families, the research question may be: To what extent does social support provided by families (as measured by the Close Persons Questionnaire (Stansfeld and Marmot, 1992)) help people to recover from depression (as measured by the Hospital Anxiety and Depression Scale (Zigmond and Snaith, 1983)) in one London borough?

T = Time frame

The time frame for the project needs to be clearly established. For some research questions this needs to be more explicit than others, but this is an important consideration in all research projects. You need to have a clear understanding of when you will begin, a realistic timetable of the various tasks that will need to be performed and an anticipated end-date. Having clearly set sub-targets within your research plan will provide deadlines to help you turn in the project on time. They serve as both motivators and reminders.

Working out a timetable can be quite difficult, particularly if this is the first piece of research that you have conducted. It is often best to allow yourself more time to allow for contingencies. One sensible rule to follow is to 'think of a number and double it' when working out how much time various tasks take. It is always best to allow yourself too much time and finish early rather than not have enough time and fall behind your schedule.

For example, our research question may now look like: To what extent does social support provided by families (as measured by the Close Persons Questionnaire (Stansfeld and Marmot, 1992)) help people to recover from depression (as measured by the Hospital Anxiety and Depression Scale (Zigmond and Snaith, 1983)) in one London borough over a 12-month period?

6 Continue refining practice question as an iterative process

Finally, you need to refine your question as an iterative process as you discuss it with your colleagues. Do not be afraid to tweak it, or ditch it completely, on the advice of others.

Where do I search for answers to my question?

Research of relevance to social work practice is published in a variety of places. Rigorous and scientific research is most likely to be published in a peer-reviewed journal such as the *British Journal of Social Work, Health and Social Care in the Community* or the *British Medical Journal*, for example. All papers in these journals have been reviewed by at least two academics, who give opinions on whether they should be published or what amendments are required prior to publication.

Each journal has a citation impact factor which indicates its provenance. These are calculated on the basis of the number of citations of papers from each journal. Journal papers which are widely cited by other academics improve the citation impact factor for the journal. Therefore, it is in the journal's best interest to publish research which is likely to be widely cited elsewhere.

In general, health journals have higher citation impact factors than social work journals. For example, the impact factors for the three journals listed above in 2006 were:

British Journal of Social Work – 0.6

Health and Social Care in the Community – 1.0

British Medical Journal – 9.2

In higher education institutions, researchers are rated according to the impact factors of the journals they publish their research in. As these institutions are rated on the provenance of their researchers there is considerable pressure for them to publish their research in the highest ranking journal possible. The implication of this for mental health social work, in particular, is that much research of relevance to practitioners can be found in psychiatric journals which have higher impact factors than social work or social science journals.

Once a peer-reviewed journal accepts a paper for publication, it assumes the copyright for it. This often means that it cannot be published elsewhere in the same form. If researchers wanted to disseminate their findings to a wider audience, they would need to present them differently and cite the main paper in the peer-reviewed journal. So, the research that finds its way into trade journals such as *Community Care, Professional Social Work* or *Mental Health Today* is often a summary or review of the original. It is not peer-reviewed and researchers are disincentivised to publish their original findings here. However, these journals are amongst those most read by practitioners (Sheldon and Chilvers, 2000).

Research conducted by voluntary sector organisations such as the Joseph Rowntree Foundation (www.jrf.org.uk) or Rethink (www.rethink.org) is available from their websites. It is increasingly common for organisations to publish their work in this way or to sell it. For example, Rethink and Mental Health Media have set up an online Mental Health Shop (www.mentalhealthshop.org) to sell their publications.

Research of relevance to social workers is also published in books or chapters in edited collections. It may also be written up in a thesis which can only be found on a university library shelf or it may not have been published at all. In order to capture the full diversity of research about a topic, and the full diversity of sources in which it may or may not have been published, it is important to devise a comprehensive search strategy encompassing a number of different options.

Devising a search strategy

The foundation of your search strategy needs to be bibliographic databases which contain citations and abstracts of papers published in peer-reviewed journals. However, your search needs to encompass other sources in addition to these because of the possibility of bias. For example, positive results are more likely to be published in peer-reviewed journals than negative or ambivalent results. This may cause a publication bias overestimating the effect of an intervention or the impact of a risk factor on a particular outcome (Sutton *et al.*, 2000). To be completely objective it is just as important to publish negative or ambivalent results as positive ones. However, researchers and journal editors alike are more likely to publish significant contributions to the evidence-base for social work than nebulous ones.

Also, there is a stronger likelihood that positive results will be published in English language journals with higher citation impact factors. This may create a form of language bias. Further, the English language journals with the highest citation impact factors are typically located in the west, particularly in the United States or United Kingdom, creating a form of international geographical bias in the research literature.

Searching the grey literature such as university theses, unpublished reports or materials produced for internal consumption inside organisations will go some way to avoiding publication bias. Library catalogue searches, Internet searches, hand searches of individual journals and citation hunting within journals will additionally help you to find the full diversity of literature relating to your topic. Each of these elements of a search strategy will now be explored in turn.

Bibliographic databases

Electronic bibliographic databases are vast repositories of resources for social workers conducting literature reviews and are the best place to start searching. There are a number of different databases of varying relevance to social work. However, for all topics the recommended starting place is Social Care Online (www.scie-socialcareonline.org.uk).

Social Care Online contains a wide range of materials from abstracts of peer-reviewed journal papers through to articles published in trade journals such as *Community Care*. It has both simple and advanced search facilities, online searching tutorials and useful help pages. There is also a browse facility to get an overview of the literature available on broad social care topics.

The next category of database to consider using is those that are freely available online such as PubMed (www.ncbi.nlm.nih.gov/sites/entrez). PubMed is an American medical database which contains millions of citations on health-related topics. It is useful for investigating research on psycho-social interventions or the aetiology of mental health conditions, for example, both of which may be of relevance to mental health social workers. There are other general medical and psychological databases which will also contain relevant references and citations. For example:

- EMBASE

- Medline

- PsycINFO

Full access to these requires an Athens Password which is obtained via membership of a university or health library. Social workers in London, for example, have full access to health libraries across London. When you hold an Athens password, this gives you access to a wide range of databases. Most universities have hundreds of different databases which you may be able to obtain access to. It is your task to be judicious and select only those that are most relevant to your topic. Here are some examples that are likely to have some relevance:

- Applied Social Sciences Index and Abstracts

- Social Science Citation Index

- Social Policy and Practice

- Social Services Abstracts

- Sociological Abstracts

Finally, it is worth checking to see whether or not a systematic review of your topic has already been completed. Systematic reviews of health interventions are conducted and reported by the Cochrane Collaboration (www.cochrane.org). Many of relevance to mental health social work practice are included in this collection. However, its sister organisation the Campbell Collaboration (www.campbellcollaboration.org) is taking the lead in publishing reviews of trials conducted in social welfare. This will increasingly become the best place to search for systematic reviews relevant to social work practice, assuming that sufficient trials have been conducted to make a review meaningful.

There are numerous advantages of using bibliographic databases. Firstly, they have inbuilt indexing systems based on keywords. These mean that common keywords are automatically recognised facilitating quick searching. It is possible to construct searches using a number of parameters. Searches can be limited to a certain time period (e.g. last 10 years) or to a certain language (e.g. English) and can be expanded again quite easily to encompass a wider selection. It is also possible to perform 'free text' searches based on any text you input and they are not restricted to the use of keywords or inbuilt indexes. You are also able to select which field or fields you would like to search – e.g. author, date, title, keyword. This flexibility helps you to find either a wide variety of papers or specific ones by one author, for example.

Unfortunately, there are some disadvantages to be aware of. Firstly, not all journals are indexed in one particular database. For example, Medline is a comprehensive database for health literature but it does not index every mental health journal. You will always need to search a selection of databases to achieve a comprehensive search. However, some journals are indexed in more than one database. This means that you are likely to come across the same papers more than once. While most journals are in English, some international journals are in other languages which will obviously create a barrier for some people to access their scholarship. Finally, the indexing itself can be quite limited, particularly if keywords are not used consistently or if slightly different keywords are attached to different papers. Valuable research could be missed if you rely entirely upon the indexing systems.

Searching bibliographic databases

1 *Identify key concepts*

To begin the process of searching bibliographic databases, or any element of your literature review, start with your research question and break it down into its constituent parts, components or concepts. Let us take the example of the research question we developed above to see how this may be done: To what extent does social support provided by families (as measured by the Close Persons Questionnaire (Stansfeld and Marmot, 1992)) help people to recover from depression (as measured by the Hospital Anxiety and Depression Scale (Zigmond and Snaith, 1983)) in one London borough over a 12-month period?

It is possible to identify five components or concepts in this research question:

• Social support

• Informal care

• Recovery

• Depression

• Longitudinal / cohort study

Alternatively, when searching for evidence about interventions, the PICO framework has been put forward as a useful way of breaking down components of questions to facilitate literature searches. This is comprised of the following elements:

Population – the group of people who you are interested in. This could be defined by demographic variables such as age, gender, ethnic group, or it could be people with a specific diagnosis such as depression or schizophrenia, for example.

Intervention – the service, therapy or treatment being investigated.

Comparison intervention – what is the intervention being compared with? This could be 'treatment as usual', a placebo or a different intervention. Quite frequently this is an optional extra in the framework, particularly in the evaluation of social interventions where there are few interventions to choose from in the first place and it would be unwise to narrow the search down too much too soon.

Outcome – what is the aim of the intervention? This may be recovery from a mental health problem, improved quality of life or social inclusion, for example.

For example, you may be interested in finding research which investigates the effectiveness of supported employment for people with mental health problems in contrast to day services in promoting their social inclusion. Breaking this question down using the PICO framework results in the following components:

Population = people with mental health problems

Intervention = supported employment

Comparison intervention = day services

Outcome = social inclusion

It is not always necessary to use all the component parts. For example, to answer a straight question about the effectiveness of an intervention you may not include the comparison intervention or outcome. There is no single right answer about what should or should not be included. However, evidence from a pilot study (Schardt et al., 2007) found a trend towards increased relevance of search results when the PICO framework was used to find evidence about interventions. This suggests that a systematic approach to breaking down a research question can improve the quality and efficiency of the searching procedure.

2 Compile search terms

From your list of key concepts and components you can now compile a list of search terms, which describe your topic, to enter into the databases.

First, consider synonyms of the concepts you have identified, that is, different ways of talking about the same thing. For example, people with depression may also be referred to as having a 'common mental disorder', 'affective disorder' or 'mood disorder', or being 'depressive' or 'depressed'.

Secondly, identify any abbreviations of the concept that may be used instead of full terms. For example, the individual placement and support model of supported employment is frequently shortened to 'IPS'.

Next, identify any terms that may be related to your concepts. For example, in the context of the research question given above, 'social support' is closely related to 'social networks', which in turn is related to 'social connections', 'social resources' and 'social capital'.

Finally, identify any transatlantic differences in spelling and terminology. For example, 'assertive outreach' in the UK is equivalent to 'assertive community treatment' in the US where it was pioneered.

3 Combine concepts using Boolean operators

Databases enable us to join together concepts to help us refine searches. They use the 'Boolean operators' of AND, OR and NOT to connect some concepts while excluding others.

The operator AND is used to narrow a search. If you entered in 'social support AND depression' into a database search it will only identify papers which contain both the concepts of social support and depression.

The operator OR is used to widen a search. If you entered in 'social support OR depression' into a database search it will identify papers which contain either the concepts of social support or depression.

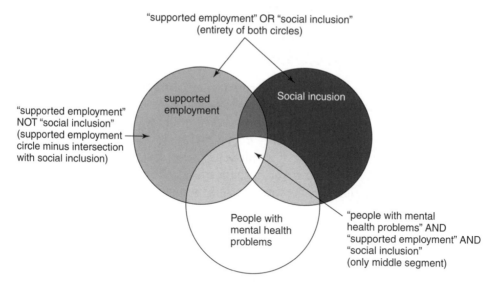

Figure 5.1 Example of use of Boolean operators

The operator NOT is used to narrow a search. If you entered in 'social support NOT depression' into a database search it will identify all the papers which contain the concept of social support except those that also contain the concept of depression. This is useful when you want to exclude a category of research. However, you need to be careful when using this that you don't inadvertently exclude papers of relevance to your question.

Figure 5.1 illustrates the use of the Boolean operators in a search for papers on supported employment for people with mental health problems and social inclusion.

4 *Some more advanced searching techniques*
There are a number of additional searching techniques that you can use within databases.

You can use brackets to clarify relationships between search terms. For example '(social support OR social capital) AND depression' will search for both 'social support AND depression' and 'social capital AND depression'.

It is also possible to use truncation or wildcards. A symbol at the end of a word stem – usually * or $ depending on the database – provides for all variants on the word stem. For example 'depress*' will search for 'depression', 'depressed', 'depressive' and so on.

A symbol within a word – usually ! or ? depending on the database – will locate different spellings or variants of the same word. For example 'wom!n' will search for both 'woman' and 'women'.

Most databases will include tutorials or help pages giving details about how to get the most out of searching them. For example, the CSA Illumina Advanced Tutorial (www.csa.com) is a nice example of an online tutorial which gives a clear demonstration about how to search its databases.

5 Document your search

It is very important to document your literature search. This is important so you can easily run the search at a later date. For example, if you were unable to complete the search all at one time, carefully documenting your search will mean that you do not have to start from scratch again. It is also important to ensure transparency in case you will need to explain to anyone else where you have searched.

For database searches you will need to include the following information:

• database name

• dates covered

• search terms used

This process will need to be replicated for each type of search you conduct.

Grey literature

In addition to searching bibliographic databases you will need to search the 'grey literature', which is work that has not been fully published such as university theses, reports or materials produced for internal consumption within organisations. Some of this may be available on the Internet or you may have to approach organisations individually to obtain it. Some places to start include:

• Google scholar (http://scholar.google.co.uk) is the best-known search engine for this kind of literature, although this contains a mixture of peer-reviewed and grey literature.

• Scirus (www.scirus.com) is the most comprehensive science-specific search engine available on the Internet. Driven by the latest search engine technology, it enables anyone searching for scientific information to find it quickly and easily.

• Index to theses (www.theses.com) is a searchable databases of abstracts of theses accepted for higher degrees by universities in the United Kingdom and Ireland.

You will need to consider searching the web pages of organisations that may publish their research online rather than in print. As previously mentioned, the Joseph Rowntree Foundation and Rethink publish their studies online.

Organisations disseminating research to social workers have well-resourced websites. These are worth searching. For example:

Social Care Institute for Excellence (www.scie.org.uk)

Research in Practice (www.rip.org.uk)

Research in Practice for Adults (www.ripfa.org.uk)

Making Research Count (http://www.uea.ac.uk/swk/MRC_web/public_html/)

Information gateways provide another option for a starting place for literature searches. The most relevant one for social work is Intute: Social Sciences (www.intute.ac.uk/socialsciences). If you select the 'social welfare' option, this lists for you broad topic areas to explore.

By definition, it is more difficult to search grey literature systematically than bibliographic databases. However, it is important to record your searches as accurately as possible to ensure that you can repeat the search at a later date should that be necessary.

Internet searching

Research is increasingly being published on the Internet outside the peer-reviewed journal arena, so it is important to include general Internet searches in your strategy. In addition to the more specific sites listed above, general search engines should also be used to look more broadly for research beyond the scope of specialist websites. For example, any of the following will get you started:

Google (www.google.co.uk)

Ask (http://uk.ask.com)

Yahoo (http://search.yahoo.com)

A very useful place to improve or consolidate your Internet searching is with Internet Social Worker (www.vts.intute.ac.uk/he/tutorial/social-worker). This is an interactive tutorial teaching you how to get the most out of the Internet for your practice.

Library catalogues

Although perhaps a little passé in the 'information age', books are still a good source of relevant information to social workers. Research can be published in either monographs (e.g. Spencer and Pahl, 2006) or edited collections (e.g. McKenzie and Harpham, 2006). A potential problem with publishing research in books is that it loses some of its timeliness because of delays in getting it into print. However, these delays are not unique to the publication of books. There is sometimes an 18-month delay in getting papers accepted by peer-reviewed journals actually published, for example.

The Copac academic and national library catalogue (www.copac.ac.uk) gives free access to the merged online catalogues of major university libraries in the UK and the British Library and provides a comprehensive database of books published in the UK. Searching this catalogue is akin to searching a bibliographic database, though it is a little simpler. If you are not able to gain access to the British Library or a university library you will be able obtain inter-library loans via your local library for a modest charge.

Your local librarian, particularly in health libraries, will also be a valuable source of information and support with your searching. If approached at a quiet time some librarians relish the opportunity to help you with your literature searches. You've nothing to lose by asking for help if you need it.

Hand searching

Another useful method, although labour intensive, is hand searching peer-reviewed or other journals. This simply involves leafing through relevant journals to identify papers relevant to your topic. An extension of this method is to search for relevant citations in papers of relevance to your topic. This snowballing approach is a useful way of finding older or obscure papers that may not be cited in bibliographic databases. Again, don't forget to note down which journals or papers you have hand-searched for relevant papers or citations as you don't want to search again in the same place six months later on.

When do I stop searching?

There are no easy answers to this question. You need to be confident that you have located the key papers about your topic which present the most relevant and up to date research. As a rule of thumb you can stop searching when you are finding nothing new. If you repeat your searches in multiple databases but are coming up with no new papers, it is likely that you have identified the key ones about the topic.

What do I do if I can't find anything on my topic?

It may be the case that there is no research at all on your topic. It could be a new or emerging area of practice and no-one has yet evaluated it. If this is the case, then think laterally and widen your search to encompass fields of practice that are connected or similar in some way. For example, if you were exploring the literature around mental health social workers' attitudes towards Asperger's Syndrome and you could find no studies that have examined this topic, then consider searching for papers on either social care workers', health professionals', or teachers' attitudes towards it. Also, you can look for papers on the prevalence of Asperger's amongst people receiving mental health services or social services, or the epidemiology of the syndrome in general.

Use the Boolean operator 'OR' to widen your search to encompass other aspects of Asperger's Syndrome which may have some bearing on your topic of interest.

What do I do if I find too much information?

Some topics have been extensively researched, both in the UK and across the world. In this case the literature search is likely to result in a vast number of relevant papers, which can be unwieldy to work with. Re-run your searches using the Boolean operators 'AND' or

'NOT' to limit the papers to only those of direct relevance. You can also restrict your searches to papers published within the last 5 years and/or in the UK, if that is an appropriate strategy for your research question, for example. Finally, you could restrict your search to the most methodologically rigorous studies. While you won't know which these are until you have had an opportunity to read them, you may be able to restrict your search to only systematic reviews and randomised controlled trials, which are both at the top of the Bandolier classification of evidence.

Critical appraisal

The process of critical appraisal will help you to 'separate the wheat from the chaff' and identify the strongest studies with the most reliable evidence. It is important for a number of reasons.

Firstly, we need to be aware of the degree to which we are persuaded by authority. Although we may not be conscious of this, it is pervasive in human nature in general and mental health social work in particular. As mentioned above, social workers whose practice is influenced by the National Service Framework should not consider themselves to be evidence-based practitioners on this basis alone. They need to critically engage with the evidence produced by academics or promoted by policy makers to question its relevance for their practice.

It is also human nature to be persuaded by emotive arguments. For example, most people in Britain believe that community care has caused an increase in the number of homicides by people with mental health problems. The evidence points in the opposite direction (Taylor and Gunn, 1999) but emotive tabloid headlines perpetuate emotive myths about mental illness which people prefer to believe. Emotive cases need to be recognised and treated with caution.

Thorough critical appraisals can take some time to complete. However, it is essential for practitioners to critically engage with the empirical literature on their topic. As a starting point, Figure 5.2 presents the PROMPT checklist which is a quick way of appraising information quality and reliability. This can be applied to non peer-reviewed research or any information relating to your practice question if you are in a rush.

Critically appraising research findings can be problematic, not least because studies have shown that scientific language can be difficult to understand (e.g. Hayes, 1992). To assist you with this process, the next six chapters present user-friendly guides to evaluating studies using common methods found within mental health research.

Presentation	How is the information presented? What is the writing style? What is the structure and layout of the information?
Relevance	Is it too detailed or specialised? Is it too basic? Does it have the wrong emphasis? Discard papers, articles or resources of marginal or no relevance.
Objectivity	What are the vested interests behind the research? Is it drug company sponsored or funded by a research council? Look out for opinions presented as fact and be aware of emotionally charged language.
Method	How robust is the method that was used in the study?
Provenance	Who produced the research and where did it come from? Are they an expert in the field? What else have they published? Is the research peer-reviewed or has it gone through a similar quality control mechanism?
Timeliness	Is it up to date? When was the research done? When was it published? Are there findings that supersede it?

Figure 5.2 PROMPT checklist of information quality and reliability

Chapter 6

How to critically appraise cross-sectional surveys

Introduction

The cross-sectional survey is perhaps the most common method used in quantitative research and is therefore an appropriate place to start our exploration of different research designs. This chapter will outline the uses and applications of cross sectional surveys, with some examples relevant to social workers. We will then explore the fundamental components of cross-sectional surveys that will facilitate the critical appraisal of studies using this design. Then we will look at the notions of validity and reliability of research instruments, followed by a brief mention of the types of analysis to expect when looking at cross-sectional surveys.

Uses and applications

Cross-sectional surveys are all around us. They are in the news, they are both welcomed and dreaded by politicians and they have even been the subject of a television topical panel quiz show.

Probably the most widely known cross-sectional surveys are opinion polls. These are repeated surveys of public opinion about given topics, most notably which political party you will vote for. Polling organisations such as Ipsos MORI provide repeated polls for the media and these are also used to predict the results of general elections, for example.

The most comprehensive cross-sectional survey in the UK is the population census. This has been conducted every 10 years since 1801 and gives a comprehensive snap-shot of the UK population. In England, for example, questions are asked on household accommodation, relationships, demographic characteristics (e.g. sex, age, marital status), migration, cultural characteristics, health and provision of care, qualifications, employment, workplace and journey to work.

The last census was conducted in 2001 and its results are used for purposes such as central and local government resource allocation, planning for the housing, education, transport and health services of the future and as comparative data within research studies. Census data for England and Wales can be viewed online at the National Statistics website (www.statistics.gov.uk), which is a veritable treasure trove of information and is well worth book-marking!

In epidemiology, the cross-sectional survey is used to measure the prevalence of a particular health problem. For example, it may be useful to know how many people in a particular locality are suffering from depression in order to plan services to meet their needs and ensure equitable access to these services.

In social work research, cross-sectional surveys serve very similar purposes. A survey of the quality of life or social inclusion of mental health service users, for example, will be useful in highlighting social factors that mental health services need to address in their planning, delivery and review of care plans. More generally, surveys assist in the planning and delivery of services, quantifying of opinions and highlighting the extent of potential difficulties.

In summary, therefore, cross-sectional surveys are useful for:

- identifying need and planning services;

- drawing attention to the extent of a particular problem;

- describing the impact of a particular health condition or social problem in a particular community.

Additionally, surveys can make comparisons with other populations. For example, recent surveys of the workload and stress of mental health social workers (Evans *et al.*, 2006) and consultant psychiatrists (Mears *et al.*, 2007) used the same standardised questionnaires to facilitate comparisons. These studies found that, amongst numerous findings, mental health social workers were more emotionally exhausted than the psychiatrists, almost twice as many social workers met the threshold for a common mental disorder than psychiatrists, but both groups of professionals on average worked the same number of hours per week.

Surveys can also chart trends over time. Repeated opinion polls in the UK are a good example of this. The polling organisation Ipsos MORI (2007) has collected together poll ratings for Tony Blair's 10 years as Prime Minister and presented them graphically to see at a glance how his poll ratings peaked and troughed from 1997 to 2007.

Surveys can also facilitate comparisons between groups within a survey. This might be those with or without a mental health problem or those with good or poor quality of life, for example. The survey of mental health social workers referred to above compared Approved Social Workers with those who did not undertake statutory duties, for example (Evans *et al.*, 2005).

The main limitation of cross-sectional surveys, however, is that they cannot determine causality. They can detect associations and highlight patterns, but they are unable to confirm whether the different variables that were measured had any causal association.

Cross-sectional surveys in social work research

Let us consider three varied examples of cross-sectional surveys that inform social work practice in a little more detail.

EXAMPLE *6.1*

Moses, T. and Kirk, S. A. (2006) Social workers' attitudes about psychotropic drug treatment with youths. Social Work, 51, 211–22

Background

In this study conducted in the United States, Moses and Kirk explored social workers' attitudes to the prescription of psychotropic drugs to young people. In studies conducted in the 1970s and 1980s the profession appeared suspicious and negative towards psychotropic medication, reflecting its resistance to the medical model. More recent studies have shown a softening in attitudes, suggesting that practitioners are more likely to see medication as one element of a care plan. However, these studies all considered the role of medication in working with adults so Moses and Kirk set out to explore social workers' attitudes to their use in young people.

Method

They used a cross-sectional self-complete postal questionnaire survey design. They selected a random sample of 2,000 members of the US National Association of Social Work and achieve a response rate of 32.7 per cent (n=563).

Results

Respondents generally agreed that psychopharmacology is generally harmful for young people. However, a majority believed that medication is a necessary component of a treatment plan for many disorders. This reflected the complexity of views held by practitioners.

Limitations

The low response rate and over-representation of more experienced practitioners may limit the generalisability of this study.

Implications for practice

Social workers need to be informed about medications that are prescribed for the young people they work with and to critically engage in discussions with those who prescribe them about their efficacy on a case-by-case basis.

Additional questions

How applicable is this study to social workers working in the UK?

If the study was conducted in the UK, would the results be vastly different?

EXAMPLE **6.2**

Evans, S., Huxley, P., Gately, C., Webber, M., Mears, A., Pajak, S., Medina, J., Kendall, T. I. M. and Katona, C. (2006) Mental health, burnout and job satisfaction among mental health social workers in England and Wales. British Journal of Psychiatry, 188, 75–80

Background

Previous research suggests that social workers experience high levels of stress and burnout but most remain committed to their work. This study aimed to investigate the prevalence of stress and burnout, and job satisfaction among mental health social workers in England and Wales and the factors responsible for this.

Method

They used a cross-sectional self-complete postal questionnaire survey design. They achieved an adjusted response rate of 49 per cent from the 610 practitioners they surveyed.

Results

Respondents reported high levels of stress and emotional exhaustion and low levels of job satisfaction. 47 per cent met the threshold for a probable common mental disorder, twice the rate for consultant psychiatrists. Feeling under valued at work, excessive job demands, limited latitude in decision-making, and unhappiness about the place of mental health social work in modern services contributed to the poor job satisfaction and most aspects of burnout.

Limitations

The study was conducted at a time of uncertainty for mental health social work due to the proposed changes in role of the Approved Social Worker. Self-selection bias cannot be ruled out with the modest response rate.

Implications for practice

Employers need to recognise the demands upon mental health social workers and to value their contribution to mental health services. Job demands, decision-making latitude and the role of social work in mental health services need to be overhauled to improve the job satisfaction of mental health social workers.

Additional questions

Do other mental health professionals such as community psychiatric nurses feel the same way? How can the role of social work be more valued in mental health services?

EXAMPLE **6.3**

Chitsabesan, P., Kroll, L. E. O., Bailey, S. U. E., Kenning, C., Sneider, S., MacDonald, W. and Theodosiou, L. (2006) Mental health needs of young offenders in custody and in the community. British Journal of Psychiatry, 188, 534–40

Background

Research has revealed high levels of mental health needs in young offenders but many previous studies have been small, focusing on specific populations. This study aimed to evaluate the mental health and psychosocial needs of a nationally representative sample of juvenile offenders in England and Wales, including female offenders and those from black and minority ethnic groups.

Method

A cross-sectional survey of 301 young offenders, 151 in custody and 150 in the community, was conducted in six geographically representative areas across England and Wales. Each young person was interviewed to obtain demographic information, mental health and social needs, and psychometric data.

Results

Young offenders were found to have high levels of needs in a number of different areas including mental health (31 per cent), education or work (36 per cent) and social relationships (48 per cent). Young offenders in the community had significantly more needs than those in secure care and needs were often unmet. One in five young offenders was also identified as having a learning disability.

Limitations

Some missing data may have resulted in lower needs ratings. Black and ethnic minority respondents were under-represented.

Implications for practice

Social workers have an important role in ensuring young offenders have access to appropriate mental health services, education and training opportunities and meaningful social relationships. The introduction of a care programme approach may improve continuity of care for young offenders.

Additional questions

Does this study suggest that young offenders not within institutions are neglected by services? How can social workers champion the needs of this group of vulnerable people?

Population

Let us now consider the fundamental components of cross-sectional surveys that will facilitate our critical appraisal of studies using this design.

The first component is the population from which the sample for the cross-sectional survey is drawn. This is also known as the base population. From the examples above, this might be young offenders (Chitsabesan *et al.*, 2006) or mental health social workers in England and Wales (Evans *et al.*, 2006), for example.

Random sampling will help to ensure that the sample is as representative of this population as possible. The findings of the survey should then be generalisable to this group. The two key words here are representative and generalisability and we will return to these throughout this chapter.

Sampling frame

The first step in conducting a cross-sectional survey is to define the eligibility criteria. This will involve defining both inclusion and exclusion criteria. Inclusion criteria may be age, gender or place of residence, for example. Exclusion criteria should be as minimal as possible so that as many people as possible are included within the survey. This will increase the potential for generalising the findings to the entire base population. Exclusion criteria may be circumstances that make participation difficult such as poor health, for example.

Those who are eligible to take part in a cross-sectional study form the sampling frame. Quite simply, the sampling frame is an accurate, up-to-date list of all those who may be asked to take part in the study. It is a list of all those in the base population from which the sample may be drawn.

Examples of sampling frames may be:

• electoral register for studies of the general population;

• community mental health team caseloads for studies of people with severe mental health problems;

• General Social Care Council list of registered social workers for studies of practitioners.

Can you envisage any potential problems with these sampling frames? Well, no sampling frame is without its difficulties. For example, researchers can only have access to the edited electoral register for research purposes. This may contain less than half of the actual population of the local area because people can choose to be left off the register available for purchase. Also, it will obviously not include those who do not have a right to vote in the first place.

Secondly, different community mental health teams may interpret eligibility criteria for services differently resulting in inconsistencies in who actually receives a service. This may provide a sampling frame consisting of people whose mental health problems vary considerably in severity.

Thirdly, the General Social Care Council list of registered social workers may be comprehensive, but there is no public access to the addresses of social workers which makes contacting them for research purposes impossible.

The survey of mental health social workers (Evans *et al.*, 2006) is an example of a study where there was no readily available sampling frame (a list of all mental health social workers in England and Wales). The study team had to develop their own by contacting all the councils with social services responsibilities and requesting lists of all their mental health social workers. A random sample of one-fifth of all eligible practitioners was selected to participate in the study. Students, managers and members of emergency duty teams were excluded from the study as their experiences were atypical of front-line mental health social workers.

Sampling strategies

As it is often not possible to obtain data from all members of a sampling frame, it is necessary to select a sample. Participants must be chosen at random to avoid bias. The most straightforward method of sampling is to select participants by using simple random sampling. As just mentioned, the survey of mental health social workers chose a sample of one in five eligible practitioners (Evans *et al.*, 2006). This is a simple random sample.

There are some situations when a simple random sample is not sufficient. Sometimes it may be necessary to stratify a sample by age, gender, ethnicity or place of residence, for example. Stratified samples are used in research of older people when it may be necessary to over-sample the oldest to ensure that there are enough in the sample, for example. In their study of social support, loneliness and life events in older people, Prince and colleagues (1997b) used variable sampling fractions. They selected one in ten of those aged 65–74, one in five of those aged 75–84 and one in two of those aged over 84.

A further sampling strategy that is sometimes employed in cross-sectional surveys is clustered random sampling. This is used to efficiently achieve nationally representative samples in populations where it is necessary to negotiate access to each participant. For example, in the case of research of people receiving services from secondary community mental health services, a random sample of mental health trusts in the UK may be initially selected. Then, in each trust a random sample of community mental health teams are selected, from which a random sample of service users is obtained. This sampling strategy minimises the number of mental health trusts whom the researcher would need to approach to gain ethical approval and the number of teams required to gain access to the service users.

Cluster random sampling is frequently used when obtaining samples from schools. For example, researchers investigating sexual abuse among girls in Istanbul first randomly selected 26 high schools, then randomly selected classes of ninth to eleventh grade students, and then randomly selected their sample from within these (Alikasifoglu *et al.*, 2006). This study necessitated negotiating access to 26 schools rather than all 348 high schools in Istanbul.

Sampling bias

The sampling procedure must be as cost-effective and efficient as possible, but it needs to avoid bias. There are a number of different ways in which sampling bias may occur in cross-sectional surveys.

Firstly, if the sampling is not random it may be possible that the sample will not be representative of the population. A non-random sample is one in which the participants are selected by convenience. At worst this is a sample of those who the researcher thinks are most likely to respond. More frequently, though, it is caused by errors of commission or omission in the sampling procedure.

Secondly, if there are errors in the sampling frame, it may be possible that the resulting sample that is drawn from it is also imperfect. It may systematically omit some people from the base population, for example. The electoral registers illustrate this as they do not include people who are disenfranchised by self-selection or law. They are an imperfect sampling frame of the general population as they are not comprehensive enough for research purposes.

Finally, sampling bias may occur if some parts of the population are less likely to participate or are hidden in some way. For example, people living within institutions such as hospitals or prisons are traditionally difficult to include within surveys. Also, young people and those from a black or ethnic minority are less likely to respond. In some situations it may be necessary to over-sample hard to reach groups to achieve representative samples. The Empiric study of psychiatric morbidity amongst people from ethnic minorities is one example of this (Sproston and Nazroo, 2002).

Response rates

In all surveys, researchers will expect a proportion of non-responders. The size of the actual sample of participants will be less than the target sample because of those who choose not to participate. There are a number of possible reasons why people may choose not to participate. For example, they may not feel that the survey is relevant to them or that it would help them in any way; they may lack the time, cognitive abilities or health to participate; or they may simply not be living at the address to which the questionnaire was sent any longer or are not contactable for any other reason. It is an important task of the researchers to ensure that as many people selected to participate are encouraged to do so.

Researchers can improve response rates to cross-sectional surveys by considering a few factors when designing their studies. Firstly, information about the survey needs to be honest and comprehensive, and set out in simple and non-threatening terms. The potential value of the survey to either themselves or people in a similar position to them should be stressed. Potential participants need to be provided with sufficient information about the study to allow them to give informed consent to participate. Respondents to surveys can easily be put off by the manner in which they are asked to participate, so this needs to be carefully considered before-hand.

Secondly, if the burden imposed by participating in the survey is too great, it will deter people from taking part. Long self-complete postal questionnaires, or lengthy interviews, may reduce the number of respondents and introduce bias into the study. However, researchers have to tread a fine line between using brief questionnaires which are not adequately measuring the concepts being studied and over-burdening respondents with lengthy, detailed and comprehensive instruments with proven validity.

Finally, the way in which data is obtained may affect response rates. Postal surveys typically achieve quite low response rates. Non responders tend to have lower socio-economic status and lower educational levels than respondents. This was illustrated in surveys we conducted when validating a questionnaire. We achieved a 34 per cent response rate from the general population in contrast to a 65 per cent response rate from academics within a university (Webber and Huxley, 2007), for example. Telephone interviews can achieve higher response rates, though there may be concerns about whether or not respondents provide meaningful answers. Face to face interviews are the most expensive method of collecting data but are effective in ensuring a response and building rapport with a respondent. Email and Internet surveys are becoming increasingly common, though researchers using this method need to be certain that responses can be attributed to individuals who are selected to participate in the study to ensure that the sample is representative.

Response bias

Response bias occurs when certain participants respond to a survey more frequently than others. For example, in our general population survey which formed part of a process of validating a research instrument measuring access to social capital, we found that more women responded than men and that one of the localities we surveyed was under-represented (Webber and Huxley, 2007). We were able to check the representativeness of the sample as we had the gender and electoral ward of each individual who was sent questionnaires from the electoral registers. Therefore, it is important for researchers to check for response bias if some data, albeit minimal in most cases, is available on all potential respondents. Systematic differences between responders and non-responders can lead to bias. Achieving high response rates is perhaps the best way of minimising the potential of response bias occurring.

Questionnaires

The questionnaires that are used in cross-sectional surveys ('research instruments') must have good validity and reliability. That is, they need to be able to accurately measure what they set out to measure (validity). They need to be validated for the population in which they are being used. For example, if an instrument is to be used in a population of people with mental health problems, but has only previously been used in general population samples, it needs to be tested first to ensure that it is has validity in measuring the same concept in the different population. Further, research instruments need to produce the same results if administered by different researchers (for non self-complete instruments) and if completed at different times (reliability).

Whilst some studies develop their own questionnaires which are piloted with a smaller sub-sample, more rigorous cross-sectional surveys will use research instruments with proven validity and reliability. The validity and reliability of research instruments is often defined statistically using psychometric tests. Prince *et al.* (2003) have a very good chapter on these issues that is worth exploring, though we will summarise the important elements of validity and reliability for you here.

Validity

Validity is defined as the extent to which a research instrument measures what it is supposed to measure. There are three essential components of the validity of research instruments – construct validity, criterion-related validity and concurrent validity. We will use the process of validating a social capital questionnaire for use in the UK general population (Webber and Huxley, 2007) to exemplify each of these.

Construct validity

Construct validity refers to the extent to which the research instrument relates to the concept being measured. In order to establish construct validity, researchers need to identify the full potential of the content to be included in the instrument. Items must then be selected which fully represent the content of the concept being measured. Key informants comment and review the appropriateness of the items selected, a phenomenon which is also referred to as establishing the face or content validity of the instrument. Qualitative methods are used to establish construct validity as it cannot be empirically proven. However, instruments could be tested at an early stage and statistical factor analysis performed to exclude items or identify internal domains.

The questionnaire we validated, the Resource Generator, was developed in the Netherlands. Therefore, we needed to develop appropriate content for the UK general population. We began with a process of exploration with people selected from the UK general population using focus groups. These groups generated a host of new ideas and items for inclusion in the questionnaire. These were refined by a panel of experts who agreed upon a list for inclusion in the instrument. Finally we conducted a field test of the draft questionnaire in the general population and analysed the data using statistical techniques derived from Item Response Theory (Mokken, 1997) to reduce the list of items to only those that were related to the concept.

Criterion-related validity

Criterion-related validity refers to the extent to which the instrument accurately measures the construct it was designed to measure. In psychiatric epidemiology, new instruments are frequently compared to existing standardised questionnaires or lengthy methods of measuring the concept such as by psychiatric diagnostic interviews (Prince *et al.*, 2003). Existing instruments are known as the 'gold standard' and there should be strong agreement between the new instrument and the gold standard when used in the same sample. An alternative method of establishing criterion-related validity is to administer the instrument to a group known to have the construct in abundance in comparison with a group deficit in it. If the results are as predicted, the questionnaire has 'known-group validity'.

As there was no gold standard for measuring access to social capital, we used a known-group validity test to establish the criterion-related validity of the Resource Generator-UK (Webber and Huxley, 2007). We administered it to a random sample of the general population and a sample of academics, as educational attainment is positively correlated with access to social capital (Van der Gaag and Snijders, 2005). We found that academics indeed had access to significantly more social capital than members of the general population.

Concurrent validity

Concurrent validity refers to the extent to which the instrument relates to other measures taken at the same time. The clearest way to demonstrate this is to select an instrument that measures a similar construct and one that measures a very different one. Then administer all three instruments to the same sample and explore the relationships between the three instruments. This is also known as 'convergent-divergent validity'.

To test the concurrent validity of the Resource Generator-UK (RG-UK), we administered it to a random sample of the general population alongside a similar instrument that we had also developed – the Position Generator-UK (PG-UK) – and a measure of locus of control (Coleman and DeLeire, 2003). We expected the RG-UK to be more closely correlated with the PG-UK, which measures a similar construct, than with locus of control, which evaluates individual beliefs about internal or external control over events (Rotter, 1972). In this test, the shared variance of the RG-UK and PG-UK was 48 per cent, in contrast to the 8 per cent shared variance of the RG-UK and locus of control. This indicated that the RG-UK and PG-UK measure a similar construct that is distinct from locus of control.

Reliability

The reliability of a research instrument refers to the extent to which it performs consistently under different conditions. This may be between different researchers, if it was an interview measure, or it may be between different time points. The test-retest method is most commonly used.

Test-retest reliability

The test-retest reliability of an instrument can be established by administering it twice to the same people after a consistent period of time has elapsed. The reliability of the instrument can be estimated by comparing the consistency of the responses between its two administrations. If the researcher obtains the same results on the two administrations, then the reliability coefficient will be 1. Normally, the correlation of measurements across time will fall short of perfection due to different experiences and attitudes that respondents may have encountered from the time of the first completion of the instrument.

In the development of the Resource Generator-UK (Webber and Huxley, 2007), we administered the questionnaire to a sample of people two weeks following its first completion. Most items had good test-retest reliability, though a few performed poorly in this test.

Internal consistency

The internal consistency of an instrument refers to the extent to which its sub-scales or internal items address a common underlying construct. Each item will correlate to a lesser or greater degree with the total score of the instrument. For the whole scale these individual correlations are frequently summarised by Cronbach's alpha (Cronbach, 1951). This is an internal consistency index designed for use with instruments that have no right or wrong answers. This is a very useful tool in social science research, particularly where respondents are asked to rate the extent to which they agree or disagree with a statement on a particular scale.

In our study (Webber and Huxley, 2007) we used a slightly different method of establishing internal consistency. Reliability statistics equivalent to Cronbach's alpha were calculated for the whole scale and four sub-scales. These were all found to have good or excellent reliability.

Analysis of cross-sectional surveys

By their very nature, cross-sectional surveys tend to be descriptive and exploratory. Frequently, they report proportions, means and other descriptive statistics. Occasionally, inter-group comparisons are made using univariate or multivariate statistics.

Prevalence

Most surveys are concerned with prevalence, which refers to the proportion of the sample with a particular condition, trait or phenomenon being measured at a particular time. For example, in psychiatric epidemiology where researchers are interested in finding out the prevalence of depression in a particular area at a particular time, this refers to the proportion of the population who meet the threshold for a clinical diagnosis of depression. This will include both people who met this threshold recently and those who have been depressed for a long time. Hence, prevalence is both a product of the speed at which new 'cases' of depression arise and the speed at which 'cases' cease to have the condition. In terms of depression, which is a relatively transient mental health problem for most people, new 'cases' are quite common, unlike schizophrenia which is less common and more enduring for most people.

Incidence

Incidence refers to the number of new 'cases' in a specified time period (for example one year). This can only be found using cohort studies.

BOX *6.1*

Critical appraisal questions

The following questions will help you to appraise the quality of cross-sectional surveys. Use them when reading research that has used a cross-sectional design.

1   *Is a cross-sectional survey design appropriate for answering the research question(s)?*

2   *What is the target population for this survey?*

3   *How did the researchers generate their sampling frame?*

4   *To what extent is the sampling frame representative of the target population?*

5   *How were participants selected from the sampling frame?*

6   *To what extent was selection bias avoided or limitations acknowledged?*

7   *What were the inclusion and exclusion criteria? To what extent do they limit the generalisability of the findings?*

8   *What was the sample size? Was this justified with a power calculation?*

9   *What was the response rate? Was response bias considered?*

10 *To what extent were the measurements used in the survey valid and reliable?*

11 *What were the main findings of the survey?*

12 *Considering the potential limitations of the study, to what extent are the findings of the survey relevant for social work practice?*

BOX 6.2

Multiple choice self-test

Test your understanding of the ideas contained within this chapter with this quick self-test. The answers can be found in Appendix 1 (pp. 184–6).

1 If you plan to conduct a cross-sectional survey of young people receiving support from Child and Adolescent Mental Health (CAMH) services in the London Borough of Southwark, which one of the following is the base/target population?

    a All young people in the London Borough of Southwark

    b All young people receiving support from CAMH services in the UK

    c All young people receiving support from CAMH services in the London Borough of Southwark

    d All young people in the UK

2 What is a sampling frame? Select the two statements that most accurately describe this.

    a All those who are eligible to take part in the survey

    b All those who respond to a survey

    c An up to date list of all those who may be asked to participate in the study

    d An up to date list of all those who are randomly selected to participate in the study

3 Which one of the following is not a reliable method of selecting a sample for a cross-sectional survey?

    a Clustered random sampling

    b Convenience sampling

    c Simple random sampling

    d Stratified random sampling

4 Which of the following can cause sampling bias? (Select all those that apply)

    a The sampling frame is not representative of the base population

    b People of African-Caribbean origin are not asked to participate as much as people of white British origin in the survey

    c The sample is not selected at random

    d The inclusion and exclusion criteria are not applied rigorously to the sampling frame

5 How can response rates to a postal self-complete questionnaire be improved? (Select all those that apply)

    a Ensure that the questionnaire is long and complex

BOX **6.2** *(CONT.)*

b Provide succinct information about how completion of the questionnaire
may benefit participants or help to improve the services they are receiving ☐

c Follow-up non-responders with reminder letters ☐

d Carefully consider the layout and design of the questionnaire,
including the colour of the paper it is printed on ☐

6 Which of the following are examples of, or could cause, response bias? (Select all
those that apply)

a People with lower educational levels do not participate in the
study as frequently as better educated people ☐

b Men and women both respond in equal proportions to a survey ☐

c Only 10 per cent of people selected to participate actually choose
to undertake the survey ☐

d The sampling frame is not representative of the base population ☐

7 The validity of a research instrument is the extent to which it measures what it is
supposed to measure. True or false.

8 Which of the following is not associated with the validity of a research instrument?

a Known-group validity ☐

b Concurrent validity ☐

c Internal consistency ☐

d Construct validity ☐

9 How might you test the reliability of a research instrument? (Select all those that
apply)

a Ask the same people the same questions again after two weeks
and compare the results ☐

b Examine the items of the instrument to see that they all relate to
the same concept ☐

c Use two different interviewers to ask the same questions to the
same people within a short space of time ☐

d Administer another instrument measuring a different concept
at the same time and compare the results with it ☐

10 You use a cross-sectional survey to find the incidence of a particular phenomenon.
True or false.

Chapter 7

How to critically appraise randomised controlled trials

Introduction

Known as the 'gold standard' method of evaluating interventions, randomised controlled trials are the most scientifically robust, and perhaps most controversial, method of evaluating whether what practitioners or services do actually makes a difference. A good understanding of the design of these studies, and an ability to critically appraise them, is a necessary prerequisite to engaging in debates about their uses in mental health social work research.

This chapter will begin with an introduction to randomised controlled trials and their importance in intervention research, giving some examples relevant to social workers. We will then explore the important aspects of their design that require careful consideration when conducting critical appraisals. Finally, we will introduce some of the controversies surrounding the method and some of their limitations.

Overview

As we have already seen in Chapter 1, randomised controlled trials (RCTs) are methodologically highly regarded. In the Bandolier classification of evidence, for example, they sit at the top with only systematic reviews of RCTs above them. John Last (2000) makes a relatively uncontroversial statement when he claims that RCTs are generally regarded as the most scientifically rigorous method of hypothesis testing available in epidemiology.

RCTs set out to find the effect of an intervention. They answer questions such as:

- Does intervention A work?

- Does intervention A work better than intervention B?

The most important feature of randomised controlled trials which distinguishes them from other studies is the random allocation of participants to the intervention and control groups.

Social work lags behind medicine in using this evaluative method for a number of reasons, including concerns about a loss of professional autonomy in a risk-averse society (Parton, 1996), scepticism about the use of empiricism in social work practice (Trinder, 1996) and the innate problems of defining complex social work interventions to achieve the consistency that is required in a randomised controlled trial. However, RCTs underpin an increasing array of social work practice, particularly within mental health services. Here are a few examples to illustrate the diversity of trials and their growing importance:

EXAMPLE *7.1*

Toroyan, T. et al. (2003) Effectiveness of out-of-home day care for disadvantaged families: randomised controlled trial. *British Medical Journal*, 327, 906–9

Introduction

Social workers routinely refer people to a variety of services, some of which have been evaluated using randomised controlled trials and others which have not. Early years' day care is an example of a social intervention that has been rigorously evaluated. A systematic review of trials found that early years day care improves child development and may reduce antisocial behaviour (Zoritch et al., 2000). However, there is little evidence of their effect on the lives of disadvantaged families. Tami Toroyan and colleagues (2003) conducted an RCT to discover whether early years day care helped to improve maternal employment rates and income in poor families in East London, in addition to outcomes for the children.

Intervention

The study was conducted at an Early Years Centre in the London Borough of Hackney where demand outstripped the supply of places. The centre provided high quality flexible day care for children under the age of five. The centre employed qualified teachers and education was integrated into the care of the children. The centre offered full time or part time places and extended care for working parents. It was even designated by the government as a centre of excellence.

Control group

Parents randomized to the control group had to secure alternative childcare arrangements, including other day care facilities. As the demand for day care was so high, it was expected that the alternative care would be provided by a mixture of nursery schools, parents and other carers.

Inclusion criteria

Families living within the catchment area who had applied for a place at the centre with a child aged between six months and three and a half years were eligible to take part.

Exclusion criteria

None

Sample

Based on a feasibility study (Oakley et al., 2002), they calculated that 140 families were required to detect an improvement in maternal employment rates of 25 per cent.

EXAMPLE **7.1** *(CONT.)*

However, they were only able to recruit 120 families due to a shortage of places at the centre.

Results

There was a non-statistically significant trend towards increased paid employment amongst mothers whose children were allocated places at the centre, but there was no difference in family income. Children in the intervention group were more likely to have otitis media with effusion (an inflammation of the middle ear often caused by respiratory infections and quite common in early years' day care) and to have used more health services.

Further work

This study demonstrated that day care alone cannot alleviate poverty amongst low-income families. Tackling low pay, changing the benefit structure and reducing the costs of day care for poorer families need to be considered as part of a wider anti-poverty strategy. The Early Years Centre is a cost-effective alternative to day care provided by other local services in Hackney, but at additional expense to the public sector (Mujica Mota et al., 2006). However, additional work needs to be conducted looking at longer-term social and educational outcomes for the children who receive early years' day care.

EXAMPLE **7.2**

Bateman, A. and Fonagy, P. (1999) Effectiveness of partial hospitalization in the treatment of borderline personality disorder: A randomized controlled trial, American Journal of Psychiatry, 156, 1563–9

Introduction

Many mental health social workers work with people with a severe borderline personality disorder whose problems are often intractable. Peter Fonagy and Anthony Bateman have developed a mentalization-based treatment which experienced social workers can use in their practice to effect positive change.

Mentalization is 'the capacity to make sense of self and of others in terms of subjective states and mental processes' (Fonagy and Bateman, 2007: 84). Fonagy and Bateman argue that a core feature of borderline personality disorder is insecure attachment relationships. They cite longitudinal evidence of an association between insecure attachment in childhood and borderline personality disorder in adulthood (Lyons-Ruth et al., 2005; Sroufe et al., 2005). As secure relationships in early childhood assist the development of an understanding of other people's behaviour in terms of their likely thoughts and feelings, many people with borderline personality disorder lack the ability to mentalize in the context of relationships with other people. This results in an inability to experience themselves as authors of their actions, for example.

EXAMPLE **7.2** *(CONT.)*

Mentalization-based treatment has been succinctly summarized by Fonagy and Bateman:

> *MBT aims to develop a therapeutic process in which the mind of the patient becomes the focus of treatment. The objective is for the patient to find out more about how he thinks and feels about himself and others, how that dictates his responses, and how errors in understanding himself and others lead to actions in an attempt to retain stability and to make sense of incomprehensible feelings. . . . We recommend an inquisitive or not-knowing stance. This is not synonymous with having no knowledge. The term is an attempt to capture a sense that mental states are opaque and that the therapist can have no more idea of what is in the patient's mind than the patient himself. When the therapist takes a different perspective to the patient this should be verbalised and explored in relation to the patient's alternative perspective, without making assumptions about whose viewpoint has greater validity. The task is to determine the mental processes that have led to alternative viewpoints and to consider each perspective in relation to the other, accepting that diverse outlooks may be acceptable. Where differences are clear and cannot initially be resolved they should be identified, stated, and accepted until resolution seems possible. . . . In MBT the principal aims are always the same – to re-instate mentalizing at the point at which it is lost, to stabilize mentalizing in the context of an attachment relationship, to minimize the likelihood of adverse effects, and to allow the patient to discover himself and others through a mind considering a mind. Careful focus on the patient's current state of mind will achieve these aims. (Fonagy and Bateman, 2007: 93)*

They have also written a fully accessible guide that is worth exploring further (Bateman and Fonagy, 2006).

Intervention

The original trial of mentalization-based treatment (MBT) was conducted in an American psychotherapy unit in the mid-1990s and the first results were published in the American Journal of Psychiatry (Bateman and Fonagy, 1999). The intervention consisted of weekly individual psychoanalytic psychotherapy, thrice weekly group analytic psychotherapy, weekly expressive therapy and a weekly community meeting. The therapy was provided by psychiatric nurses who were trained in MBT but did not have any formal psychotherapy qualifications. The participants in the study attended the psychotherapy unit as day patients.

Control group

The control group received 'standard' treatment from mental health services, which comprised regular review with a senior psychiatrist, inpatient admission as appropriate with aftercare provided by community psychiatric nurses as required.

EXAMPLE 7.2 (CONT.)

Inclusion criteria

A clinical diagnosis of borderline personality disorder as assessed by the Structured Clinical Interview for DSM-III-R (Spitzer et al., 1990) and the Diagnostic Interview for Borderline Patients (Gunderson et al., 1981).

Exclusion criteria

Participants were excluded from the study if they also met the criteria for schizophrenia, bipolar disorder, substance misuse, or mental impairment based on the SCID (Spitzer et al., 1990) or had evidence of organic brain disorder.

Sample

Fourty-four people were randomized to either the intervention or control group. Three participants in the control group crossed over to the intervention group after serious suicide attempts and three participants dropped out of the intervention group. Data on these six participants was not included in the final analysis leaving a total of nineteen in each group.

Results

After 18 months, the number of incidents of self-harming behaviour reduced in the intervention group, but remained constant in the control group. The average length of hospital in-patient admission in the control group at 18 months was significantly more than the intervention group, though there was no difference at 12 months. Further, levels of depression and anxiety in the intervention group decreased while they remained stable in the control group, and significant improvements to the social adjustment and interpersonal problems of the intervention group were also noted after 18 months. A subsequent economic evaluation demonstrated that these improvements were made at no greater cost than standard care (Bateman and Fonagy, 2003).

Further work

It is unclear which component or combination of components of the intervention was effective, although mentalization was a common feature. A further trial is underway of outpatient individual and group psychotherapy to people with a less severe borderline personality disorder to explore whether a more modest programme has equal results. There is also potential to study whether mentalization approaches integrated into routine care provided by mental health social workers are also effective.

EXAMPLE *7.3*

Johnson, S. et al. (2005) Randomised controlled trial of acute mental health care by a crisis resolution team: the north Islington crisis study. British Medical Journal, 331, 599–603

Introduction

The recent 'modernisation' of mental health services in the UK has introduced a range of new services, of which crisis resolution teams are a core component. These teams were largely created by re-allocating psychiatric inpatient resources to community mental health services with the purpose of reducing hospital admissions. They operate predominantly within a medical model of practitioners visiting people in their own homes, maybe several times a day, to administer medication and monitor their mental state. The interventions are usually quite brief and last up to a few weeks at a time. Continuing care is provided by a community mental health team if it is required.

Social workers within these teams can find themselves isolated and unable to implement social models or interventions. There is also a paradox that these services are being run out across the country but evidence for their effectiveness in the UK is somewhat lacking (Pelosi and Jackson, 2000). The trial by Sonia Johnson and colleagues (2005b) was one of the first UK studies to demonstrate its effectiveness in reducing hospital admissions.

Intervention

The intervention group received support from a crisis resolution team that was available 24 hours a day. This team aimed to support people within their own home.

Control group

The control group received 'standard' care from the mental health services which included access to community mental health care, crisis houses and in-patient facilities.

Inclusion criteria

People living within the catchment area aged between 18 and 65 experiencing a mental health crisis severe enough for mental health professionals to consider admission were eligible for entry into the trial. Obtaining informed consent from people in the midst of a crisis is a challenge and poses a number of ethical dilemmas. The researchers gave information to people already in contact with services about the study and gave them the opportunity to opt out of randomisation in the event of a mental health crisis. People who lacked the capacity to consent to the study in a crisis were included if their carer assented for their entry. Consent for the follow-up research interview was obtained separately when the participants had regained their capacity.

Exclusion criteria

People in a mental health crisis who lacked the capacity to consent for randomisation, and lacked a carer to assent for them, were not eligible for the study.

EXAMPLE **7.3** *(CONT.)*

Sample

A total of 260 people were randomised to either the crisis resolution team or treatment as usual, just short of the 268 the research team had aimed to recruit. In comparison with a previous naturalistic study in the same borough (Johnson et al., 2005a), people within this sample were significantly less likely to have been compulsorily admitted in the previous two years, to be rated by staff as uncooperative at initial assessment, to be psychotic or manic, but were more likely to be depressed.

Results

The study found that people receiving support from the crisis resolution team were less likely to be admitted to hospital in the eight weeks following the crisis and were more satisfied with their care. However, the crisis resolution team did not reduce the likelihood of compulsory admission in the six months after the crisis.

Further work

This study gave an indication of the likely effectiveness of crisis resolution teams in terms of reducing hospital admissions, but few other outcomes were measured. More research is required on other outcomes of crisis intervention teams and in particular the role of social work with them.

Essential components of randomised controlled trials

The essential components of randomised controlled trials are summarised in Figure 7.1.

Before the study begins there needs to be a convincing rationale for the trial. This is established from a thorough literature review. A clearly focused research question or hypothesis is required to ensure that outcomes are defined at the outset, which provides clarity and transparency in the design of the trial. The study population needs to be defined with clear inclusion and exclusion criteria for the sample. The sample is then recruited and randomised to one of two or more groups. Often there is only one control group, but some trials test two interventions and have a third group receiving standard care in a control group. In terms of the research procedures at baseline and follow-up, control and intervention groups are treated in exactly the same way. The same measures are taken from both groups at the same time in the same way. The only difference between the groups is the intervention that they receive. The measures taken from the two groups are compared and conclusions about differences between the groups are obtained.

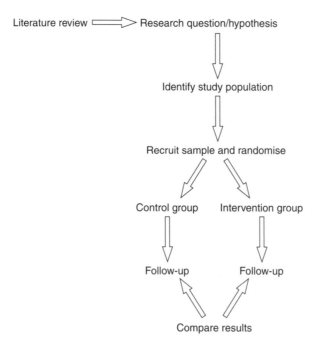

Figure 7.1 Essential components of a randomised controlled trial

Let us explore each of these stages in a little more detail.

Literature review

A comprehensive literature review is required before a trial can begin to be planned. The main purpose of this is to discover if the intervention has been evaluated before. If the search illustrates that there is compelling evidence in the public domain of the effectiveness of the intervention in the population in question, it may not be necessary or ethical to carry out the trial. In the field of social interventions, this is rarely the case as there are comparatively few trials.

The dilemma whether to undertake a trial and randomise people to either the intervention or control group is known as 'equipoise' (Lilford and Jackson, 1995). This describes the state of being equally poised between different interventions and there is genuine uncertainty about which is the most effective in any particular practice situation. It would be unethical to randomise someone to a control group if there was already convincing evidence that the intervention was effective. Similarly, it may be unethical to provide an intervention which has not been rigorously evaluated and its effectiveness demonstrated. If the intervention is likely to lead to improved outcomes, but there is insufficient evidence of this, an RCT may be justified.

Aims and objectives

The trial needs to have a clearly focused research question. It needs to state a primary hypothesis to be tested with a primary outcome measure. There can be secondary research questions and hypotheses, but these need to be limited so as to avoid 'data dredging' (exploring results for a statistically significant result with no clear rationale for doing so).

Small pilots are often conducted prior to trials to provide estimates of the likely effect of the intervention in the particular population the researchers wish to evaluate it in. These studies provide information for power calculations which determine how many people need to be recruited to demonstrate the effectiveness of an intervention. All this information needs to be written into the aims and objectives of the study and provided to the ethics committee before the trial commences. This helps to ensure that no more people are recruited than are needed.

Population and sample

The target population, as in cross-sectional studies, is the group of people to whom you would like to be able to generalise the findings of the study. So, for the three examples we have provided above, the target populations are:

Example 1: families with children aged between six months and three and a half years.

Example 2: people with a clinical diagnosis of borderline personality disorder but no other severe mental health problem.

Example 3: people aged between 18 and 65 experiencing a mental health crisis severe enough for mental health professionals to consider admission.

It is a matter of critical judgement whether the results of a trial conducted in a deprived location such as the London Borough of Hackney, for example, could be generalised to a wealthier location such as the Royal Borough of Kensington & Chelsea. Also, it is a matter of debate whether trials conducted in America or other developed countries could be generalised to the UK. As part of the critical appraisal process, it is important to consider the composition of the study population and the socio-economic environment they are drawn from.

The study population is the group of people from whom you will select your sample. It needs to be as representative of the target population as possible. However, it is frequently not possible to develop accurate sampling frames. This is particularly true when conducting trials which have diagnostic inclusion criteria. These inclusion criteria often need to be applied by researchers and it is often not possible to interview everyone with a particular mental health problem to determine their potential eligibility for a trial. For this reason, it can be very difficult to develop accurate lists of potentially eligible people and recruitment often relies on strong working relationships with practitioners who may be able to refer people they are working with for assessment for eligibility for the trial. This is one of the reasons why trials are often conducted in single sites, although organisations such as the Mental Health Research Network can facilitate recruitment to trials in a number of different locations across the UK.

The sample is the group of people who participate in the study. Ideally, they will be as representative as possible of the target population. The size of the sample is determined by a power calculation.

Inclusion and exclusion criteria

Randomised controlled trials have strict eligibility criteria which clearly define who can and cannot be included in the study. The inclusion and exclusion criteria for the RCT of mentalization-based treatment for borderline personality disorder (Bateman and Fonagy, 1999), for example, are typical of trials for a particular disorder. They state clearly that people with other mental health problems cannot be included.

Inclusion criteria in mental health trials often insist on homogenous samples. To achieve this they screen out people who may have more than one mental health problem, known as co-morbidity. Co-morbidity in trials makes it difficult for researchers to interpret the findings as they will not know if the other mental health problems have influenced the effectiveness of the intervention or not. Interestingly, a naturalistic study of psychological therapies found that people with depression and other mental health problems required about twice as many therapy sessions to recover as those with just depression (Morrison *et al.*, 2003).

The difficulty with over-restrictive inclusion and exclusion criteria is that they can limit the generalisability of a trial. In their systematic review of treatments for depression, panic and generalised panic disorder, Westen & Morrison (2001) found that up to 70 per cent of people screened for entry into the trials were excluded. Including such a select group of people in trials raises questions about their generalisability, as they could only be generalised to people who often have only one diagnosed condition which frequently does not apply to many people with mental health problems.

It may be useful at this point to make a distinction between efficacy and effectiveness trials. Broadly speaking, efficacy trials test whether interventions work in a specific population. They usually have restrictive eligibility criteria and exclude people with co-morbid mental health problems. In contrast, effectiveness trials have less restrictive eligibility criteria and test whether the intervention will work in the real world. As you will see from the following examples, efficacy trials include very a select group of participants (Box 7.1), whereas effectiveness trials are more likely to reflect real life clinical populations (Box 7.2).

BOX **7.1**

Efficacy trial inclusion and exclusion criteria
Efficacy of paroxetine in the treatment of adolescent depression (Keller et al., 2001)

Inclusion criteria

- *medically healthy young people aged 12 to 18 fulfilling the DSM-IV (American Psychiatric Association, 1994) criteria for a current episode of major depression of at least 8 weeks' duration;*

- *total score of at least 12 on the 17-item Hamilton Rating Scale for depression;*

- *score of less than 60 on the Children's Global Assessment Scale;*

- *score of at least 80 on the Peabody Picture Vocabulary Test.*

Exclusion criteria

- *a current or lifetime DSM-IV diagnosis of bipolar disorder, schizoaffective disorder, eating disorder, alcohol or substance use disorder, obsessive-compulsive disorder, autism/pervasive developmental disorder, or organic brain disorder;*

- *a diagnosis of post-traumatic stress disorder within 12 months of recruitment;*

- *current suicidal ideation with intent or specific plan or a history of suicide attempts by drug overdose;*

- *any medical condition in which the use of an antidepressant was contraindicated;*

- *current psychotropic drug use;*

- *an adequate trial of antidepressant medication within six months of study entry, or exposure to investigational drug use either within 30 days of study entry or within five half-lives of the drug;*

- *females who were pregnant or breastfeeding and those who were sexually active and not using reliable contraception.*

Informed consent

Gaining informed consent from participants is a key ethical issue in conducting a trial. Informed consent is defined as:

A person gives informed consent to take part in a clinical trial only if his decision:

(a) *is given freely after that person is informed of the nature, significance, implications and risks of the trial; and*

(b) *either:*

   (i) *is evidenced in writing, dated and signed, or otherwise marked, by that person so as to indicate his consent, or*

89

BOX *7.2*

Effectiveness trial inclusion and exclusion criteria
Antenatal structured psychosocial intervention for postnatal depression (Brugha et al., 2000)

Inclusion criteria

- *women aged over 16 at booking for obstetric care in a first pregnancy;*

- *residing within a reasonable travelling distance of the hospital;*

- *capable of understanding and completing screening questionnaires in English;*

- *presence of any one of six depression items on a modified General Health Questionnaire (GHQ-D) (Surtees and Miller, 1990);*

capable of giving written, informed consent.

Exclusion criteria

None

(ii) *if the person is unable to sign or to mark a document so as to indicate his consent, is given orally in the presence of at least one witness and recorded in writing. (National Research Ethics Service, 2007)*

Potential participants always need to have time to consider written and verbal information on the trial, to ask any questions and consult with family. If they agree to participate it is on the understanding that withdrawal from the trial will not affect their health or social care in any way. Additionally, they are not required to give a reason for their withdrawal.

Randomisation

Randomisation is the single most important component of a randomised controlled trial and distinguishes it from other methods of studying interventions. Its purpose is to ensure that all variables that may have an effect on the outcome, other than the intervention being evaluated, are distributed as equally as possible between the intervention and control groups. This will help researchers to measure the effect of the intervention more accurately.

The process of randomisation is not undertaken by researchers working on the trial to avoid any potential for bias. This is often out-sourced to specialist randomisation centres such as the Institute of Psychiatry's Clinical Trials Unit. Researchers can telephone these centres 24 hours a day to randomise participants to either the intervention or control group, a process which is conducted by computer to ensure equal numbers in both groups and a complete random selection of group.

Studies indicate that if the process is not concealed, the effect of the intervention is overestimated (Kunz and Oxman, 1998; Schultz *et al.*, 1995). This may occur if a doctor was recruiting her own patients for her own study and was conducting her own randomisation, for example. In a scenario such as this there would be no safeguards to prevent the potential for bias in group allocation.

Randomisation in trials is not always at the unit of an individual. It may be at a higher level such as a GP practice, local authority or mental health trust. One such example of this is the first randomised controlled trial of the new graduate primary care mental health workers (Lester *et al.*, 2007). This was a cluster randomised controlled trial in which 19 GP practices in Birmingham were allocated at random to the intervention group, which had access to a graduate worker, or the control group, which didn't.

Intervention and control groups

The intervention group receives the new intervention being evaluated and the control group receives an alternative intervention. The choice of an alternative intervention is crucial for demonstrating the effectiveness of the new intervention.

In pharmacological trials, the control group may receive a placebo, which is an inactive drug. This would be the case for health problems which have no established treatments. Complex interventions addressing novel problems with no established intervention with which to compare them with may have to develop a neutral intervention for the control group. A trial of joint crisis plans which aimed to reduce compulsory psychiatric admissions, for example, gave information sessions to the control group (Henderson *et al.*, 2004).

If there was already an established intervention for the health or social problem, it would be unethical to withhold this. In these cases the trial will test a new intervention against the standard treatment. For example, in trials of assertive outreach in mental health services the control group receive treatment as usual from the community mental health team (e.g. Burns *et al.*, 1999).

Another alternative is to give the intervention group an existing intervention supplemented with a new one, with the control group having just the standard treatment. For example, a trial of cognitive behavioural therapy (CBT) for psychosis provided CBT in addition to standard mental health services to the intervention group, whereas the control group just received the standard mental health services (Kuipers *et al.*, 1997).

A trial which ensures that everyone receives the intervention – eventually – is the waiting-list controlled trial. Participants are randomised to receiving the intervention now or later on. Those who receive it at a later point form the control group. An example of this is a trial of befriending for women with depression (Harris *et al.*, 1999).

Blinding

Blinding is the degree to which participants and / or researchers are aware of group allocation. The scientific justification for blinding in randomised controlled trials is to minimise the possibility of bias. If a participant knew which group they were in it would possible that they may over-emphasise their symptoms or problems, or answer questions differently to demonstrate how effective the intervention has been, or not been, for example. If a researcher knew which group a participant was in, they may probe for different responses or follow-up those who received the intervention more rigorously to find the desired effect, for example.

The most scientifically rigorous method is a double blind trial, in which both the participants and researchers are unaware of which group they are in. This is usually only achievable in pharmacological trials in which a placebo could be disguised as the drug being tested.

The most common method found in social care trials, or those involving complex health and social care interventions, is single blinding. This means that either the participants or the researchers do not know who is in which group. Often it is difficult to disguise the intervention from participants, so all attempts are made to keep it hidden from researchers. Different researchers conduct the baseline and follow-up interviews from those involved in informing the participants which group they are in and they ask the participants not to disclose which intervention they received. The degree of concealment of group allocation is tested by asking the researchers afterwards which group they thought the participants were in. If they guessed correctly each time then it is likely that the group concealment process did not work in some way. Interventions where the group allocation can be hidden from the participants, but not from the researchers, are also known as single blind trials.

Measurements

Researchers take measurements at baseline (at the point of group allocation before the intervention begins) and at the end of the intervention (follow-up). Occasionally intermediate measurements are taken during the intervention. Additionally, longer-term follow-up measurements are taken after completion of the trial. Each trial will vary in the number and frequency of its follow-ups and, in appraising papers, it is important to see whether the intervention is tested after a short or long follow-up period.

At baseline various socio-demographic data is obtained from the participants. This may be income, ethnic origin, employment status, service use, to name but a few. The intervention and control groups are compared on these variables to see if the randomisation process has worked. If it was successful then both groups should be comparable. This means that other variables which may affect the results of the trial are distributed equally between the groups.

The outcome measures are also taken at baseline to facilitate comparisons at follow-up. Outcome measures could be anything as diverse as mental health, quality of life or number of hospital admissions in the previous six months, for example. In large trials, several outcome measures are frequently taken. In the UK 700 trial of intensive case management (Burns et al., 1999), for example, the following outcome measures were taken:

- days in hospital with psychiatric disorders*;

- comprehensive psychiatric rating scale (Asberg *et al.*, 1978);

- scale for the assessment of negative symptoms (Andreasen, 1989);

- abnormal involuntary movement scale (Guy, 1996);

- WHO disability assessment schedule (Jablensky *et al.*, 1980);

- Lancashire Quality of Life Profile (Oliver *et al.*, 1997);

- Camberwell Assessment of Need (Phelan *et al.*, 1995);

- Satisfaction with health services (Tyrer and Remington, 1979).

* Primary outcome measure

The research instruments that are used need to have proven reliability and validity. This is particularly important in trials where several researchers administer interviews to different participants in different sites. Sometimes trials will use several instruments to measure the primary outcome, although only one of these will be the primary outcome measure. In Brugha and colleagues' (2000) trial of an antenatal intervention, for example, they used three measures of depression: the modified GHQ-D (Surtees and Miller, 1990) (primary outcome measure), the Edinburgh Post-Natal Depression Scale (Cox *et al.*, 1987) and the Schedules for Clinical Assessment in Neuropsychiatry (Wing *et al.*, 1990).

Follow-up

Following up, and obtaining complete measurements, from as many participants as possible is a crucial aspect to any longitudinal study. It is particularly important in a randomised controlled trial where loss to follow-up may reduce the statistical power that is required to evaluate the intervention. Incomplete data sets may also introduce bias into the study, particularly if the people who dropped out were similar in some way or were all from the control group, for example. This could introduce a form of selection bias into the study as the composition of the groups starting the trial may be different from those completing it.

As we have seen previously, the measurements at both baseline and follow-up are taken by researchers who are blind to the participant's group allocation, where possible, to avoid any potential for researcher bias.

Analysis

On completion of the trial, outcomes of the intervention and control groups are collated and compared using multivariate analysis, which controls for the effect of any potential confounding variables. The analysis strategy is specified prior to the commencement of the trial to avoid researcher bias whereby there may be a temptation to amend the analysis to favour the outcomes of the intervention group, for example.

Intention to treat analysis

An 'intention to treat' analysis is frequently used in randomised controlled trials. This means that all those in the intervention and control groups are included in the analysis, regardless of whether or not they completed the trial, dropped out or died. It is the offer of the intervention that is being evaluated and not whether it was completed in full by everyone.

An intention to treat analysis helps to evaluate an intervention's effectiveness in real-life situations. It also guards against conscious or unconscious attempts to influence the results of the study by excluding odd outcomes. Further, it also guards against bias being introduced when dropping-out is related to the outcome. For example, in Brugha and colleagues' (2000) trial of an antenatal intervention which had depression as its primary outcome, it may be possible that those who were depressed dropped out more frequently from the trial. Although this wasn't the case, if those who dropped out were excluded, this may have led to the over-estimation of the effect of the intervention.

Number needed to treat

Quite often trials will report the 'number needed to treat'. This is the number of participants from the study population who need to be given the new intervention in order to achieve the desired outcome in one participant. It is a measure of the effectiveness of the intervention. Ideally, the number needed to treat will be small so that as few people as possible do not achieve the desired outcome.

The number needed to treat (NNT) is the reciprocal of the difference between the proportion achieving the outcome in the intervention group and the proportion achieving the outcome in the control group. Or, expressed as a formula, it is:

$$NNT = \frac{1}{(\% \text{ benefiting from the intervention} - \% \text{ benefiting in the control group})}$$

For example, if the outcome of a trial was recovery from depression and there was a 4 per cent recovery rate in the control group and a 10 per cent recovery rate in the intervention group, then 17 people would need to be treated in order that one person recovers. Recovery in this one person can be attributed to the intervention and not to chance.

$$NNT = \frac{1}{(0.10 - 0.04)} = \frac{1}{0.06} = 17$$

Patient preference trials

Before we conclude this chapter, it is worth mentioning some of the criticisms and limitations of the randomised controlled trial methodology.

Firstly, contemporary randomised controlled trials in mental health face difficulties in recruiting participants. Despite the facilitation role provided by the Mental Health Research Network, there is still a potential for trials to under-represent the population (Slade and Priebe, 2001). Samples may be biased towards enthusiastic volunteers who do not have a strong preference for which intervention they receive.

The notion of 'patient preference trials' in mental health research has been developed to improve their generalisability and to overcome potential confounding factors such as the perceptions, preferences and experiences of potential participants (Howard and Thornicroft, 2006).

Strong preferences deter people from entering randomised controlled trials as they do not wish to be randomised. As Howard and Thornicroft (2006) observe, the absence of these people may limit the generalisability of the findings of the trial. If people with strong preferences do enter a trial but are not randomised to their preferred intervention, they may withdraw from the study. If they do receive their preference, they may have a better outcome irrespective of the effectiveness of the intervention itself.

Patient preference trials are a way around this problem. People with strong preferences are allowed to choose which intervention they would like. Those with no preference are randomised as usual to either the intervention or the control group. If the randomised participants are otherwise similar to those who express a strong preference, this will boost the external validity and representativeness of the randomised sample, as demonstrated by Ward and colleagues (2000) in their trial of non-directive counselling, cognitive behavioural therapy and GP care for depression.

Processes within complex interventions

It can be difficult to understand how complex interventions evaluated using the randomised controlled trial methodology actually work and produce an effect. In response to this, the Medical Research Council developed a framework for the development and evaluation of RCTs for complex interventions which recommended that qualitative methods are embedded within the trial to explore the processes at work within the intervention (Medical Research Council, 2000).

Qualitative methods such as ethnography help to provide insights into the inner workings of an intervention and the interactions between clinicians and service users. As an example of the insights that ethnography can provide, John Larsen (2007) conducted a person-centred ethnographic study of a Danish early intervention in psychosis service, which involved two years' participant observation and repeated interviews with 15 service users.

He concluded that:

> *The study of the Danish early intervention in psychosis service suggests a need*
> *to carefully examine the ways in which staff interact with clients to negotiate*
> *meaning in respect to the psychotic experiences and how these may be influenced*
> *by the overall therapeutic theoretical framework in the individual services, as well as*

staff training and management support structures. But equally important, the study points to the importance of the type and quality of the personal relationship between staff and clients, and whether the staff adopts an authoritative or an equalitarian attitude to negotiate meanings and life directions. (Larsen, 2007: 343)

Evidence 'biased' health and social care

As a result of the hegemony of the RCT method of evaluating interventions, the evidence base within health and social care has become biased towards the 'easily measurable'. A quick search of any database will reveal that pharmacological treatments and brief psychological interventions such as cognitive behavioural therapy have well developed bodies of evidence of their effectiveness from systematic reviews of a number of randomised controlled trials. Unfortunately this is not the case for social care.

The social care evidence base is vastly under-developed in comparison to health or psychology. Quite simply, social interventions are inherently complex and are much less amendable to the randomised controlled trial methodology. Statutory work conducted by mental health social workers cannot be subjected to the rigours of an RCT, for example.

The result is that social care and social interventions figure very poorly in clinical guidelines. For example, in the National Institute for Health and Clinical Excellence guidelines for the treatment of depression (National Collaborating Centre for Mental Health, 2004), there is reference to only one social intervention. The guidelines suggest that befriending may be an effective intervention, a recommendation based on the previously mentioned trial conducted by Tirril Harris and colleagues' (1999).

It is possible to argue that this doesn't really matter as clinical guidelines are not important for social workers. However, in a climate of evidence-based practice, effective interventions are more likely to attract funding and social workers may be losers in this if they are unable to demonstrate that their interventions work. Herein lies a challenge for social work practitioners and researchers who need to collaborate to carefully define the various components of the complex interventions they deliver and evaluate them using robust randomised controlled trials that measure appropriate outcomes. Only then can a comparable body of knowledge be developed that will inform policy-makers about the effectiveness or otherwise of social work.

BOX 7·3

Critical appraisal questions

The following questions will help you to appraise the quality of randomised controlled trials (RCTs). Use them when reading a paper reporting the results of an RCT.

1 Did the study ask a clearly focused question?

2 Was this a RCT and was it appropriately so?

3 Were participants appropriately allocated to intervention and control groups?

4 Were participants, staff and study personnel 'blind' to participants' study group?

5 Were all of the participants who entered the trial accounted for at its conclusion?

6 Were all the participants in all groups followed up and data collected in the same way?

7 Did the study have enough participants to minimise the play of chance?

8 How are the results presented and what is the main result?

9 How precise are the results?

10 Were all important outcomes considered so the results can be applied?

BOX 7·4

Multiple choice self-test

Test your understanding of the ideas contained within this chapter with this quick self-test. The answers can be found in Appendix 1.

1 Which of the following questions can an RCT answer? (Select all those that apply)

  a Is intervention X more effective than intervention Y?

  b Is intervention Y effective in population A?

  c How does intervention Y work?

  d Is intervention X more effective than intervention Y or intervention Z?

2 What is equipoise? (Select one option only)

  a An intervention that has been rigorously evaluated before

  b The state of genuine uncertainty about the effectiveness of an intervention

  c An intervention that has not been rigorously evaluated before

  d The process of randomising participants to either the intervention or control group

3 Which one of the following statements is not true?

  a The target population is the group of people to whom you would like to be able to generalise the findings of the study

BOX 7.4 *(CONT.)*

b The study population needs to be as representative of the target population as possible ☐

c The size of the study population is determined by a power calculation ☐

d The sample is the group of people who participate in the study ☐

4 Which of the following are true of efficacy trials? (Select all that apply)

a They often have numerous inclusion and exclusion criteria ☐

b They test whether interventions work in real-life settings ☐

c They often exclude people with co-morbid mental health problems ☐

d They are often conducted before effectiveness trials ☐

5 Why is randomisation so important in RCTs? (Select the most important reason only)

a It is a convenient way of deciding who should receive the intervention and who shouldn't ☐

b It ensures that variables which may have an impact on the outcome are distributed equally between the intervention and control group ☐

c It reduces the potential for selection bias ☐

d It ensures that the outcome is measured more accurately ☐

6 Blinding in randomised controlled trials reduces the potential for researcher bias. True or false?

7 Why is it important to follow-up as many participants in a RCT as possible? (Select all those that apply)

a To increase the statistical power of the study ☐

b To minimise the potential for selection bias ☐

c To minimise the potential for researcher bias ☐

d To ensure follow-up data is as complete as possible ☐

8 A large 'number needed to treat' (NNT) indicates a more effective intervention than one with a small NNT. True or false?

9 Which of the following are limitations of RCTs? (Select all those that apply)

a RCTs often face recruitment difficulties leading to questions about their representativeness ☐

b RCTs of complex interventions don't always tell you how the interventions actually work ☐

c RCTs bias the evidence base in favour of interventions that are easier to deliver and evaluate ☐

d RCTs give limited information about the experience of receiving the intervention ☐

Chapter 8

How to critically appraise cohort studies

Cohort studies are frequently used in mental health research which informs the practice of mental health social workers, in particular by exploring cause-and-effect relationships. This chapter will explore the essential features of cohort studies and three different types – classical, population and historical – with examples of each. It will then examine the individual components in a little more detail and the key questions to ask when appraising them.

Essential features

Cohort studies are longitudinal, that is they track change over time. In common with randomised controlled trials (RCTs) they obtain data about individuals or groups from at least two points in time. However, where they differ from RCTs is that they are observational in nature and not necessarily associated with an intervention of any sort.

Their essential purpose is to examine cause-effect relationships. They can answer questions such as:

- Does variable A result in outcome B?

- Does expressed emotion cause people with schizophrenia to relapse?

- Does social support help people to recover from depression?

A key feature is that cohort study participants are defined, or selected, on the basis of the hypothesised risk factor. In the case of these three examples, risk factors are variable A, expressed emotion and social support. A risk factor doesn't have to be a negative thing, as implied in the notion of 'risk'. It is a description of a phenomenon that may have an influence on something else such as the course of a mental health problem, for example. Therefore, if we were answering these questions, we would select participants on the basis of their possession, or otherwise, of variable A, expressed emotion or social support. As we will see in Chapter 9, this is the main difference between cohort studies and case control studies.

It is important to ascertain the risk factor separately from the outcome. For example, it is important to know the nature and extent of social support before discovering its effect on recovery from depression. This may sound obvious, but it is possible in the design of some cohort studies to know the outcome first. In these cases, bias may be introduced into the study through the possibility of manipulating the risk factor in some way.

Cohort studies allow researchers to estimate the incidence of a particular outcome, unlike the prevalence which can be found using a cross-sectional design. This may be the onset of schizophrenia, for example, which may be investigated alongside a number of potential risk factors with minimal information bias.

Before we explore these key features in a little more detail, let us look at some different types of cohort studies and some examples of these.

Classical cohort study

The classical cohort study is the 'purest' form of cohort study where a single risk factor is studied. Participants are selected on the basis of this single risk factor, which can be quite rare, and then followed up over a period of time to see if a particular outcome occurs. One group of people who have been exposed to the risk factor is selected alongside a similar group of people who have not come into contact with it. It is important that neither group contains any individuals with the outcome at the beginning of the study. If this is a mental health problem, for example, it is important for all the participants to be mentally healthy if the study is determining incidence rates for a particular disorder.

Both the group who have been exposed to the risk factor and the control group are followed up for a certain period of time to see if the outcome of interest has developed more in one group than the other. As the exposure to a risk factor is determined at the start of the study, a cohort study can clarify the temporal sequence between the occurrence of a risk factor and an outcome with minimal information bias.

A limitation of the classical cohort study design is that it is limited to the study of a single risk factor. It is also typically very expensive and it can take many years to produce a result as researchers have to wait for the follow-up period to elapse. Further, this type of cohort study is prone to selection bias arising from loss-to-follow-up and is generally not suited to the study of rare outcomes as very large cohorts would need to be recruited and followed-up.

A good example is Peter Warr and Paul Jackson's (1985) study of the psychological impact of unemployment, although this is a slight variation on the classical cohort study design as it does not have a comparison group (example 8.1).

Population cohort study

The most prevalent type of cohort study in the mental health social science literature is the population cohort study. Population cohorts are large representative groups of people who are followed up numerous times over many years. They are often representative of the general population, or other large populations. Participants, who provide data for a population cohort, or a 'panel', answer numerous questions about many aspects of their lives. This allows researchers to test numerous hypotheses involving a range of risk factors

EXAMPLE *8.1*

Unemployment and mental health (Warr and Jackson, 1985)

Background

Cross sectional studies have indicated that the psychological health of men who have been unemployed for more than three months is significantly worse than those out of work for shorter periods. Both groups were significantly less healthy than men in jobs (Jackson and Warr, 1984). However, it is difficult to discern patterns of causality from these cross-sectional findings.

Method

Nine-month cohort study of 954 unemployed men who were registered at 41 Unemployment Benefit Offices throughout the UK in 1982. Seventy-five per cent (n = 711) were followed up at time two. Psychological ill-health was measured using the General Health Questionnaire (GHQ) (Goldberg, 1981) at both time points in addition to questions about physical health, their commitment to employment, job seeking, income, financial strain, number of dependants, financial support and social contact. All men had held their previous job for at least three months and had been engaged in unskilled or semi-skilled manual work. Of the 711 who were followed up, 11 were excluded from the analysis as they had retired and a further 71 were excluded as they had worked and then became unemployed again.

Results

Participants who had been unemployed for less than three months at time one had significantly poorer psychological health at time two if they remained unemployed. However, the psychological health of those who had initially been unemployed for longer than three months at time one did not worsen at time two if they were still unemployed. Those who were re-employed at time two experienced improved psychological health and less financial strain than those who were continuously unemployed.

Conclusions

This study supports previous cross-sectional research which found a plateau effect for psychological health resulting from unemployment. The most significant damaging effect on psychological health comes during the first few months of unemployment. Re-employment has the opposite effect.

Implications for practice

Although this study is rather dated, it remains important in the literature on unemployment and mental health as it was the first to test these hypotheses longitudinally in a large sample. It suggests that interventions should be targeted towards assisting people to re-enter the labour market at an early point to improve their psychological health.

and outcomes. It is the ability of the population cohort to address a range of research questions that forms the main difference between this design and a classical cohort study. Also, the ability to assess multiple outcomes distinguishes this type of cohort study from a case-control study.

The Millennium Cohort Study is an example of a 'live' cohort. It is collecting data on over 18,000 children who were born in 2000. Its aim is to understand how the social conditions surrounding birth and early childhood affect people throughout their lives. It also aims to explore advantage and disadvantage in education, health, employment and the parenting of the next generation.

Other examples of population cohorts in the UK are:

1946 – National Survey of Health and Development

1958 – National Child Development Study

1970 – British Cohort Study

1991 – Avon Longitudinal Study of Parents and Children

2006 – Born in Bradford

An example of a population cohort study is a study by Stephen Stansfeld and colleagues (1998) which used data from a cohort of civil servants (Whitehall II study, Example 8.2).

EXAMPLE 8.2

Social support and common mental disorders (Stansfeld et al., 1998)

Background

Social support is hypothesised to be beneficial for mental health in two ways. Firstly, it can have a direct effect on well-being and, secondly, it can moderate the impact of stressors on health. Few studies have examined the associations between the different types of social support and mental health using a longitudinal design.

Method

This study used data from the Whitehall II study of British civil servants (n = 7,697). Social support was measured using the Close Persons Questionnaire (Stansfeld and Marmot, 1992) and common mental disorders were measured using the General Health Questionnaire (Goldberg and Williams, 1988). Social support at baseline was used to predict the likelihood of a common mental disorder about five years later.

Results

The analysis showed that low emotional support in men at baseline significantly increased the likelihood of having a common mental disorder at follow-up. A similar trend was not found for women. However, having negative social relationships was a predictor of

EXAMPLE 8.2 (CONT.)

common mental disorder for both men and women at follow-up. There was no evidence of social support acting as a buffer against stressful life events for men or women in the sample.

Conclusions

Different types of social support are risk factors for common mental disorders such as anxiety and depression, but work differently for men and women. A limitation to this study is that the sample is occupationally defined and is not representative of the general population. It is likely that civil servants had more access to social support than the general population. This study needs to be replicated in other general population cohorts.

Implications for practice

Interventions that support people who have difficulties in their relationships with others are likely to prevent the onset of depression and anxiety.

Historical cohort study

Both the classical and population cohort studies collect data prospectively. That is they collect information about the risk factor first and then about the outcome at a later date. However, it is also possible to collect data for a cohort study retrospectively and this is known as a historical cohort study. In this design researchers collect data about both the risk factor and the outcome by looking back at pre-existing data sets.

Historical cohorts are particularly convenient for researchers as they don't have to wait lengthy periods of time to collect the follow-up data as it would have occurred already. Also, data about the risk factors is already present and doesn't need to be obtained through original research. Information bias shouldn't be a problem if the data about the risk factor was collected independently of the outcome. Finally, historical cohorts are particularly useful for answering questions that require a long period of time to elapse between the risk factor and the outcome occurring.

The main limitation of this method is that the data used in these studies is often collected for other purposes and may be incomplete or not measure the concept adequately.

A good use of the historical cohort study design is in the study of cannabis use and schizophrenia (e.g. Zammit *et al.*, 2002, Example 8.3). As very few people in the general population suffer from schizophrenia, researchers would have to recruit a very large sample to study this prospectively. However, using data that has already been collected for other purposes allows researchers to study a relatively rare outcome such as onset of psychosis and schizophrenia.

Let us now examine the essential ingredients of cohort studies.

EXAMPLE *8.3*

Cannabis use and onset of schizophrenia (Zammit et al., 2002)

Background

The relationship between cannabis use and onset of psychosis is complex. While previous studies indicate that heavy cannabis usage leads to brief psychotic episodes, it is unclear whether cannabis increases the risk of psychosis persisting after abstention from using the drug. No other cohort studies have investigated this risk.

Method

The cohort consisted of 50,087 Swedish men who were conscripted for compulsory military training in 1969–70. Only 2–3 per cent of the male population were excused conscription on health grounds, increasing the generalisability of the findings of this study. Data on the risk factor (cannabis use) were obtained at the time of conscription in 1969–70. Outcome data was obtained from the Swedish national hospital discharge register which has a virtually complete record of all psychiatric admissions up to 1996. This is a reliable record of the incidence of schizophrenia as over 90 per cent of people with this diagnosis were admitted to hospital for treatment at this time (Geddes and Kendell, 1995). People with psychosis at baseline (conscription in 1969–70) were excluded.

Results

Frequent cannabis use is associated with an increased risk of developing schizophrenia. Men who had used cannabis over 50 times were at the highest risk. This association is not explained by other illicit drug use or personality traits relating to social integration.

Conclusions

This study suggests that cannabis increases the risk of schizophrenia by 30 per cent. Although occasional use does not appear harmful, heavy use could be detrimental to mental health. This study needs to be replicated in more recent cohorts to see if a similar effect is still present. The effects on women also need to be similarly tested.

Implications for practice

Practitioners can advise men that they work with that frequent and heavy cannabis use increases the risk of developing schizophrenia in later life.

Population

The first aspect of a cohort study to consider is the study population, as this determines who the results could be generalised to. For example, the cohort of British civil servants in the Whitehall II study has been used to answer a number of research questions but it is questionable whom these results could be generalised to. It is possible that they may be generalised to other non-industrial working populations aged between 35 and 55, but probably not to people who are not in work.

Occupational cohorts are frequently used because they are often easier to achieve a more complete follow-up. To a certain extent they are a 'captive audience' and easier to track down for follow-up. Having a high response rate at follow-up makes the findings more valid. The results would not be able to be generalised at all if there was a low follow-up rate. Therefore occupational groups are used to secure participation with the possible trade-off that results from these studies may not be generalised to all parts of the general population.

Comparison group

It is important for cohort studies to have a comparison group in which the risk factor was not present in order to calculate the relative risk of the outcome occurring in the study group. Population cohort studies often have a comparison group within the cohort as they often contain both those with the risk factor and those without. However, when it comes to selecting a comparison group for a prospective cohort study, it is important to consider whether or not the comparison group selected is appropriate.

The comparison group must be as similar to the study group as possible. The only difference between the groups should be exposure to the risk factor that is being evaluated. Comparison groups may be people living in the same region of the same age and sex, or those living in the same neighbourhood or working in the same setting as the study group, for example.

A key problem to be aware of is 'contamination'. This refers to people in the comparison group who have been exposed to the risk factor. In the case of the cannabis and schizophrenia example given earlier, the comparison group were those who said at the time of conscription that they did not use cannabis. If they had lied and in fact did use cannabis, this may have caused 'contamination' of the comparison group. The effect of this on the results is to minimise any difference between the groups.

A frequently cited study to exemplify the use of comparison groups in cohort studies is an investigation into Gulf War Syndrome (chronic fatigue syndrome) (Unwin *et al.*, 1999), in which two comparison groups were used to compare with the veterans of the 1990–1 Gulf War. One was a group of personnel serving in Bosnia on peace-keeping duties between 1992 and 1997 and the other was a group of military personnel in the UK who were not deployed to the Gulf War in 1990–1 (an 'era control'). Having two comparison groups was necessary because the group of serving military personnel in Bosnia were deployed later than those who served in the Gulf War. An 'era control' group of military personnel who were not deployed eliminated the problem of possible differences within the armed forces between the turn of the 1990s and later in the decade when the Bosnian veterans were serving.

The researchers found that those serving in the Gulf developed symptoms of chronic fatigue to a significantly greater degree than those who served later in Bosnia and those who were not deployed, demonstrating that this was likely to be associated with serving in the Gulf War. It is important to note that this study is generalisable to veterans of the first Gulf War but not those who served in the more recent conflict.

Sample

The samples selected for the cohort study need to be as representative as possible of the population from which they are drawn. Representative samples can then be generalised to their populations and appropriate inferences made about the results of the study. One of the potential constraints to achieving a representative sample is non-participation.

Scott Weich and Martin Prince (2003) note that:

> Non-participants are, in general, likely to be less well educated, less affluent, less healthy and more likely to be out of work than participants. (p. 167)

For example, in their study of data from the British household panel survey which explored the effect of poverty and unemployment on the incidence of common mental disorders, Scott Weich and Glyn Lewis (1998) found that non-participation was associated with low socioeconomic status. Those living in very large households or with no access to a car or a van within their household were under-represented in the cohort. The implication of this is that their findings could not be generalised to these groups.

Weich and Lewis were able to deduce who did not respond to the panel survey at baseline as they had some very basic information about all those who were asked to participate. This information was used to make a comparison of participants and non-participants. Often this information is limited to the age or sex of non-participants, but in panel surveys this information is usually more extensive as some participants may have responded to previous waves of the survey.

It is an enduring challenge of researchers to engage more marginalised, or socially excluded, people in research to enable studies to be generalised to the whole population.

Data collection

There are several important principles of data collection in cohort studies to ensure that bias is minimised (Weich and Prince, 2003). Firstly, data must be collected in exactly the same way for participants in both the study group and the comparison group. This is to minimise information bias.

Secondly, collection of data about the outcome should ideally be conducted blind to whether the participant is in the study group or the comparison group. This will help to guard against misclassification of the outcome which may occur if researchers wanted to bias the results in favour of their hypothesis. For example, if it was hypothesised that social support was associated with recovery from depression, if researchers were aware whether the participants had low or high social support at baseline, they may be tempted to rate their recovery from depression accordingly.

Thirdly, both the risk factor and the outcome being measured need to be clearly defined and operationalised consistently between groups. Ideally all concepts will be measured using standardised research instruments with established psychometric properties that are reported in other peer-reviewed journals. This helps to ensure that the risk factor and outcome are both measured accurately and as consistently as possible.

Finally, other variables which may explain the outcomes in a cohort study, known as 'confounding variables', also need to be measured accurately. Confounders explain the difference in outcomes between a study group and comparison group that has not been caused by the risk factor. Confounders are associated with both the risk factor and outcome. For example, in a study of social support and recovery from depression, personality may be a potential confounding variable. An individual who had a personality that enabled him or her to accept the support of others and to make use of it may recover quicker from depression than someone who finds it difficult to accept the support they have on offer. Also the former person is more likely to have access to more social support than the latter. All potential confounding variables need to measured as accurately and comprehensively as possible in both groups. In Chapter 10 we describe how multivariate analysis controls for the effect of potential confounding variables.

Follow-up

Obtaining data from the whole cohort at all time points is particularly important for the success of a cohort study. Complete data will facilitate generalisation and it is essential to follow-up all participants through all data collection points to achieve this.

Loss to follow-up can reduce the generalisability of study findings. For example if particular groups did not complete the study, the results could not be generalised to them. For example in Scott Weich and Glyn Lewis' (1998) study referred to earlier, people who were unemployed or with the lowest income were less likely to participate at follow-up. The response rate at follow-up of those unemployed was 79 per cent in contrast to 86 per cent of those who were in work. Although these are generally good follow-up rates, if the loss to follow-up of those who were unemployed became any greater it would limit the generalisability of the findings of the study.

Loss to follow-up can also undermine the validity of the findings. For example, in Weich and Lewis' (1998) study, unemployment at baseline was associated with maintenance of common mental disorders at follow-up. Or, in other words, those who were unemployed and had a common mental disorder such as anxiety or depression at time one, remained unwell at time two. If unemployed people dropped out of the study at a greater rate than people in work, which they did in this study, it is possible that rates of common mental disorder at time two could be mis-represented. It would also be more difficult to draw conclusions about the association between the risk factor and the outcome if there was too much missing data from the study group. A careful examination of the follow-up rates to see whether they differed between the study and comparison group will reveal if this is a potential limitation of the study.

Also, if those who develop the outcome being studied are less likely to participate at follow-up, this may also bias the results and lead to an under-estimation of the outcome. For example, if participants who became depressed were less likely to complete the study, it is possible that the estimate of the incidence of depression in the sample may be biased. In Weich and Lewis' (1998) study, where unemployment at baseline was not associated with the onset of a common mental disorder at follow-up, it is possible that those who became unwell during the study dropped out at a greater rate than those who were healthy. If all those who dropped out of the study before follow-up were included, it is possible that the incidence rates of common mental disorder may be higher and the study may have had statistical power to find an association between unemployment and onset of illness.

Loss to follow-up can be assessed by comparing the characteristics of those completing the study with those who withdraw, using their baseline data. When appraising studies it is important to check whether researchers have done this and commented upon it in their discussion of the results. If not, they could be concealing some potential sources of bias which may make the results misleading.

Incidence rate

The unique and important feature of cohort studies is that they can tell you the incidence rate of a particular outcome. In psychiatric epidemiology, for example, they can tell you the rate at which people develop a mental health problem according to exposure to particular risk factors.

The incidence rate is the number of people who develop the outcome during a particular time period, usually one year. The incidence rate is the statistic that is most frequently cited in papers reporting the results of cohort studies. This is calculated using the following formula:

$$\text{Incidence rate} = \frac{\text{Number of people developing outcome in a specified period}}{\text{Person-years at risk}}$$

The 'number of people developing outcome in a specified period' is quite straightforward to calculate. It is quite simply the number of people in the cohort as a whole who have developed the outcome, such as a mental health problem. The time period is the length of time between baseline and follow-up.

The 'person-years at risk' is the number of participants who are at risk of developing the outcome, or the total number of people in the cohort, multiplied by the length of time they remain at risk. Or, in other words, this is the period of time until they develop the outcome (e.g. become unwell), drop out of the study or the entire length of the study if they still have not developed the outcome at follow-up.

The incidence rate is expressed in terms of 'person-years'. A good example of the use of incidence rates can be found in a large cohort study of over 4 million Swedes (Sundquist *et al.*, 2004). This study found, for example, an incidence rate for psychosis amongst women living in the most urbanised areas of 84 (95 per cent CI=81–86) per 100,000 person-years, in contrast to 30 (95 per cent CI=29–32) from the least urbanised areas. Or in other words, 84 in every 100,000 women developed psychosis in the most urbanised areas in contrast to 30 in the least urbanised areas over the period of one year. Comparable rates were found for men.

The incidence rate forms the basis for statistical comparisons between study groups to estimate the effect of a risk factor on an outcome. This is known as the relative risk.

Relative risk

The relative risk describes the relative likelihood of an outcome occurring in one group in relation to another. Quite simply the relative risk (RR) is calculated by dividing the incidence rate in the study group by the comparison group:

$$RR = \frac{\text{Incidence rate in study group}}{\text{Incidence rate in comparison group}}$$

The relative risk can be easily interpreted:

- A relative risk of 1 means that there is no difference between the study group and the comparison group.

- A relative risk of more than 1 means that the outcome is more likely to occur in the study group than the comparison group.

- A relative risk of less than 1 means that the outcome is less likely to occur in the study group than the comparison group.

Relative risk – an example

Let us look at an example to illustrate how relative risks work in practice.

Kathryn Abel and colleagues (2005) explored the parenting outcomes of mothers with schizophrenia who were admitted to a psychiatric mother and baby unit. They studied mothers with schizophrenia (study group), bi-polar affective disorder and depression (comparison groups).

Abel and colleagues presented the relative risks of the parenting outcomes occurring in the mothers with schizophrenia in relation to the two comparison groups in Table 2 on page 785 of their paper. They have used the term 'risk ratio' to describe the relative risks. This was calculated from incidence risks rather than incidence rates, but it still refers to the relative risk of the outcome occurring in one group in comparison to another. The last two columns of data from this table are summarised in Table 8.1 below.

Table 8.1 Relative risk of outcomes from Table 2, Abel et al., 2005

Outcome	Risk ratio (95% CI) Schizophrenia vs Bi-polar	Risk ratio (95% CI) Schizophrenia vs Depression
Under social services supervision	2.5 (1.8 to 3.5)	5.4 (4.0 to 7.4)
Significant problems caring for infant	2.4 (1.6 to 3.6)	3.4 (2.5 to 4.6)
Significant problems of emotional response	3.2 (2.1 to 4.8)	3.0 (2.3 to 3.9)
Significant risk of harm to child	3.5 (1.8 to 6.7)	3.4 (2.2 to 5.3)
At least 1 staff-rated poor outcome	2.4 (1.7 to 3.2)	2.6 (2.1 to 3.2)
Actual harm to child (pre or during admission)	1.7 (0.5 to 6.6)	0.8 (0.4 to 2.0)
Any clinical evidence (thoughts or acts)	1.0 (0.6 to 1.8)	0.5 (0.3 to 0.7)

Table 8.1 presents two sets of risk ratios comparing mothers with schizophrenia firstly with those with bi-polar affective disorder and then with those with depression. Let us take three of the cells to exemplify how relative risks work.

Firstly, ignoring the confidence intervals for a moment (the figures within brackets), the figure of 2.5 in the first row of the middle column is the risk of women with schizophrenia having their children under social services supervision relative to that of women with bi-polar affective disorder. Or, in other words, women with schizophrenia were 2.5 times more likely to have their children under social services supervision than women with bi-polar affective disorder.

Secondly, the figure of 0.5 in the last row of the far right hand column is the risk of women with schizophrenia presenting any clinical evidence of harm to their child relative to that of women with depression. As this figure is less than 1 it means that the study group (women with schizophrenia) have a lower risk of developing the outcome than the comparison group (women with depression). Or, in other words, women with schizophrenia were 0.5 times less likely to present any clinical evidence of harm to their child than women with depression.

Thirdly, the figure of 1.0 in the last row of the middle column is the risk of women with schizophrenia presenting any clinical evidence of harm to their child relative to that of women with bi-polar affective disorder. A relative risk of 1 indicates that there is no difference between the two groups. Or, in other words, women with schizophrenia were no more likely to present any clinical evidence of harm to their child than women with bi-polar affective disorder.

Relative risk and confidence intervals

As you will read in Chapter 10, confidence intervals can tell us whether particular findings hold statistical significance. In this regard they work in a similar way to p-values, although provide us with arguably more useful information. In terms of relative risks, 95 per cent confidence intervals provide us with a range of values in which the true population relative risk will lie on 95 occasions if the study were replicated 100 times.

To interpret their statistical significance simply follow these three rules:

- If the two figures in the confidence interval are both above 1, then it means that the outcome is statistically significantly more likely to occur in the study group than the comparison group.

- If the two figures in the confidence interval are both below 1, then it means that the outcome is statistically significantly more likely to occur in the comparison group than the study group.

- If the two figures are either side of 1 (one is below 1 and the other is above 1), then it means that there is no statistically significant difference between the two groups. This is the case because it is likely that the relative risk could equal 1, which means that there is equal likelihood of the outcome occurring in either the study group or comparison group.

The confidence intervals for the first relative risk we discussed above (2.5) are 1.8 to 3.5. Both these figures are above 1 so we can conclude that mothers with schizophrenia have a statistically significant greater risk of having their children under social services supervision than mothers with bi-polar affective disorder.

The second confidence interval ranges from 0.3 to 0.7. These figures are both below 1, indicating that the finding is statistically significant, but that the mothers with schizophrenia were less likely than the mothers with depression to present with any clinical evidence of harm to their child.

Finally, the third confidence interval ranges from 0.6 to 1.8. This range encompasses the value of 1, which is in fact the estimated relative risk in this sample. This confirms that there is no statistically significant difference between mothers with schizophrenia and those with bi-polar affective disorder on the likelihood of presenting with any clinical evidence of harm to their child.

Population attributable fraction

The final statistical device to briefly mention that can be found in cohort studies is the population attributable fraction (PAF). This refers to the proportion of incident cases in the population that would be prevented if a risk factor were removed, assuming that the causal association is not confounded by any other variables. This puts into perspective the relative importance of various risk factors on an outcome.

It is calculated using this formula:

$$PAF = p \left(\frac{RR}{RR + 1} \right)$$

where:

PAF   is the population attributable fraction

p   is the prevalence of the risk factor in the population

RR   is the relative risk

Examples of the use of the PAF can be found in Table 5 of Abel and colleagues' (2005) paper. This indicates, for example, that the risk factor of lower social class has a PAF of 51.2 per cent for the outcome of social services intervention at discharge for the mothers from the mother and baby unit. This means that over half of these social services interventions could be avoided if the mothers were not of a lower social class. While this may be of limited practical use, it does indicate the relative importance of different variables on various outcomes.

BOX *8.4*

Critical appraisal questions

The following questions will help you to appraise the quality of cohort studies. Use them when reading a paper reporting the results of a cohort study.

1 Was the cohort recruited in an acceptable way?

2 Was the risk factor accurately measured to minimise bias?

3 Was the outcome accurately measured to minimise bias?

4 Have the researchers identified all the relevant confounding factors?

5 Have the confounding factors been accounted for in the design or analysis of the study?

6 Was the follow-up of the participants complete and long enough?

7 What are the results of the study?

8 How precise are the results?

9 Do you believe the results?

10 Can the results be applied to my local population?

11 Do the results of this study fit with other available evidence?

BOX *8.5*

Multiple choice self-test

Test your understanding of the ideas contained within this chapter with this quick self-test. The answers can be found in Appendix 1.

1 What is the main difference between a classical cohort study and a case-control study? (Select one option only)

a Classical cohort studies examine the impact of risk factors on outcomes

b Classical cohort studies are longitudinal

c Classical cohort studies select the participants on the basis of their exposure to a risk factor rather than an outcome

d Classical cohort studies are expensive

2 Cohort studies find 'incidence' and cross-sectional studies find 'prevalence'. True or false?

3 Classical cohort studies are useful for: (Select all those that apply)

a The study of rare risk factors

BOX 8.5 *(CONT.)*

   b The study of rare outcomes

   c Exploring the connection between the occurrence of a risk factor and an outcome

   d Researchers on a tight budget

4 Which of the following are advantages of a population cohort study? (Select all those that apply)

   a They are often representative of a specific population

   b If the data is complete, results from occupational cohorts can always be generalised to the general population

   c Numerous hypotheses could be tested about a range of risk factors and outcomes

   d Data from population cohort studies can be used for secondary data analysis

5 What is the main limitation of historical cohort studies? (Select one option only)

   a You have to wait a long time for the outcome to occur

   b The data used may have been collected for other purposes and may be incomplete or inaccurate

   c It can get confusing collecting data on both outcomes and risk factors simultaneously

   d Retrospective data is less relevant than prospective data

6 What is 'contamination' in cohort studies? (Select one option only)

   a Researchers contracting illnesses from participants while collecting data

   b People in the comparison group who are also in the study group

   c People in the comparison group who have been 'exposed' to the risk factor

   d People in the study group who have been 'exposed' to the risk factor

7 Which of the following are non-participants in cohort studies more likely to be (according to Weich and Lewis (2003))? (Select all that apply)

   a Less well educated

   b Less affluent

   c Less healthy

   d Employed

BOX 8.5 (CONT.)

8 Why is it important to follow-up all participants in cohort studies? (Select all that apply)

a Loss to follow-up could limit the generalisability of the findings ☐

b Loss to follow-up could undermine the validity of the study ☐

c If one group is followed up more than another it may bias the results ☐

d To use up all the research grant ☐

9 A relative risk of less than 1 means that the outcome is more likely to occur in the study group than the comparison group. True or false?

10 If the two figures in the confidence interval surrounding a relative risk are both above 1, then it means that the outcome is statistically significantly more likely to occur in the study group than the comparison group. True or false?

Chapter 9
How to critically appraise case-control studies

Introduction

Like cohort studies, case-control studies have great potential for establishing the relationship between risk factors and outcomes. They are often easier to conduct than cohort studies, making them feasible for social work practitioners to undertake small case-control studies to answer practice-based research questions. This chapter will discuss the purpose of case-control studies, outlining why and when this method is used. We will then explore three examples of case-control studies which provide useful evidence for social work practice and highlight the relevance of this research design to the profession. This will be followed by an exploration of the various components of this method to provide some helpful hints when it comes to appraising case-control studies.

Why use a case-control design?

Case-control studies are used when the outcome being studied is rare. Rare outcomes in mental health research, for example, might be suicide or the onset of schizophrenia. These are both quite rare phenomena in the general population:

- The male suicide rate was 18 per 100,000 men and the equivalent figure was 6 per 100,000 women in the UK in 2004 (Brock *et al.*, 2006).

- The incidence rate for schizophrenia is between 7 and 17 per 100,000 people each year in London (Boydell *et al.*, 2003).

To generate a sample of 100 people in one year who have a new onset of schizophrenia, researchers would need a population of 1 million if the annual incidence rate was 10 per 100,000 people. This makes a prospective cohort study of risk factors involved in the onset of schizophrenia virtually impossible.

The case-control study takes the opposite approach to the classical cohort study. Instead of waiting for the outcome to occur, it starts with the outcome and works backwards. Researchers identify people who have the outcome, such as a new diagnosis of schizophrenia, and then 'looks back' to examine risk factors. They also select a group of people who don't have the outcome, known as controls, and collect the same data about them. This distinction can be illustrated by Figure 9.1.

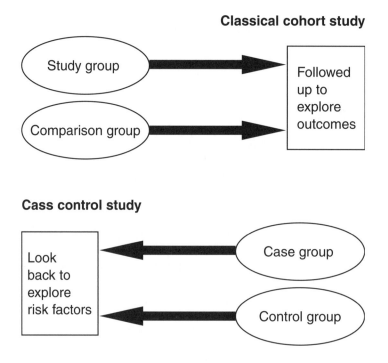

Figure 9.1 Main differences between a classical cohort study and a case-control study

In addition to the case-control method being appropriate when the outcome is rare, it is also used when there is a long period of time between the risk factor occurring and the outcome developing. In a cohort study there would be a huge potential for loss to follow-up if researchers had to collect data from participants over a long period of time. In a case-control study it doesn't matter how far back the researchers need to look for the data, as long as it is complete and accurate.

Further, case-control studies are used when the risk factors are common. This is in contrast to cohort studies when the risk factor is frequently rare. Additionally, the outcome is common in cohort studies and the period of time elapsing between the risk factor occurring and outcome developing is relatively brief.

Finally, the method has been used to evaluate interventions where random allocation is not possible. For example, mental health promotion interventions frequently use a control group who have not received the intervention (e.g. Rickwood *et al.*, 2004). However, these studies may be best described as 'quasi-experimental' rather than true case-control studies.

Let us look at three examples of case-control studies which have implications for social work practice to explore the design a little further.

EXAMPLE **9.1**

Child maltreatment following return from substitute care (Fuller, 2005)

Background

There is an inherent risk in returning children home from substitute care, such as foster care, and it is likely that some families will fail to keep the child safe from additional harm. Social workers are faced with the difficulty of predicting whether the child will be harmed on return to the family. Previous studies have not adequately explored predictors of short-term child maltreatment when they return home to their families.

Outcome

Maltreatment recurrence within 60 days of reunification

Risk factors

A whole range of potential risk factors were explored – child, carer, and placement characteristics, family environment, service provision, caseworker behaviours.

Case group

Children who experienced a substantiated maltreatment recurrence within 60 days of reunification with their families, identified from the Illinois Child and Youth-Centred Information System (n = 82).

Control group

Children from the same child welfare agencies as those in the case group who had not experienced maltreatment recurrence (n = 92).

Results

Seven risk factors were significantly associated with maltreatment recurrence: child age (below one had highest odds, and this reduced as age increased); presence of a mental health problem in the carer; having five or more placements; being in a placement for over three years; being placed in a kinship foster home; having four or more children in the home at reunification; and having both a single parent and siblings returned home at the same time.

---

*EXAMPLE **9.1** (CONT.)*

Discussion

Maltreatment upon reunification can be understood within a parenting stress framework. Having a young child with multiple siblings who all return home at the same time, a mental health problem and no partner to gain support from all contribute to carer stress which puts the child at increased risk of maltreatment. A longer period of time in place-ment suggests more intractable problems on behalf of the child or carer which may be reflected in the increased risk of maltreatment recurrence.

Implications for practice

Social workers should give careful consideration to the number and types of stressors that would be present in the family environment if the child was returned home. Support should be provided to ameliorate the impact of potential stressors. Further, recent carer behaviour does not adequately predict the impact of the cumulative stress of having their child returned home. The potential impact of this cumulative stress needs to be consid-ered in decision-making about reunifications.

Further questions

This study was conducted in the US and it would be instructive to see if similar risk factors are present in the UK: further research is required.

---

*EXAMPLE **9.2***

Depression in Irish migrants living in London (Ryan et al., 2006)

Background

Irish-born people living in England have high rates of mental distress. Circumstances lead-ing up to migration and migration itself may contribute to some of this. In particular, it is possible that unplanned migration may be associated with rates of depression, but this has not previously been investigated.

Outcome

The presence of depression as measured by a score of 14 or more on the Beck Depression Inventory (Beck and Steer, 1984).

Risk factors

Unplanned migration was the primary risk factor assessed. Data was also collected on a range of pre- and post-migration factors such as cultural integration, discrimination, alco-hol misuse and social support, for example, which may modify the relationship between migration and depression.

EXAMPLE **9.2** *(CONT.)*

Case group

People aged 18 or over who were born in Ireland but lived in north London within the catchment area of 11 participating GP practices and were currently suffering from depression.

Control group

People who were born in Ireland but lived in north London without depression were matched to the case group by age, gender and general practice.

Results

The risk of depression was greater for those whose migration was unplanned. When factors such as childhood trauma and previous history of depression were taken into consideration, this relationship only held for Irish men. When post-migration risk factors (such as social support and employment) were considered the odds ratios for depression associated with poorly planned migration failed to reach significance for men or women.

Discussion

Poorly planned migration appears to be a significant predictor of depression in Irish migrants to London. However, social support and employment were protective against depression, particularly for men.

Implications for practice

This study suggests that depression in recently arrived migrants could be alleviated by the provision of social support or employment. In liaison with other social care workers and employment advisors, social workers can lead on assessing and meeting the social needs of these potentially vulnerable people.

Further questions

London is home to many thousands of migrants from across the world. It would be instructive to replicate this study in other migrant populations to explore whether these results could be generalised to different ethnic groups.

EXAMPLE **9.3**

Physical health as a risk factor for suicide in older people (Préville et al., 2005)

Background

Physical illness and frailty are reported as significant factors in suicide of older people. However, few controlled studies have been conducted exploring this relationship as the choice of a control group has been problematic. This study aimed to use the psychological autopsy approach with a control group of people who had died of natural causes to rigorously investigate this relationship.

EXAMPLE *9.3* (CONT.)

Outcome

Suicide in people aged over 60.

Risk factors

Socio-demographic status, mental and physical health, stressful life events, social integration and religious practice were all considered as potential risk factors.

Case group

People aged over 60 who had committed suicide that was registered by the Quebec Chief Coroner's Office in 1998–9.

Control group

People aged over 60 who had died in 1998–9 from non-accidental causes were matched for age, sex, area of residence and date of death.

Results

42.1 per cent of those committing suicide had a mental health problem in the six months prior to their death in contrast to 10.5 per cent of the controls. There was no difference between the two groups in terms of the number of physical health problems, although the control group experienced a greater deterioration in their functional autonomy in the six months prior to their death.

Discussion

Similar to other studies (e.g. Harwood et al. (2001) in the UK), this Canadian case-control psychological autopsy study found that older people who committed suicide presented a higher risk of suffering from a mental health problem. No association was found between physical illness and suicide.

Implications for practice

Social workers need to be alert to the presence of mental health problems amongst older people and to consider effective strategies for minimising the potential for suicide in high risk cases. Although mental illness increases the risk of suicide in older people, only a small minority with a mental health problem will commit suicide. Therefore careful risk assessment is required to highlight those at greatest risk to facilitate the provision of the necessary support or protection.

Further questions

This study raises the question of which suicide prevention strategies are the most effective for older people. How can social workers work effectively with those at greatest risk? Are there effective public health interventions to reach those at risk who are not currently in contact with services?

Case group

In mental health research, the case group is frequently composed of people with a particular diagnosis. However, it could be any particular group which has a particular issue that requires investigation.

Accurate definitions of the case group are important to clarify exactly who the study could be generalised to. Clear inclusion and exclusion criteria will help to achieve this. As in study designs previously discussed, having a large number of exclusion criteria will restrict the generalisability of a study's findings, as they could potentially apply to fewer people. For example, a recent case-control study in Leicestershire that explored memory impairments in people with a diagnosis of schizophrenia (Al-Uzri *et al.*, 2006) had several exclusion criteria which limited the population it could be generalised to. People with the following were excluded:

- organic brain disease;

- head injuries;

- co-morbidity (other mental health problems);

- English not a first language;

- electro-convulsive therapy within previous year;

- those aged over 60.

As a result of these exclusion criteria, 30 per cent of those potentially eligible were excluded (Al-Uzri *et al.*, 2006). If the study had been conducted in London or another major conurbation this figure would increase due to greater concentrations of people who do not have English as their first language.

The source of the cases should be clearly defined as this will determine who the study could be generalised to. In mental health research, case-control studies of people with schizophrenia frequently recruit participants from secondary mental health services. Most people receiving treatment for schizophrenia would be known to secondary mental health services so this recruitment strategy should ensure that the sample would be broadly representative of the whole population. However, it will not be representative of those with the diagnosis but not receiving treatment from secondary care.

In contrast, if the case group consisted of people with depression, it would be more appropriate to recruit the sample from primary care as only the most severely depressed people would be known to secondary mental health services. However, this would mean that the sample would not be representative of those who were suffering from depression but not receiving any treatment from their GP. This group are effectively invisible to services and, by definition, difficult to research.

The cases are selected for the study after the inclusion and exclusion criteria have been clearly defined. The study cases need to be representative of the population from which they are drawn and efforts to demonstrate this should be made in papers reporting case-control studies.

Finally, it is important to understand the distinction between cases selected from incident and prevalent samples in mental health research. Incident cases are those who have just become unwell and prevalent cases are those who are already unwell.

Case-control studies using incident cases are often interested in exploring factors associated with the onset of ill-health. For example, the ÆSOP study used incident cases of first episode psychosis to study a number of risk factors such as ethnicity and social isolation (Morgan *et al.*, 2006). The main difficulty with using incident cases is that they can be difficult and expensive to identify. Although it was large and very highly regarded, the ÆSOP study cost many millions of pounds to conduct, for example.

Case-control studies using prevalent cases, in contrast, are often interested in recovery or maintenance of mental health problems. For example, in their study of Irish migrants, Louise Ryan and colleagues (2006) recruited people who were already depressed ('prevalent cases'). Prevalent cases are easier to find than incident cases, though using them will mean that the risk factors would be associated with the maintenance of the mental health problem rather than its inception. Further it may be possible that prevalent samples may not be representative of the entire population as people who develop the outcome for a brief period of time may be under-represented.

Control group

The control group must be similar in all regards to the case group except its members must not have the 'outcome' of interest in the study. If the outcome is a mental health problem, for example, then they must be screened beforehand to discover whether or not they have it. The key question to ask of the control group is: 'Could they become a "case" if they were to develop the outcome?' If they are similar in all regards except for the outcome, they are suitable for inclusion in the control group.

The control group must be recruited from the same source population as the case group. The same inclusion and exclusion criteria need to be applied to it. The control group must be as representative as possible of the source population. The control group for the ÆSOP study (Morgan *et al.*, 2006), for example, were randomly selected from the general population using the postal address file that was used in the National Psychiatric Morbidity Survey (Jenkins and Meltzer, 1995). Ten randomly selected addresses were approached for each case to recruit potential controls. Although they were broadly matched by area of residence, they were otherwise unmatched. This process achieved a broadly representative control group.

Many case-control studies match controls with cases on a range of demographic variables such as age, gender, social class or ethnic group. This is done in order to avoid these variables – potential 'confounders' of the relationship between the risk factor and outcome – affecting the results. However, this may occasionally lead to recruitment difficulties and complexities in the data analysis. Multivariate analysis can account for the effect of confounding variables if matching was not possible or desirable.

Occasionally, studies will recruit more controls than cases when the outcome being investigated is particularly rare. This helps to increase the statistical power of the study. For example, in a study of increasing severity of self-harm as a risk factor for suicide (Carter *et al.*, 2005) controls were selected in a 3:1 ratio to cases (93:31).

Sometimes it may be relevant to include more than one control group. This can provide a more rigorous test of a hypothesised connection between a risk factor and outcome. For example, Woodbury-Smith and colleagues (2005) explored the association between high functioning autistic spectrum disorders and offending in a case-control study. They recruited two control groups to compare with a case group of people with high functioning autistic spectrum disorders and a history of offending. One consisted of people with high functioning autistic spectrum disorders and no history of offending, and the other control group was recruited from the general population with neither autism nor an offending history.

Selection bias

Selection bias is a potential problem in case-control studies. This occurs when the risk factor being studied influences the likelihood of cases or controls being entered into the study. All cases or controls should have an equal likelihood of being included in a case-control study. If inclusion or exclusion criteria are related to the risk factor being studied, the results will be biased.

For example, if we were to conduct a case-control study of severity of cognitive impairment in older people as a predictor of respite care usage, we might encounter problems with selection bias if we were to recruit participants from an older person's mental health inpatient setting. As cognitive impairment is associated with admission to hospital for older people with dementia, we are likely to find higher levels of cognitive impairment than equivalent cases from the general population. This becomes a problem if we were to select controls not using respite care from the general population, who would be likely to have less severe cognitive impairment than cases in hospital. This would lead to an overestimation of the effect of cognitive impairment on respite care usage.

Selection bias can be avoided by paying careful attention to the details of the selection process for cases and controls. Further examples of selection bias, and a concise description of the phenomena, is provided by Max Henderson and Lisa Page (2007) in a brief article in *Evidence Based Mental Health*.

Recall bias

An underlying principle of data collection in case-control studies is that information should be collected in exactly the same way for cases and controls. However, case-control studies are prone to two forms of information bias – recall bias and investigator bias.

Firstly, recall bias occurs when experience of the outcome affects the process of recalling the risk factor. On the one hand it may be possible that the recall of the risk factor is underestimated in the case group if the outcome is dementia, for example, because of memory loss.

On the other hand, it may be possible that the recall of the risk factor is overestimated in the case group because of 'effort after meaning'. This refers to a process of intense concentration on potential risk factors to explain an outcome. For example, parents of people with schizophrenia may spend considerably more time recalling childhood events or other potential risk factors to explain their child's diagnosis to themselves than people whose son or daughter did not have the same diagnosis.

Recall bias can be minimised by using records that do not rely on the memory of participants, for example, health and social care records.

Investigator bias

Investigator bias can occur when the interviewer knows whether the participant is in the case or control group. It is possible that they may – either consciously or unconsciously – pursue questions about the risk factor more vigorously amongst the cases than controls to demonstrate an association between the risk factor and the outcome.

Investigator bias may be overcome by disguising which group the participants belong to from the interviewers. However, this may be very difficult to achieve when it is obvious when the participant has the outcome or not. People with severe depression, for example, may find this very difficult to disguise from interviewers.

Alternative approaches include disguising the hypothesis being tested from the interviewer by including other questions in addition to ones about the risk factor under investigation. Also, structured interviews which do not allow interviewers to deviate from the questions set could minimise the potential for investigator bias. Finally, asking participants to self-complete questionnaires about the risk factor will avoid the necessity for interviewers altogether.

Data analysis

The analysis of data from case-control studies usually consists of a series of steps. To illustrate these I will use our paper which explores the association between social exclusion and emergency compulsory detention in hospital following a Mental Health Act assessment (Webber and Huxley, 2004).

Firstly the sample, and the population it came from, is described. We described where the sample came from (p.1002) and then provided details about the age, gender and ethnicity of the sample (p.1003).

Secondly, the socio-demographic characteristics of the cases and controls are compared through statistical testing. This evaluates whether or not these variables are risk factors in their own right, or potential confounding variables in the association between the risk factor and outcome. In our study we found that a number of variables (non-white British ethnicity, bi-polar affective disorder and presenting a risk to self or others at a Mental Health Act assessment) were associated with the outcome (Table 2, Webber and Huxley, 2004). These may be potential confounding variables in the association between social exclusion and emergency compulsory detention and are entered into the multivariate analysis in the final stage of data analysis.

The next step is to examine the relationship between the risk factor and outcome, and calculate odds ratios (see Chapter 10). In our study we found that the only dimension of social exclusion to increase the odds of admission under section 4 of the Mental Health Act 1983 was low social support (Table 3, Webber and Huxley, 2004).

Finally, multivariate analysis controls for the effect of potential confounding variables. Confounding variables have a causal association with the outcome and a relationship with the risk factor. However, they are not simply on a causal pathway between the risk factor and outcome and can confuse the researcher into believing that the risk factor causes the outcome (see Chapter 10).

To discover whether the other variables associated with the outcome (in addition to low social support) were confounders in our study, we examined the difference between the odds ratio for low social support in the multivariate analysis (OR=2.04 (95%CI=1.12 to 3.71)) and the univariate analysis (OR=2.16 (95%CI=1.22 to 3.83)) (tables 3 and 4, Webber and Huxley, 2004). If the odds ratio for the risk factor hypothesised to be associated with the outcome becomes non-significant with the inclusion of additional variables, it means that the new variables entered into the model are confounders. In our case, the odds ratio became only marginally smaller and remained significant (both the lower and upper limits of the 95 per cent confidence interval were above 1). This indicated that low social support was associated with an increased risk of emergency compulsory detention.

The other variables – non-white British ethnicity, a diagnosis of bi-polar affective disorder and presenting a risk to self or others at a Mental Health Act assessment – were also all independently associated with an increased risk of emergency compulsory admission. They did not confound the relationship between low social support and emergency compulsory admission.

Interpreting results of a case-control study

There are a number of possible ways to interpret the results of case-control studies.

Firstly, there may be a causal relationship between the risk factor and the outcome. It is the ultimate aim of a case-control study to find this, but a careful consideration of the variables needs to be made to deduce whether this is true. In the case of the example cited above (Webber and Huxley, 2004), it is entirely plausible that there is a causal relationship between low social support and emergency compulsory admission. If there were relatives or friends available to offer support to the individual being assessed it would decrease the likelihood of their emergency detention under the Mental Health Act 1983.

An alternative explanation may be 'reverse causality'. In this case, the association works in the opposite direction and the outcome causes the risk factor instead of the other way round. For example, in studies of depression and severe life events, it is possible that people who were depressed, or prone to depression, were more likely to have severe life events because of the effects of the condition. Careful timing of the onset of the mental health problem (if used as an outcome in case-control studies) is essential to avoid this possibility.

The role of chance in the causal relationship must not be forgotten. The confidence intervals around the odds ratio must not straddle 1 in order to reach the conclusion that the finding was not due to chance. Even though an odds ratio may be above 1, it should not be assumed that this demonstrates a causal relationship if the confidence intervals are wide and straddle 1.

Finally, the role of confounding and bias as discussed previously, needs to be considered when assessing the findings of a case-control study.

BOX **9.1**

Critical appraisal questions

The following questions will help you to appraise the quality of case-control studies. Use them when reading a paper reporting the results of a case-control study.

1 *Were the cases recruited in an acceptable way?*

2 *Were the controls selected in an appropriate way?*

3 *Was the risk factor accurately measured to minimise bias?*

4 *Have the researchers identified all the relevant confounding factors?*

5 *Have the confounding factors been accounted for in the design or analysis of the study?*

6 *What are the results of the study?*

7 *How precise are the results?*

8 *Do you believe the results?*

9 *Can the results be applied to your local population?*

10 *Do the results of this study fit with other available evidence?*

BOX **9.2**

Multiple choice self-test

Test your understanding of the ideas contained within this chapter with this quick self-test. The answers can be found in Appendix 1.

1 *Are case-control studies used when the risk factor or the outcome is rare?*

2 *Which type of study does the case-control study take an opposite approach to? (Select one)*

a *Cross-sectional study* ☐

b *Classical cohort study* ☐

c *Randomised controlled study* ☐

d *Qualitative study* ☐

BOX 9.2 (CONT.)

3 Case-control studies are appropriate when: (Select all that apply)

a outcome is rare ⬜

b risk factor is rare ⬜

c there is a long period of time between the risk factor occurring and the outcome developing ⬜

d you want to explore the relationship between risk factors and an outcome ⬜

4 If you were studying factors associated with the onset of ill-health in a case-control study, would you be recruiting incident or prevalent cases?

5 The control group must be similar in all regards to the case group except for having the risk factor being studied. True or false?

6 Which of the following are features of the control group in case-control studies? (Select all that apply)

a They are similar to the case group in all regards except for the outcome being studied ⬜

b They are recruited from a different source population than the case group ⬜

c They may be matched to cases using set criteria ⬜

d There may be more controls than cases in the study ⬜

7 Name three potential sources of bias in case-control studies

8 Which of the following can be reported in the analysis of case-control studies? (Select all that apply)

a relative risks ⬜

b odds ratios ⬜

c t-tests ⬜

d multivariate analysis ⬜

9 If an apparent causal relationship appears in the results of a case-control study, which of the following may be possible alternative explanations? (Select all that apply)

a reverse causality ⬜

b chance ⬜

c confounding ⬜

d bias ⬜

Chapter 10

Demystifying *p*-values: A user-friendly introduction to statistics used in mental health research

Reading papers presenting quantitative research can be a challenging enterprise without a basic understanding of the statistics that have been used. This chapter will cover some of the elementary statistical concepts used in research relevant to mental health social work. It is possible that you will not understand it all at the first reading, but this chapter will become a useful reference source if you become stuck whilst reading quantitative research papers.

Descriptive statistics

Statistical methods can be used to summarise or describe a collection of data. These methods are known as descriptive statistics and are particularly useful in everyday social work practice. Both categorical and continuous data are frequently and routinely used.

Categorical data

Categorical data is anything that can be categorised. For example, gender, ethnicity and mental health diagnosis are all categories. To describe these concepts – or variables as they are referred to in statistical language – we use percentages or proportions. Here are some examples:

- 60 per cent of community mental health team service users are female.

- 10 per cent of service users are in employment.

- 70 per cent of people assessed under the Mental Health Act 1983 were subsequently detained.

A percentage is the number within a particular category divided by the total number and multiplied by 100. Let's take the first example above. If you wanted to calculate the proportion of female service users in your team you simply take the number of female services users (e.g. 180) and divide it by the total number of services users (e.g. 300). This gives you the figure of 0.6, which is the proportion of service users who are female. To convert this to a percentage, multiply it by 100, which will give you 60 per cent. Expressed as a formula this looks like:

$$\frac{\text{Number within category}}{\text{Total overall}} \times 100$$

Percentages are very useful for summarising categorical variables as they illuminate patterns within data.

Continuous data

Continuous data is information captured numerically or on a scale. For example, age (in years), scores on a depression scale or subjective quality of life scores are all continuous data. Continuous data needs to be treated differently from categorical data. It has more statistical power than categorical data and more inferences can often be drawn from it. Much of the research conducted within mental health services relies on this kind of data.

There are three summary measures of continuous data – the mean, median and mode.

Mean

The mean is the average of a range of values. It is calculated by adding up (or summing) all the values and then dividing by the number of values. Expressed as a formula this is:

$$\frac{\text{Sum of values}}{\text{Number of values}}$$

For example you may like to summarise the average age of a group of 15 people. Their ages (in years) are:

49, 35, 43, 52, 60, 25, 31, 48, 52, 60, 25, 49, 43, 29, 43

$$Mean = \frac{49 + 35 + 43 + 52 + 60 + 25 + 31 + 48 + 52 + 60 + 25 + 49 + 43 + 29 + 43}{15} = 42.9$$

The mean age is 42.9 years, or approximately 43 years.

Median

The median is the mid-point of any group of data, or distribution. If all the data were lined up in ascending order, the median is the middle value. The median is particularly useful when there are a few very high or very low values which may make the mean either higher or lower, giving a distorted impression of the average.

Using our group of 15 people as an example, we arrange their ages in ascending order:

25, 25, 29, 31, 35, 43, 43, 43, 48, 49, 49, 52, 52, 60, 60

The median is the middle value, or 43 years, in this distribution. In this case the median is the same as the mean, but it does not always work out this way. The median is particularly important in skewed distributions (see below), but the mean forms the basis of more powerful statistical tests.

Mode

The mode is an average that is used much less often, but is simply the most frequent value. In our example the mode is also 43, because there are 3 people with that age.

These three measures of the average give only limited summary information about a data set. For example, they don't tell us anything about the spread of the data. You could report minimum and maximum values, e.g.

Minimum = 25

Maximum = 60

Additionally, you could report the range of values, e.g.

Maximum – minimum = 60 – 25 = 35 years

However, this still doesn't tell you whether most of the people were closer to the mean age of 43, or were closer to the minimum or maximum values. This is where standard deviations and inter-quartile ranges are useful.

Standard deviation

The standard deviation is a summary measure of the average distance of all the values from the mean. The standard deviation is routinely reported in the results of quantitative research papers and is a useful measure of the spread of the data.

To conceptualise the importance of the standard deviation, consider this example. Imagine there are three teams of parachutists with 15 members in each team. The three teams are competing on the accuracy of their landing skills. Each team has a target in a field which they are required to land on, or as close to as possible. The team which, on average, lands closest to their target is the winner. Figure 10.1 illustrates the results.

The black team have aimed for target 1, the light-grey team for target 2 and the dark grey team for target 3. Which do you think is the winner?

The black team have consistently landed close to their target. The light-grey team have done quite well as they have all landed in the correct corner of the field. However, the dark grey team have landed all over the field, with some parachutists landing closer to the other targets than their own!

To calculate which team was the winner, and to confirm the black team as gold medallists, you would need to calculate the average distance from the target of the parachutists in each team. Imagine that the centre of the target is the mean, then the average distance of the parachutists from the target is equivalent to the standard deviation. A small standard deviation indicates that the data is all close to the mean – or that the parachutists have all landed on or very close to their target. A large standard deviation indicates that the data is

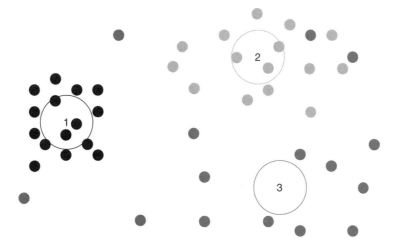

Figure 10.1 Parachutists on and off target

more spread and is less close to the mean – or that the parachutists have not landed very close to their target.

The standard deviation is slightly complicated to compute, but is worth knowing about as it is widely used in statistical tests. The formula to calculate it for any given set of values is:

$$\sigma = \sqrt{\frac{\Sigma (x_i - \bar{x})^2}{(n - 1)}}$$

Where:

σ = standard deviation

n = number of values

x_i = represents each individual value

$\bar{x}$ = mean

As a worked example, here is how to calculate the standard deviation of the ages of the group of people referred to above (p. 129). It can be calculated easily on a calculator or using a program such as Microsoft Excel.

s.d. = square root of ((49 – 43)² + (35 – 43)² + (43 – 43)² + (52 – 43)2 + (60 – 43)² + (25 – 43)² + (31 – 43)² + (48 – 43)2 + (52 – 43)2 + (60 – 43)² + (25 – 43)² + (49 – 43)² + (43 – 43)² + (29 – 43)² + (43 – 43)²) / (15 – 1)

s.d. = square root of (36 + 64 + 0 + 81 + 289 + 324 + 144 + 25 + 81 + 289 + 324 + 36 + 0 + 196 + 0) / 14

s.d. = 11.6

A large standard deviation in relation to the mean indicates that the values are spread out. A small standard deviation means the scores are similar. If the standard deviation is more than half the mean, as a rule of thumb, this tells you that the distribution is spread out. The median is likely to be the best average to give in these circumstances.

In our example, the standard deviation (11.6) is small in comparison to the mean (43) indicating that these ages are relatively close together and that the mean is a good description of the average of the sample.

Inter-quartile range

The inter-quartile range is reported alongside the median when the latter is used in preference to the mean. When all the values are laid out in ascending order, the median is the middle value. The inter-quartile range is the difference between the value three-quarters of the way up the distribution and the value one-quarter up the distribution. Here is an example of the inter-quartile range of the ages of the group of 15 people:

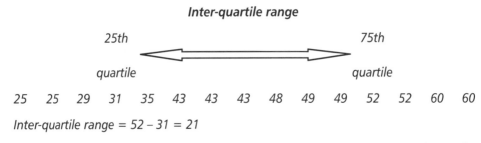

Inter-quartile range

| 25th | | | | | | | | | | | 75th | | | |
| quartile | | | | | | | | | | | quartile | | | |

25   25   29   31   35   43   43   43   48   49   49   52   52   60   60

Inter-quartile range = 52 – 31 = 21

The inter-quartile range and standard deviation statistics help you to interpret the results reported in research papers. They are particularly useful for helping you to decide whether the results can be generalised to the group of people you are interested in.

For example, in a recent national study of the mental health, burnout and job satisfaction of mental health social workers (Evans *et al.*, 2006), the mean and standard deviation of the age of the sample was 46 and 9.2 respectively. As the standard deviation is low in proportion to the age, we can expect most of the sample to be quite close to the mean. As we discuss below, most are within one standard deviation of the mean so the majority will be in the range of approximately 37 to 55 years of age. While this reflects the ageing social work workforce in England and Wales, the survey is not necessarily representative of newly qualified social workers who are in their 20s or early 30s.

Normal distribution

Continuous data can be plotted on a histogram such as the one in Figure 10.2.

Histograms show at a glance whether the distribution of data is squashed up or spread out. They also help us to observe whether or not the variable follows a normal distribution. This is important to deduce because it determines which statistical tests can or cannot be performed on it. The data shown in Figure 10.2 of ages of a sample of people with depression participating in a study on social capital is approximately normally distributed. We can draw this conclusion because it has the four essential characteristics of the normal distribution:

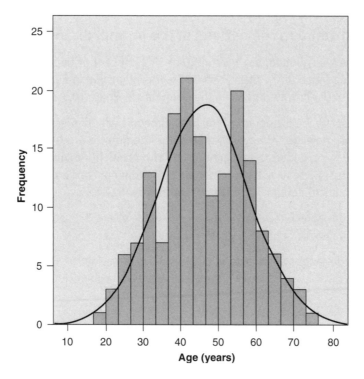

Figure 10.2 Histogram of ages of people with depression in a social capital study

1 It is symmetrical. If you were to draw a line down the middle, both sides of the distribution (or 'tails') are similar.

2 The shape of the curve is like a bell.

3 Its mean, median and mode are very close in the middle of the distribution. In the 'real' data shown in Figure 10.2 the mean is 46.0 and the median is 45.8. There are two peaks (modes) in the distribution in the early 40s and mid 50s, but they are close enough to the mean and median for us to conclude that this distribution is 'normal'. The normal distribution has very few high scores or very few low scores, with the majority in the middle and close to the average.

4 The two tails of the distribution never actually touch the horizontal, or x, axis. This is a mathematical property of the distribution and not one that is reflected in real life.

How can you tell that a distribution is 'normal'? Although there is a mathematical procedure for determining this, the most common method is by inspecting, or 'eye-balling', the histogram to see if it is bell-shaped and symmetrical.

It is important to establish whether or not the distribution is normal as this determines which statistical tests you can perform on it – either parametric for normal distributions or non-parametric for non-normal distributions. We will return to this throughout this chapter.

Means and standard deviations in the normal distribution

In a true normal distribution, you will find that 68.2 per cent of the values will fall within one standard deviation of the mean, and 95.4 per cent are within two standard deviations of the mean. Let us illustrate this using the histogram in Figure 10.3:

Figure 10.3 displays the histogram of the ages of people with depression in the social capital study again. However, it now indicates where the mean is located on the distribution (in the middle). Also, it indicates where one and two standard deviations either side of the mean are located. These have been calculated by quite simply adding and subtracting multiples of the standard deviation (12.2) from the mean (46.0).

One standard deviation either side of the mean are the values 33.8 and 58.2. About 68 per cent of all the values lie between these two points.

Two standard deviations either side of the mean are the values 21.6 and 70.4. About 95 per cent of all the values lie between these two points. There are very few people at either

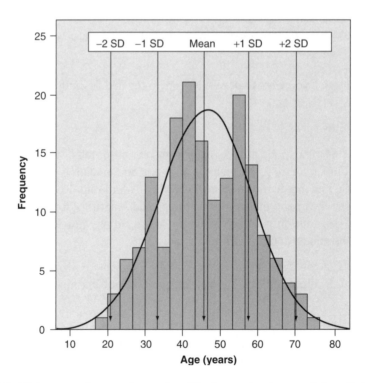

Figure 10.3 Histogram of ages of people with depression in a social capital study with mean and standard deviations

extreme of the age distribution – only a few below 21.6 or above 70.4 years of age. Knowing this is very useful as you can see at a glance where a particular individual may fit on a distribution and it provides some more information about whom you could generalise the findings of the study to.

Skewed distributions

A non-normal, or skewed, distribution of values is one with significant clustering at one end of the distribution. Distributions in which the majority of values are low, or clustered towards the left hand side, are termed 'positively skewed'. Alternatively, distributions in which the majority of values are high, or clustered towards the right hand side, are termed 'negatively skewed'. The use of 'positive' and 'negative' in this context refers to the direction of the tail.

An example of a positively skewed distribution is the General Health Questionnaire (GHQ) (Goldberg and Williams, 1988) when used in the general population. The GHQ is used as a screening tool for common mental disorder, such as depression or anxiety. The 12-item version has a cut-off of 3 or 4 on the scale for a probable common mental disorder. Anyone scoring above these thresholds is likely to suffer from a common mental disorder. In the general population, as the majority of people at any one time do not suffer from a common mental disorder, we would expect most people to score very low on the screen. As Figure 10.4 illustrates from data gathered in Croydon and Doncaster (Webber and Huxley, 2007), the GHQ scale has a positively skewed distribution. We call this a positive skew because the tail points to the right, or in a 'positive' direction.

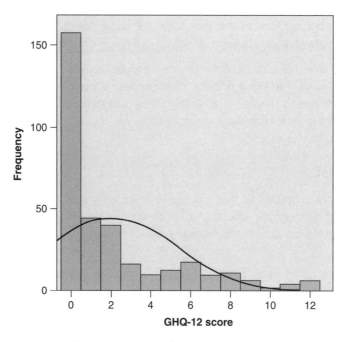

Figure 10.4 Histogram of GHQ-12 scores in a general population sample

This distribution is not normal because the curve is definitely not bell-shaped, but asymmetrical with a long tail to the right. Also, the mean (2.1), median (1) and mode (0) are quite different. In this case, it will be more important to quote the median as a reflection of the average of the distribution and use non-parametric statistical tests, which we will discuss later in this chapter.

Evaluating change

Social workers need to know about changes for their clients, whether things have improved for them or not. It is also important to know whether these changes can be attributed to a particular service or intervention. Finally, it is important to know whether any changes or improvements are *real* improvements, or whether they are just due to chance.

For example, imagine that a voluntary sector befriending scheme has just started in your area and you wanted to find out whether it helps to reduce the social isolation of people with enduring mental health problems such as schizophrenia. The most scientific methodology for evaluating the effectiveness of this service is the randomised controlled trial (Chapter 7).

Firstly, by asking questions about how many people they regularly see and how isolated they feel both before and after a period of time with a befriender, we will be able to evaluate whether or not there has been any change for this group of people. If they see more people and feel less isolated, we may conclude that things have improved for them.

Secondly, if we used a randomised controlled trial method of evaluating the befriending service, we will have a comparison group of people with schizophrenia who did not receive the service. We can then compare the social isolation of both groups to see whether those with a befriender became less isolated than the other group over time. This will help us to evaluate whether any changes could be attributed to the befriending service.

Finally, changes over time, or between the two groups, may be either small or large. However, it is important to know whether changes or improvements are real, or significant, and not just due to chance. To evaluate this we use statistical tests. Statistical tests help us to decide whether changes or improvements are *statistically significant*. This is a concept we will return to shortly.

Statistical tests

Statistical tests are important as they help us to reach a number of conclusions. Firstly, they tell us whether things are different. So, in the previous example, they will help us to evaluate whether the group with a befriender were less isolated than the group without a befriender.

Secondly, they tell us whether things are related. For example, they will tell us whether social isolation was related to a different variable, such as age.

Thirdly, and perhaps most importantly, statistical tests tell us whether these differences or associations were significant or due to chance. They tell us whether the people with a befriender were significantly less isolated than the group without a befriender. They also tell us whether or not there was a significant association between social isolation and age.

The significant differences or associations we are referring to here relate to statistical significance. The notion of statistical significance underlies all quantitative research and is a concept that is important to understand.

Statistical significance

Statistical significance is the probability that an observed difference may have arisen by chance. Using the above example, you may find that people who had a befriender became less isolated over time than those who did not. It is possible that this difference between the two groups may have arisen purely by chance. Statistical significance in this context relates to the probability that the difference in social isolation between the group who had befrienders and the group who did not was due to chance. Or, in other words, statistical significance tells us how sure we can be that this difference is real, that it is not as a result of a fluke – caused by an unusual sample or the impact of another variable, for example.

Statistical significance is expressed as a probability, which is called a *p*-value.

p-values

The probability that a statistical finding (a difference or association between groups or variables) is due to chance can range from 0 to 1:

- A *p*-value of 0 indicates that there is no possibility that the finding was caused by chance.

- A *p*-value of 1 indicates that there is absolute certainty that the finding was caused by chance.

A *p*-value can be any figure between 0 and 1. In our example of befrienders of people with enduring mental health problems, the *p*-value would tell you the probability that any difference in social isolation between the group who had befrienders and the group who did not was due to chance. For example:

- If $p = 0.9$, this means that nine in ten times the difference would be due to chance. Or, put another way, if the study was repeated 100 times, a similar difference would be found on only ten occasions.

- If $p = 0.5$, this means that one in two times the difference would be due to chance. Or, put another way, if the study was repeated 100 times, a similar difference would be found on 50 occasions.

- If $p = 0.1$, this means that one in ten times the difference would be due to chance. Or, put another way, if the study was repeated 100 times, a similar difference would be found on 90 occasions.

- If $p = 0.05$ this means that one in twenty times the difference would be due to chance. Or, put another way, if the study was repeated 100 times, a similar difference would be found on 95 occasions.

A result with a p-value of 0.05 has much more statistical significance than one with a p-value of 0.9 as the likelihood of the result being a fluke is much lower. The closer the p-value gets to 0, the greater the statistical significance of the result becomes.

In statistics, a p-value of 0.05 is conventionally used as the cut-off for deciding whether a result is statistically significant or not. Any difference or association with a p-value greater than 0.05 is not statistically significant. However, a difference or association with a p-value less than 0.05 is statistically significant.

Imagine that there is a difference in social isolation between the group who had befriending and the one that didn't. If the p-value for this difference is above 0.05 ($p>0.05$ or ns – not significant), we would conclude that the difference is not statistically significant and is likely to have been caused by chance. However, if the p-value for this difference was less than 0.05 ($p<0.05$), we would conclude that the difference is statistically significant and is unlikely to have been caused by chance.

The p-value of 0.05 is the conventional cut-off, but sometimes we want to be even more certain that a result did not occur by chance. In these cases we may choose a p-value of 0.01 or even 0.001.

Here is an example of how p-values are reported in research taken from our study referred to above:

> *Significantly more women completed the questionnaire than men ($\chi^2(2) = 11.00$, $p<0.01$). (Webber and Huxley, 2007: 485)*

The concepts of statistical significance and p-values can be a little confusing and you may need to re-read this section a few times to grasp it. Don't worry about this – this is quite common. Both Clegg (1990) and Newman and colleagues (2005) provide user-friendly introductions to these concepts if you want to look for further examples.

Statistical significance using confidence intervals

Confidence intervals are frequently reported by researchers to indicate the precision of their results and it is important to understand their purpose.

Point estimates

Research studies select a sample from a population to study as it is usually not possible to gather data from the entire population. Researchers must carefully select their sample to ensure that it is as representative of the population as possible. This will help to ensure that their results are as close to the reality in the target population as possible. If a different sample was taken within the same population, a slightly different result may be found. These results are called 'point estimates'. Let us illustrate this with an example.

Let us imagine that we were interested in finding out the mean age of people with a diagnosis of schizophrenia in the UK. The target population comprises 500,000 people, let us say. However, it is not possible to find the mean for the entire population as it is not feasible to survey half a million people. Instead, we select a random sample of 1,000 that is representative of this target population and obtain data from them. The mean age of this sample is known as a 'point estimate' of the population as a whole. If a different representative random sample of 1,000 people were taken from the same population and asked the same question, slightly different results, or point estimates, will emerge.

Sampling distribution

Staying with the previous example, if we were to repeat the study a number of times within the same population, a whole range of mean ages will emerge. Although they are likely to be quite close together, they will differ slightly. If these mean ages were all put together and plotted in a histogram they would form a distribution in their own right. This hypothetical distribution is referred to as the 'sampling distribution'.

The sampling distribution is normally distributed and this becomes evident when the means from each sample are plotted in a histogram. The mean of the sampling distribution is the population mean.

Sample size is closely related to the accuracy of the point estimates. Small samples are likely to produce estimates further away from the population mean and will lead to a larger spread in the sampling distribution. Larger samples will be more accurate and will be closer to the population mean.

Standard errors

Just as the sampling distribution has a mean, it also has a standard deviation. However, the standard deviation for the sampling distribution is known as the 'standard error'.

As we saw above, the standard deviation gives us some information about the spread of data within the distribution. In normal distributions, 95 per cent of values lie within about two standard deviations of the mean. In the same way, in sampling distributions, 95 per cent of sample means obtained by repeated sampling lie within about two standard errors of the population mean. This information can be used to estimate how precise a sample mean is, giving the range of likely values for the population mean.

Confidence intervals

Confidence intervals are the range of values that are likely to contain the unknown value for the population. In the case of the mean age of people with schizophrenia, the confidence intervals around a sample mean are likely to contain the population mean. For large samples, which are more likely to be closer to the population mean, the confidence intervals will be small. The opposite will be true for small samples.

It is convention to calculate 95 per cent confidence intervals. These represent the range in which 95 per cent of mean values would lie if numerous samples were collected from the same population. Or, put another way, if the same study was repeated with 100 samples, the confidence interval will contain the population mean on 95 occasions.

Calculating confidence intervals

Confidence intervals can be calculated for a whole range of statistics – means, differences in means, proportions, odds ratios to name but a few. Although these calculations can easily be performed by a computer, it is useful to be familiar with the formulae that are used to calculate them.

Confidence intervals for a mean

To calculate a confidence interval for a mean of sample size 'n' and standard deviation 'sd', first calculate the standard error (se) of the sampling distribution:

$$se = \frac{sd}{\sqrt{n}}$$

Then, calculate the 95 per cent confidence intervals (CI) around the mean:

$$95\%CI = mean \pm 1.96 \times se$$

Confidence intervals for a proportion

To calculate a confidence interval for a single proportion 'p' in a sample of size 'n', first calculate the standard error (se) of the sampling distribution:

$$se = \sqrt{\frac{p\,(1-p)}{n}}$$

Then, calculate the 95 per cent confidence intervals (CI) around the proportion:

$$95\%CI = p \pm 1.96 \times se$$

Additional formulae for calculating confidence intervals around other statistics can be found in most good statistics text books.

Reporting confidence intervals

In the results sections of papers, you will see the confidence intervals reported in brackets following the statistics. Here are some examples taken from the paper describing the validation of the Resource Generator-UK (Webber and Huxley, 2007):

> *Respondents in the second general population pilot (n = 335) had access to a mean of 17.24 out of 27 social resources (95%CI = 16.54 to 17.93) on the RG-UK scale.*
> *(p. 487)*

This means that if the study was repeated with other samples from the same population, the population mean will lie between 16.54 and 17.93 social resources in 95 per cent of the samples.

> *Adjusted for age, academics had access to a mean of 1.53 (95%CI = 0.93 to 2.13) more resources in the expert advice sub-scale and 0.58 (95%CI = 0.31 to 0.86) in the problem-solving sub-scale (than the general population sample). (p. 487)*

This means that if the study was repeated with other samples from the same populations, the difference in population means will lie between 0.93 and 2.13 social resources for the expert advice sub-scale and between 0.31 and 0.86 social resources for the problem-solving sub-scale.

Confidence intervals and *p*-values

As we saw above, *p*-values are important in telling us the probability that a result occurred through chance. Confidence intervals can also do this, and more.

The size of the *p*-value gives little indication of the strength of an association or a difference as it is highly dependent upon sample size. Large samples may return highly significant (i.e. very small) *p*-values for weak associations or small differences.

On the other hand confidence intervals can describe the magnitude of the association, by giving the likely parameters of the population value, as well as indicating whether the association or difference is statistically significant. Let us take the following extract from the same paper (Webber and Huxley, 2007) to illustrate this:

> *Adjusted for age, the difference between the group of academics and the general population in the RG-UK scale was 1.48 (95%CI = 0.01 to 2.96) resources (p = 0.049). (paraphrased from p. 487)*

The *p*-value of 0.049 indicates a marginally statistically significant difference in means between the two groups. The confidence intervals indicate that the difference in means could be as low as 0.01 resources or as high as 2.96 resources. If the lower figure went below 0, there would be no statistically significant difference between the groups as this would indicate that the academics had access to fewer resources than the general population. As it stands, however, if the study was repeated with other samples, on 95 per cent of occasions the difference in population means will lie between 0.01 and 2.96.

The value of '0' is known as the 'null' value for a difference in means. If the confidence interval includes the value '0' (i.e. if the lower figure is negative and the higher figure is positive), there is no statistically significant difference. For example if the difference in means reported above was 1.3 (95% CI = −1.5 to 2.7), this would not be a statistically significant difference.

Pearson's chi-square test

The Pearson's chi-square test is one of the most common statistical tests used in social science. It tests a null hypothesis that the relative frequencies of occurrence of observed events follow a specified frequency distribution. The events are assumed to be independent and have the same distribution, and the outcomes of each event must be mutually exclusive. The chi-square test is used with variables which have frequencies, otherwise known as categorical variables. It is not used with continuous variables which have a mean and standard deviation.

Before we explain the test in a little more detail, let us take a look at what the null hypothesis is all about.

Null hypothesis

A null hypothesis is a hypothesis set up to be refuted in order to support an alternative hypothesis. When used, the null hypothesis is presumed to be true until statistical evidence in the form of a hypothesis test indicates otherwise. The null hypothesis proposes something initially presumed true. It is rejected only when it becomes evidently false.

Let us illustrate this with an example. We may wish to test the effectiveness of an intervention on recovery from depression. We have an intervention group and a control group. The null hypothesis would be that the number recovered in the intervention group was the same as the control group. Expressed as a formula, this is:

$$H_o : n_{int} = n_{con}$$

where

H_o is the null hypothesis

n_{int} is the number recovered in the intervention group

n_{con} is the number recovered in the control group

We assume that the numbers who have recovered will be the same in both groups because the intervention is as yet untested. The null hypothesis is typically of no difference between groups or variables, or that an intervention has no effect on an outcome. It is typically that there is no difference between the value of a particular variable and that of a prediction.

It is the researcher's task to disprove the null hypothesis and propose an alternative hypothesis. The simplest alternative hypothesis is that the number recovered in the intervention group will be different from in the control group. This alternative hypothesis is referred to as:

$$H_1 : n_{int} \neq n_{con}$$

where

H_1 is the alternative hypothesis

n_{int} is the number recovered in the intervention group

n_{con} is the number recovered in the control group

Three types of chi-square test

Pearson's chi-square is commonly used to assess three types of comparison:

- **Chi-square test for independence**: used when you have two categorical variables from a single population. It is used to determine whether there is a significant association between the two variables.

- **Chi-square test of goodness of fit**: used with one categorical variable from a single population. It is used to determine whether the sample data is consistent with a hypothesised distribution.

- **Chi-square test for homogeneity**: used with one categorical variable from two different populations. It is used to determine whether frequency counts are distributed identically across different populations.

Calculating the chi-square statistic

The chi-square statistic (χ^2) is calculated by exploring the difference between observed values and the expected values if the null hypothesis were true. The formula for calculating χ^2 is the same for each of the different types of chi-square test:

$$\chi^2 = \sum \frac{(O_i - E_i)^2}{E_i}$$

where

O_i is an observed frequency

E_i is an expected frequency if the null hypothesis of no difference were true

For example, to test the hypothesis that a random sample of 100 people has been drawn from a population in which men and women are equal in frequency, the observed number of men and women would be compared to the frequencies expected if the null hypothesis were true. The null hypothesis would be that there are equal numbers in each group (50).

If there were 45 men in the sample and 55 women, then:

$$\chi^2 = \frac{(45 - 50)^2}{50} + \frac{(55 - 50)^2}{50} = 0.5 + 0.5 = 1$$

Degrees of freedom

Degrees of freedom is a measure of the number of independent pieces of information on which the precision of a parameter estimate is based. The number of degrees of freedom generally refers to the number of independent observations in a sample, minus the number of population parameters that must be estimated from the sample data. It can also be thought of as the number of observations, or values, which are freely available to vary given the additional parameters estimated.

The calculation for the degrees of freedom varies slightly according to which chi-square test you are performing.

When you are calculating the chi-square test of goodness of fit with one categorical variable from a single population, degrees of freedom (*df*) is the number of levels of the categorical variable (the number of categories it has) minus one:

$$df = k - 1$$

where

k = number of levels/categories

When you are calculating the chi-square test for independence with two categorical variables from a single population, degrees of freedom (df) is the number of levels/categories of one categorical variable minus one, multiplied by the number of levels/categories in the other categorical variable minus one:

$$df = (k_a - 1) \times (k_b - 1)$$

where

k_a = number of levels/categories in variable *a*

k_b = number of levels/categories in variable *b*

When you are calculating the chi-square test for homogeneity with one categorical variable from two or more populations, degrees of freedom is the number of populations minus one, multiplied by the number of levels/categories in the categorical variable minus one:

$$df = (n - 1) \times (k - 1)$$

where

n = number of populations

k = number of levels/categories in the variable

Let us use the example of our random sample of 100 people. We have one variable (gender) with two categories (men and women). Therefore, the degrees of freedom are the number of categories minus one:

$$df = k - 1 = 2 - 1 = 1$$

Chi-square distribution and *p*-values

The chi-square distribution of values varies according to degrees of freedom. As Figure 10.5 shows, the shape of the curve varies according to degrees of freedom (*k*).

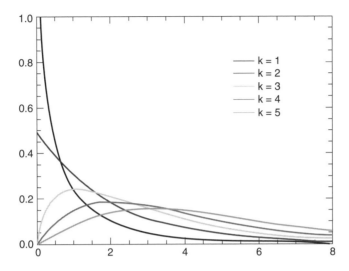

Figure 10.5 Chi-square distribution

It is not necessary to know the complex statistics involved in the chi-square distribution. However, it is important to understand that it is useful because, under reasonable assumptions, easily calculated quantities can be proven to have distributions that approximate to the chi-square distribution if the null hypothesis is true. Or, in other words, knowing the chi-square statistic and degrees of freedom is sufficient to test a null hypothesis and obtain a p-value for the statistical significance of a chi-square test.

Therefore, in our example, we have a chi-square value of 1 and 1 degree of freedom. Consulting the chi-square distribution above (x axis is the chi-square statistic and y axis is the *p*-value), we can see that the value of 1 on the x axis hits the black curve (where degrees of freedom = 1) somewhere in the region of the p-value of 0.3.

A more accurate way of determining the *p*-value is to consult statistical tables which can be found in any standard statistics text book (e.g. Clegg, 1990, p. 175). This can also be done using statistical software to arrive at the precise p-value of 0.3173. This means that the probability of observing a difference of 45 men and 55 women in our sample of 100, if men and women are equally numerous in the population is approximately 0.3. This probability is higher than the conventional criteria for statistical significance (0.05). Therefore, we would not reject the null hypothesis that the number of men in the population is the same as the number of women.

This is reported as:

There is no statistically significant difference between the numbers of men and women in the sample ($\chi^2 = 1$, df = 1, p = 0.32).

If the p-value had been 0.03 instead of 0.3, we would have rejected the null hypothesis and accepted an alternative hypothesis that the number of men is not the same as the number of women.

Example

The chi-square test is best understood by examining real data. Let us use the results of the befriending trial (Harris *et al.*, 1999) that we have previously referred to.

Table 1 of this paper (p. 221) contains the key results of the study: 65 per cent of those in the intervention group (befriending) experienced remission from depression at follow-up in contrast to 39 per cent in the waiting list control group. The authors report this as a statistically significant difference. Let us illustrate how their chi-squared calculation was performed.

Firstly, let us reproduce table 1 in full:

Table 10.1 Percentage of chronically depressed women with remission within 13 months of interview (Harris et al., *1999: 221)*

Remitted?	Befriending		Controls		Total	
	%	n	%	n	%	n
Yes	65	**28**	39	**17**	52	45
No	35	**15**	61	**26**	48	41
Total	100	43	100	43	100	86

Secondly, let us consider the null hypothesis. The null hypothesis is that there is no difference between the befriending and control groups in the number of women who remitted. Or, in other words, if remission was unrelated to receiving the befriending intervention, we would expect the same proportion in each group to have got better.

Now we can calculate the expected frequencies for both groups by applying the figures from the sample as a whole. In this sample 52 per cent remitted. If remission was unrelated to receiving the befriending intervention, we would expect 52 per cent of both the intervention and control groups to recover. Tabulating this information looks like this (Table 10.2):

Table 10.2 Expected frequencies according to null hypothesis

Remitted?	Befriending (expected)		Controls (expected)		Total (expected)	
	%	n	%	n	%	n
Yes	52	**22.5**	52	**22.5**	52	45
No	48	**20.5**	48	**20.5**	48	41
Total	100	43	100	43	100	86

With both the observed (Table 10.1) and expected (Table 10.2) frequencies, we can calculate the χ^2 value. We apply the formula to each cell with frequencies for the two groups (highlighted in bold in both tables).

$$\chi^2 = \frac{(28-22.5)^2}{22.5} + \frac{(15-20.5)^2}{20.5} + \frac{(17-22.5)^2}{22.5} + \frac{(26-20.5)^2}{20.5} = 1.3 + 1.5 + 1.3 + 1.5 = 5.6$$

The more the observed figures depart from the expected, the higher the χ^2 value will be. If there is no systematic association between the two variables, then departures between observed and expected values are likely to be very small and represent only chance fluctuations. Conversely a large value for χ^2 will suggest that there is some systematic relationship between the two measures.

Next, we calculate the degrees of freedom. For a chi-square test for independence the formula is:

$$df = (k_a - 1) \times (k_b - 1) = (2-1) \times (2-1) = 1 \times 1 = 1$$

Finally, consulting a table for the chi-square distribution or using statistical software, find the p-value. The result is 0.018. This is below the conventional threshold of 0.05 and therefore we can reject the null hypothesis of no difference. Our conclusion is that the number experiencing remission in the befriending group is significantly more than those in the control group ($\chi^2 = 5.6$, df = 1, p=0.018). In reality this calculation will be performed in a flash by a statistical software programme, but it is useful to know something about the theory behind it to fully understand its purpose.

Odds ratios

Odds ratios are widely used in a variety of research designs to describe the impact of a risk factor on an outcome. The odds ratio is the ratio of the odds of an event occurring in one group to the odds of it occurring in another group. These groups might be men or women, a study or comparison group or a case or control group, for example.

The higher the odds ratio is, the more likely the event is to occur in one group in comparison to another. The odds ratio can be interpreted in the following way:

- If the odds ratio is greater than 1, the event is more likely to occur in one group than another.

- If the odds ratio is less than 1, the event is less likely to occur in one group than another.

- If the odds ratio equals 1 the event is just as likely to occur in one group as another.

Calculating the odds ratio

To calculate the odds ratio, first calculate the odds of the outcome occurring in each group by dividing the number of occurrences of the outcome by the number of non-occurrences. Secondly, you divide the odds for one group by the other to find the odds ratio. This is best described through an example.

Let us imagine a cross-sectional study which has found the prevalence of depression in men and women in a particular population. We can calculate the odds of women being depressed in comparison to men (the odds ratio) from these results.

Firstly, tabulate the results in the format as suggested in Table 10.3, which shows the number of women who are depressed or not depressed and similar figures for men. We have supplanted the actual figures with letters to demonstrate how to calculate the odds ratio. This table is known as a 2 × 2 table as it has two cells of data for each of the two categories.

Table 10.3 2 × 2 table for calculating the odds ratio

	Depressed	Not depressed
Female	A	B
Male	C	D

Next, we calculate the odds of the outcome occurring (being depressed) in each group.

The odds of women being depressed is calculated by dividing the number of women who are depressed by the number who are not depressed: A/B.

The odds of men being depressed is calculated by dividing the number of men who are depressed by the number who are not depressed: C/D.

To calculate the odds ratio (OR) simply divide one by the other:

$$OR = \frac{A/B}{C/D} = \frac{A \times D}{B \times C}$$

Let us put some figures into this table to see it working in practice (Table 10.4).

Table 10.4 Cross-sectional study results

	Depressed	Not depressed	Total
Female	81	315	396
Male	35	223	258
Total	116	538	654

The odds of being depressed if a woman = 81/315 = 0.26

The odds of being depressed if a man = 35/223 = 0.16

The odds ratio (OR) of being depressed if a woman compared to a man = 0.26/0.16 = 1.64

This odds ratio of 1.64 means that women have increased odds of being depressed in contrast to men.

Odds ratios and confidence intervals

As we know, confidence intervals tell us whether particular findings hold statistical significance. They work in a similar way for odds ratios as they do for relative risks (Chapter 8).

Ninety-five per cent confidence intervals around odds ratios provide us with a range of values in which the true population odds ratio will lie on 95 occasions if the study were replicated 100 times, for example.

To interpret their statistical significance simply follow these three rules (which are exactly the same as relative risks):

- If the two figures in the confidence interval are both above 1, then it means that the odds of the outcome occurring in the first group is statistically significantly higher than the second group.

- If the two figures in the confidence interval are both below 1, then it means that the odds of the outcome occurring in the first group is statistically significantly lower than the second group.

- If the two figures are either side of 1 (one is below 1 and the other is above 1), then it means that the odds of the outcome occurring in one group is not statistically significantly different from the other group. This is the case because it is possible that the odds ratio could equal 1, which means that there is equal likelihood of the outcome occurring in either group.

Example: odds ratios in case-control studies

Odds ratios are frequently used in reporting the findings of case-control studies. They give us the odds likelihood of the outcome occurring in one group in contrast to the other. Let us look at some results of a case-control study I conducted on the outcomes of Mental Health Act assessments (Webber and Huxley, 2004) as an example of how odds ratios are used.

The paper explored risk factors for emergency detention under section 4 of the Mental Health Act 1983. The data given in Table 10.5 summarises some of the associations between risk factors and the outcome of admission under section 4 following a Mental Health Act assessment. This data is extracted from Table 2 of Webber and Huxley (2004) (p.1004).

Table 10.5 Odds ratios of risk factors for emergency compulsory admissions (from Table 2, Webber and Huxley, 2004)

	Odds ratio	95% Confidence Interval	*p*-value
Non-white British	1.71	0.96 to 3.02	0.07
Bi-polar affective disorder	2.60	1.34 to 5.02	0.004
Present risk identified by ASW	3.06	1.57 – 5.95	0.001

To interpret these findings look at the confidence intervals and p-values in Table 10.5. Firstly, although the odds ratio for the 'non-white British' row (1.71) is greater than 1, the confidence interval includes the value 1. The lower figure (0.96) is slightly smaller than 1 and the higher figure (3.02) is above 1. This denotes a non-significant odds ratio and is reflected in the p-value which is slightly more than 0.05. This result indicates that there is no significant difference in the odds likelihood of non-white British people being admitted under section 4 (as opposed to other outcomes of a Mental Health Act assessment) in contrast to people of white British origin.

The second row of data (Table 10.5) gives the odds ratio for people with a diagnosis of bi-polar affective disorder being admitted under section 4 in contrast to people with other diagnoses. Here the odds ratio is 2.60 with its confidence intervals both above 1. This indicates that people with a diagnosis of bi-polar affective disorder have a statistically significant greater odds likelihood of being admitted under section 4 than other assessment outcomes.

Now try this out for yourself: do people who present a risk that is identified by an ASW have higher odds of being admitted under section 4 than any other outcome of a Mental Health Act assessment (Table 10.5)? Write a sentence explaining the statistical significance of this result.

FURTHER READING

Martin Bland and Douglas Altman (2000) provide a succinct introduction to odds ratios that is worth reading for additional clarification, should it be required.

Student's t-test

The *t* statistic was introduced by William Sealy Gosset for cheaply monitoring the quality of the beer he brewed. He used the pen name 'student' when he published the *t* distribution in 1908, hence the *t*-test being referred to as 'Student's *t*-test' (Student, 1908).

Student's *t*-test is used to compare the means of two normally distributed populations. It is used with continuous variables such as the scores on a depression scale or age in years which have a mean and standard deviation.

There are two types of *t*-tests. Firstly, the *t*-test is used with two *independent samples*. This may be the case and control groups in a case-control study or the intervention and control groups in a randomised-controlled trial, for example. Also, the independent groups may be defined by a binary variable (one which has two options) such as gender (men/women) or Approved Social Worker (yes/no).

The second type of *t*-test is *paired*. The paired *t*-test is used when there is a relationship between the two groups. For example, it is used to compare the means on a depression scale administered before and after an intervention. Here, the two groups are the baseline and follow-up scores which are taken from the same scale.

In order to perform a *t*-test, three assumptions need to be met:

• Both the samples must be normally distributed. This can be checked by inspecting a histogram and looking for the bell-shaped curve.

• The variances of both samples must be similar. The variance is the square of the standard deviation. Hence the standard deviations of the two samples need to be similar.

• The samples need to be either independent (for the independent samples t-test) or related (for the paired t-test).

The Student's *t*-test is used in any research design in which it is necessary to compare the means of two groups, hence its wide application. Let us look at some examples of independent samples *t*-tests and paired *t*-tests.

In our cross-sectional survey of mental health social workers, we compared those who were practising as an Approved Social Worker (ASW) and those who were not (Evans *et al.*, 2005). Table 4 of this paper (Evans *et al.*, 2005) presents the differences in attitudes towards work and policy of these two groups. The *t*-test was used to evaluate the difference in means on the terrible-delighted scale (Andrews and Withey, 1976) for a range of questions. A higher score on the terrible-delighted scale indicates greater satisfaction. Two of the questions from Table 4 (Evans *et al.*, 2005) are reproduced here in Table 10.6.

Table 10.6 Attitudes to work and policy of ASWs and non-ASWs (from Table 4, Evans et al., 2005)

	Group	Mean (s.d.)	*t*-test results
Feelings about current job	Non-ASW	4.8 (1.2)	$t = 3.29$, d.f.$=233$, $p = 0.001$
	ASW	4.2 (1.2)	
Place of mental health social work in mental health services	Non-ASW	3.5 (1.2)	$t = 0.72$, d.f.$=231$, $p = 0.47$
	ASW	3.4 (1.3)	

Looking at the first line of data in Table 10.6 we can see that non-ASWs have a higher mean satisfaction with their current job (4.8) than ASWs (4.2). The *t*-test helps us to evaluate whether this difference is statistically significant. In the final column of Table 10.6 these results are presented. The key figure to look at is the *p*-value, which is 0.001. This figure is well below the customary cut-off for statistical significance (0.05) and we can therefore conclude that non-ASWs feel more satisfied than ASWs with their current job.

The second line of data (Table 10.6) shows the mean satisfaction scores for ASWs and non-ASWs about the place of mental health social work in mental health services. Non-ASWs were slightly more satisfied on average (3.5) than ASWs (3.4). However, the *p*-value was 0.47, which is above the threshold for statistical significance. This indicates a strong likelihood that this difference was caused by chance alone and it was not a real difference between the ASWs and non-ASWs. Hence we cannot conclude that non-ASWs feel any different about the place of mental health social work in mental health services from ASWs.

For an example of paired *t*-tests, let us look at Alison Wood and colleagues' (1996) trial of cognitive behavioural therapy for depression in adolescents. They used paired *t*-tests to examine differences in ratings between parents and adolescents. For example, they found that parental ratings of depressive symptoms in their son or daughter were significantly lower than their child's ratings ($t=4.2$, df$=46$, p<0.001) (Wood *et al.*, 1996: 741). They used paired *t*-tests as the depression ratings of the parents and adolescents were related.

They also used paired *t*-tests to evaluate change in study participants between baseline and follow-up. For example, they found that anxiety decreased significantly between baseline and immediately following the intervention for both groups ($t=3.4$, df$=42$, p<0.01) (Wood *et al.*, 1996: 742). Paired *t*-tests were used here as the baseline and follow-up scores for individuals are related.

Non-parametric tests

The Student's *t*-test is known as a 'parametric' test. It is used with continuous variables that are normally distributed. However, if a variable is skewed or otherwise does not follow a normal distribution, it would not be appropriate to use a parametric test.

Additionally, variables that are derived from ranks also cannot be evaluated using parametric tests. An example of a ranking variable is the Indices of Deprivation (Noble *et al.*, 2004) which rank local authorities in England from the highest to the least deprived areas.

Skewed variables and ranking variables are analysed using a 'family' of tests known as 'non-parametric tests'. All parametric tests will have a non-parametric equivalent. For example, the non-parametric equivalents of Student's *t*-test are:

• Mann-Whitney U test (for independent samples)

• Wilcoxon Signed Rank test (for related samples)

The Mann-Whitney U test is frequently used to evaluate inter-group differences in the General Health Questionnaire (GHQ) (Goldberg and Williams, 1988), for example. The GHQ was administered to mental health social workers to measure common mental disorder in our national survey (Evans *et al.*, 2005). As the GHQ was skewed, we tested the difference between the median scores of ASWs and non-ASWs using the Mann-Whitney U test. We found that the median ASW score on the GHQ (4) was significantly higher than non-ASWs (2) (U=-2.05, $p<0.04$).

So far we have looked at how to test for associations between:

• two categorical variables (chi-square);

• one categorical variable (with two categories) and one continuous variable (t-test or non-parametric equivalent).

There are two more types of tests to be familiar with:

• two continuous variables (correlation);

• one categorical variable (with more than two categories) and one continuous variable (one-way ANOVA or non-parametric equivalent).

Correlations

The association between two continuous variables can be represented pictorially using scatterplots. Scatterplots plot one variable on the horizontal (x) axis and the other on the vertical (y) axis. Here are some examples.

Figure 10.6 is a scatterplot demonstrating a positive association between two continuous variables. This means that as one variable increases, the other variable also increases.

Figure 10.7 is a scatterplot demonstrating a negative association between two continuous variables. This means that as one variable increases, the other variable decreases.

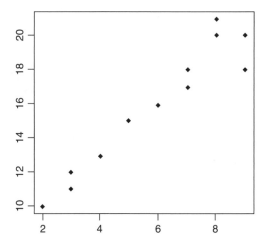

Figure 10.6 Positive association

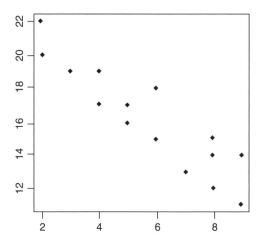

Figure 10.7 Negative association

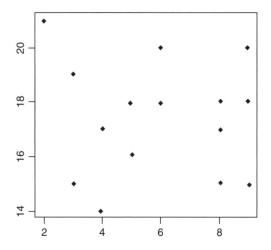

Figure 10.8 No association

Figure 10.8 is a scatterplot demonstrating no association between two continuous variables. The data points are randomly scattered across the plot and there is no systematic association between the two variables.

Correlations are used to quantify the linear relationship between two continuous variables that can be illustrated in scatterplots. There are two types of correlations that are most relevant:

● Pearson product-moment correlation coefficient (parametric)

● Spearman's rank correlation coefficient (non-parametric)

Pearson's and Spearman's correlation coefficient can both be interpreted in the same way. The correlation coefficient (ρ) is a figure between –1 and 1.

● –1 denotes a perfect negative correlation (i.e. as one variable goes up, the other goes down);

● 1 denotes a perfect positive correlation (i.e. as one variable goes up, the other goes up);

● 0 denotes no correlation.

The proximity of the correlation to either 0 or 1 helps you to understand the strength of the correlation, or how strongly the two variables are associated. A correlation between –0.5 and 0.5 is a weak correlation in contrast to one below –0.5 or above 0.5 which is strong. The closer the correlation gets to 1 or –1, the stronger the correlation is. Let us give an example to explore this a little further.

In the development of our measure of an individual's access to social capital (the Resource Generator-UK (RG-UK)) (Webber and Huxley, 2007), we evaluated how closely it was associated with different concepts. We compared it with the GHQ (Goldberg and Williams, 1988) and a measure of locus of control (Coleman and DeLeire, 2003). As all three instruments were continuous measures, we calculated correlation coefficients to evaluate the strength of association between them. We found that the RG-UK had a weak negative correlation with the GHQ (ρ =-0.11, p<0.05). This meant that as people had access to more social capital, their score on the GHQ fell. Lower GHQ scores indicate a lower likelihood of common mental disorder, so this pattern shows a weak association between access to social capital and mental health.

We also found that locus of control was associated with the RG-UK and the correlation was stronger than with the GHQ: ρ =-0.45, p<0.0001. This is only a moderate correlation, but it tells us that access to social capital is associated with external locus of control in a negative direction (i.e. access to more social capital is associated with a stronger sense that the world is controlled from within the individual than by external factors). That this correlation is stronger than with the GHQ tells us that access to social capital is more strongly associated with locus of control than with GHQ scores. Further examples can be found elsewhere in the paper (e.g. Table 4, Webber and Huxley, 2007: 490).

FURTHER READING

Although quite dated and wordy, a useful introduction to correlation is provided by Rummel (1976).

One-way analysis of variance (ANOVA)

Analysis of variance is a family of statistical techniques which are used for a multitude of different purposes. Here we will introduce you to only one, the one-way analysis of variance (ANOVA). The one-way ANOVA is equivalent to Student's *t*-test, but is used when the categorical variable has more than two categories. It is a parametric test, so can only be used when the continuous variable is normally distributed and the other assumptions for the *t*-test are met. Therefore the one-way ANOVA tests for differences in the means of at least three groups at one time. It does this by calculating the F statistic.

We used the one-way ANOVA in our sub-group analysis of the mental health social work national survey (Evans *et al.*, 2006). Table 10.7 shows some data extracted from this paper.

Table 10.7 Burnout and job demands of mental health social workers (from Table 2, Evans et al., 2006)

	Job demands			
	Low (n=63)	Medium (n=81)	High (n=85)	One-way ANOVA
Emotional exhaustion MBI mean (s.d.)	21.5 (10.0)	24.1 (9.7)	31.8 (7.9)	$F=25.44$, d.f.=2, 219, $p<0.001$
Personal accomplishment MBI mean (s.d.)	32.4 (7.8)	34.1 (6.7)	34.5 (5.9)	$F = 1.76$, d.f.=2, 216, $p = 0.174$

Table 10.7 has split the sample of mental health social workers into three groups according to the demands of their job (low, medium and high), as measured by the Karasek Job Content Questionnaire (Karasek, 1979). The two rows of data are the emotional exhaustion and personal accomplishment sub scales of the Maslach Burnout Inventory (Maslach and Jackson, 1986). The one-way ANOVA results inform us of differences between these groups.

In the first line of data, the *p*-value of the F-test is very small ($p<0.001$), indicating that there are significant differences between the groups. We can see that the emotional exhaustion score for those with high job demands (31.8) is much higher than the other two groups (21.5 and 24.1 respectively). The F-test confirms that this is a significant difference and unlikely to be a chance finding.

In the second line of data, in contrast, the *p*-value is above the threshold of 0.05, indicating that any differences are likely to be caused by chance. On inspecting the data, we can see that those with high job demands have marginally more personal accomplishment, on average, than those with low or medium job demands. However, it is likely that this difference was caused by chance so we cannot conclude that this is a statistically significant difference. Therefore, personal accomplishment is not associated with job demands in this sample.

The non-parametric equivalent of the one-way ANOVA is the Kruskal-Wallis one-way analysis of variance by ranks, which compares the medians of at least three groups.

Summary of univariate statistical tests

Within this chapter we have introduced you to a number of different statistical tests. Table 10.8 brings them all together and groups them under the headings of parametric and non-parametric as a reference point for you.

Table 10.8 Summary of univariate statistical tests

Purpose of test	Parametric test	Non-parametric test
Compares two categorical variables	N/A	Chi-Square test
Compares two independent samples	t test for independent samples	Mann-Whitney U test
Compares two related samples	Paired t test	Wilcoxon signed-rank test
Assesses the linear association between two continuous variables	Pearson correlation coefficient	Spearman rank correlation coefficient
Compares three or more groups	One way analysis of variance (F test)	Kruskal-Wallis one way analysis of variance by ranks

An introduction to multivariate analysis

Analysis involving more than one predictor variable can become quite complex, and a full description is beyond the scope of this chapter. However, we will provide an accessible introduction to the topic here. In short, we will explore the rationale for multivariate analysis. Then we will introduce two common types – linear and logistic regression. We will highlight the important statistics to extract from tables reporting the results of multivariate analysis and describe how to interpret them.

Confounding

Quantitative research of relevance to mental health social work frequently explores associations between risk factors and outcomes, as we have found in previous chapters. Studies frequently test a hypothesis that a specific risk factor leads to a specified outcome. For example, a cohort study may test the hypothesis that social support is associated with recovery from depression.

Quite frequently, there is more than one possible explanation for the outcome. In this example, an individual's personality may hinder their recovery from depression, particularly when it is anxious or avoidant, as this may prevent them taking the necessary risks that are involved in the recovery process. When personality is also associated with the predictor variable (social support in our example here), then it is known as a 'confounding variable'. In this case it is entirely plausible that the two are associated as people with an anxious or avoidant personality may shun social contact and receive less social support from other people.

Confounding variables provide alternative explanations for the outcome. They are associated with both the risk factor and outcome. If there is an association between the risk factor and outcome, and confounding variables are not considered, the perceived relationship between the risk factor and outcome will be inaccurate. The effect of confounding

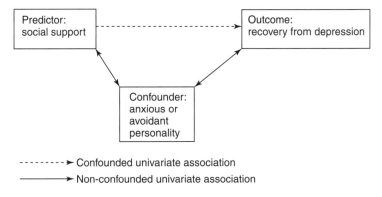

Figure 10.9 Effect of confounding variable on relationship between a predictor and outcome

variables is described in Figure 10.9. It shows that a univariate association between a predictor variable (e.g. social support) and an outcome (e.g. recovery from depression) may become confounded when a third variable (e.g. anxious or avoidant personality) is introduced.

Multivariate analysis is used to determine if the third variable is a confounder of the relationship or not. Here we will introduce you to two common forms of multivariate analysis – linear and logistic regression.

Linear regression

Linear regression is a multivariate method used for modelling a number of potential risk factors associated with a particular outcome. The outcome used in linear regression must be a continuous variable, such as the score on a depression scale (e.g. Hospital Anxiety and Depression Scale (Zigmond and Snaith, 1983)) or a quality of life measure (e.g. Manchester Short Assessment of Quality of Life (Priebe *et al.*, 1999)).

In its simplest form linear regression models the relationship between two continuous variables, a risk factor and an outcome. This relationship is described in the following equation:

$$y = \beta_0 + \beta_1 x + \varepsilon$$

where:

y is the outcome variable (also known as the dependent variable)

x is the risk factor or predictor variable (also known as the independent variable)

β_0 is the intercept, or 'constant'

β_1 is the coefficient for variable x

ε is the unexplained variation in y

In this equation, variables y and x must be approximately normally distributed continuous variables for a linear regression to be accurate.

The purpose of the equation is to predict values of y given values of x. More specifically, it is used to draw a regression line to indicate a linear relationship between two variables. The value for β_0 is where the regression line crosses the y axis and the value for β_1 is the gradient of the slope of the line. β_1 is important because it describes the relationship between x and y. It works in a similar way to the correlation coefficients described above:

- If β_1 is above 0, it indicates a positive relationship between x and y.

- If β_1 is below 0, it indicates a negative relationship between x and y.

β_1 is sometimes referred to as the 'Beta coefficient' or simply 'B'. It is very useful in interpreting the results of a regression analysis, as we shall shortly see.

Figure 10.10 illustrates the various components of the regression equation and the resulting regression line. The predictor (independent) variable is plotted along the x axis (access to social capital). The outcome (dependent) variable is plotted along the y axis (depression score). The relationship between the two is summarised in the regression line. The slope of the line (β_1) is –0.13 and the intercept (β_0) is 13.8. This line shows a negative association between access to social capital and depression scores. In particular, it shows that, on average, depression scores decrease by 1 point for every extra 0.13 social resource that is accessed (our measure of social capital), not including the effect of other unmeasured variables.

Controlling for confounders with linear regression

So far, we have considered the linear relationship between two continuous variables. The regression equation allows us to include any number of additional variables which enables us to account for the effect of potential confounders:

$$y = \beta_0 + \beta_1 x_1 + \beta_2 x_2 \ldots + \beta_p x_p + \varepsilon$$

Within this equation each subsequent variable added to the model (x_p) has a coefficient (β_p),

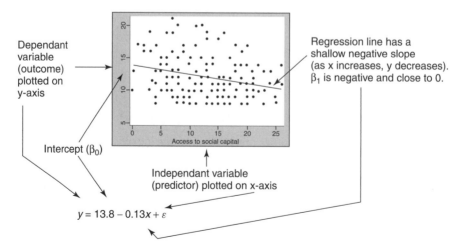

Figure 10.10 *Graphical illustration of a regression line and equation*

and it is these coefficients which are the key to identifying confounding variables. This is best illustrated through an example.

Table 10.9 is an extract of the results of our national survey of mental health social workers. It shows the variables that are associated with job satisfaction in the linear regression model (Table 3, Evans *et al.*, 2006, p. 79). Each of these variables – feeling valued, job demands, decision latitude, active as an ASW and feelings about the social work role – has an independent association with the outcome (job satisfaction). The two columns labelled 'Beta' and '*p*' inform us of the direction and significance of the association.

Table 10.9 Linear regression model for predictors of job satisfaction of mental health social workers (from Table 3, Evans et al., 2006)

Variable	Beta	*p*
Feeling valued	0.25	0.002
Job demands	−0.22	0.002
Decision latitude	0.21	0.003
Active as an ASW	−0.15	0.029
Feelings about the social work role	0.15	0.047

Firstly, a quick glance down the column of *p*-values on the right hand side of Table 10.9 indicates that each are statistically significant as they are smaller than 0.05. This means that the likelihood of these being associated with job satisfaction by chance alone is acceptably small.

Secondly, the 'Beta' column contains the standardised beta coefficients from the linear regression model. As they have been standardised, we know that higher beta values (irrespective of whether they are positive or negative) indicate more important variables in the model. Hence, 'feeling valued' has been listed at the top as its beta value is the highest. The beta coefficients determine the gradient of the regression line (Figure 10.10), so higher values will indicate steeper gradients, which indicate stronger associations.

The presence or absence of a minus sign indicates the direction of the slope of the regression line and the direction of the association. So, the interpretation of these beta values is as follows:

• Job satisfaction is greater when workers feel more valued.

• Job satisfaction is lower when job demands are higher.

• Job satisfaction is greater when workers have greater decision latitude.

• Job satisfaction is lower for those active as an ASW (this variable is categorical and 'dummy' variables were used in the regression equation to compare the categories with).

• Job satisfaction is greater when workers feel more positive about the social work role in mental health services.

Table 10.9 presents the final multivariate model for job satisfaction. But we have missed a step – the univariate analysis. In the univariate analysis job-related social support, as measured by the Karasek Job Content Questionnaire (Karasek, 1979), was related to job satisfaction (Table 2, Evans *et al.*, 2006, p.78). Mental health social workers with greater social support in the workplace had better job satisfaction. However, social support does not appear in the multivariate model in Table 10.9. So where has it gone?

When the other variables that appear in Table 10.9 were entered into the linear regression model, the *p*-value for the association between job satisfaction and social support rose above 0.05. This is called 'dropping out of the model'. Variables drop out of the model when other confounding variables are entered into it. If the *p*-value for the association between job satisfaction and social support stayed below 0.05 after the inclusion of additional variables, we could have concluded that their association was independent of other variables. However, these variables are *confounders* for the association between social support and job satisfaction. As we state in the paper:

> *These results suggest that personal characteristics, aspects of the working environment or feelings about that environment might confound the univariate association between job satisfaction and social support. (Evans et al., 2006, p.78)*

The linear regression results given in Table 10.9 only present the variables with an independent association with job satisfaction. They do not include other variables such as social support, whose univariate association with job satisfaction can be explained by other variables. These variables are dropped from the model when confounding variables are entered. The confounders have independent associations with job satisfaction in their own right and are the important ones to refer to when discussing results such as this.

Logistic regression

So far, we have considered multivariate analysis for continuous outcomes. A different method – logistic regression – is used when the outcome is binary, that is, is formed of two categories. In mental health research, for example, it is often used to determine risk factors for the presence or absence of mental disorders. It is also used in the analysis of case-control studies to compare the case and control groups.

The results of logistic regression are presented as odds ratios which are interpreted in the same way as in univariate analysis. We shall look at an example below which illustrates this.

Logistic regression is a useful alternative for a range of circumstances in which linear regression is not appropriate. For example:

- Unlike linear regression, logistic regression does not assume a linear association between predictors (independent variables) and outcome (dependent variable) so it can be used to model non-linear relationships.

- Unlike linear regression, logistic regression can be used when the dependent variable is not normally distributed – it is frequently converted into a binary variable in these circumstances.

- Unlike linear regression, logistic regression can include independent variables that are not normally distributed.

Controlling for confounders with logistic regression

The best way of understanding logistic regression is through an example. Let us look again at the case-control study we referred to above (Webber and Huxley, 2004). Instead of look-ing at the results for the outcome of section 4 of the Mental Health Act 1983 (MHA), let us consider the results for all detentions under the MHA (sections 2, 3 and 4) in contrast to the other assessment outcomes (informal or no admission). The purpose of this analysis is to tell us which risk factors are associated with compulsory admissions under the MHA fol-lowing a MHA assessment.

The univariate analysis in this study found that being of non-white British ethnicity, having a diagnosis of psychosis, presenting a risk to self or others at the time of the MHA assess-ment, having insecure housing and multiple social exclusion were all risk factors for compulsory admission. However, a different picture emerged in the multivariate logistic regression, which is summarised in Table 10.10.

Table 10.10 Logistic regression model for predictors of compulsory psychiatric admissions (from Table 7, Webber and Huxley, 2004)

Variable	Odds ratio	95% confidence intervals	*p*
Non-white British ethnicity	2.16	1.16 – 4.02	0.016
Psychosis diagnosis	2.22	1.21 – 4.07	0.010
Present risk	11.14	6.18 – 20.09	<0.001
Insecure housing	1.51	0.82 – 2.76	ns
Multiple social exclusion	1.59	0.87 – 2.91	ns

The first thing to notice in Table 10.10 is that two of the variables have become non-signifi-cant in the logistic regression model – insecure housing and multiple social exclusion. These variables were 'dropped' from the model when the others were entered. Or, in other words, non-white British ethnicity, having a diagnosis of psychosis or presenting a risk at the time of the MHA assessment were all *confounders* for the variables of insecure housing and mul-tiple social exclusion. Insecure housing and multiple social exclusion therefore do not have an independent association with compulsory detention following a MHA assessment.

The top three variables in Table 10.10 all have an independent association with the outcome (compulsory detention under s.2, 3 or 4 of the MHA) because their p-values have remained below 0.05. None of the other variables confound their relationships with the outcome.

The odds ratios can be interpreted in exactly the same way as in a univariate analysis and as previously described. The confidence intervals for all three variables are above 1, which indicates an increased odds likelihood, and can be interpreted thus:

• People of non-white British ethnicity have a higher odds of being compulsorily detained following a MHA assessment.

• People with a diagnosis of psychosis have a higher odds of being compulsorily detained following a MHA assessment.

• People presenting a risk at the time of the MHA assessment have a higher odds of being compulsorily detained following a MHA assessment.

Other forms of multivariate analysis

There are many different types of multivariate analysis that are used in research. One of the new techniques that is becoming more widely used is multi-level modelling. This allows for researchers to distinguish between effects at different levels within samples. For example, it is possible to investigate the effect of variables at the level of individuals and groups using multi-level modelling techniques. Social capital is a concept that is frequently measured at the level of individuals and communities. Multi-level modelling is often used

---

BOX **10.1**

Multiple choice self-test

Test your understanding of the ideas contained within this chapter with this self-test. The answers can be found in Appendix 1.

1 *Which one of the following is the closest description of a population mean age?*

   a *The average age of a sample*

   b *The average age of a population*

   c *The average age of a sampling frame*

   d *The average age of non-responders*

2 *Which one of the following is not true?*

   a *95 per cent confidence intervals are a range of values that are likely to contain the unknown value for the population*

   b *95 per cent confidence intervals are a range of values that always contain the unknown value for the population*

   c *95 per cent confidence intervals always contain the sample mean (or whichever statistic they are surrounding)*

   d *95 per cent confidence intervals represent the range in which 95 per cent of population mean values (or whichever statistic they are surrounding) would lie if numerous samples were collected from the same population*

3 *Confidence intervals can tell you whether or not a difference in means is statistically significant. True or false.*

4 *Which one of the following values must the confidence intervals for a difference in means not include for the difference to be statistically significant?*

   a *0*

   b *1*

   c *2*

   d *3*

BOX ***10.1*** *(CONT.)*

5 Which of the following are statistically significant results for a difference in means? *(Select all those that apply)*

  a The difference in mean age between men and women in the sample was 1.3 (95% CI = −1.5 to 2.7) years ☐

  b The difference in mean age between men and women in the sample was 1.3 (95% CI = 0.3 to 2.7) years ☐

  c The difference in mean age between men and women in the sample was −1.3 (95% CI = −2.7 to −0.3) years ☐

  d The difference in mean age between men and women in the sample was −1.3 (95% CI = −2.7 to 2.7) years ☐

6 The chi-squared test can only be used with categorical variables. True or false?

7 Which one of the following is not a type of chi-squared test?

  a Chi-squared test of goodness of fit ☐

  b Chi-squared test for independence ☐

  c Chi-squared test of the null hypothesis ☐

  d Chi-squared test for homogeneity ☐

8 Large chi-squared values are required to reject the null hypothesis of no difference between variables. True or false?

9 If the odds ratio is greater than 1, the event is less likely to occur in one group than another. True or false?

10 If the upper and lower figures in a confidence interval around an odds ratio are either side of 1, then it means that the odds of the outcome occurring in one group is not statistically significantly different from the other group. True or false?

11 Which of the following assumptions need to be met for a t-test? (Select all that apply)

  a Both the samples must be normally distributed ☐

  b The variances of both samples must be similar ☐

  c The samples need to be independent or related, depending on the type of t-test being performed ☐

  d The categorical variable defining the groups for comparison must be a binary variable (i.e. have two groups) ☐

12 The customary threshold (0.05) for p-values applies to all statistical tests. True or false?

BOX 10.1 (CONT.)

13 When are non-parametric tests used? (Select all that apply)

   a When you have two categorical variables

   b When you have a skewed continuous variable

   c When you have a ranking variable

   d When you don't know what else to do

14 When do you calculate a correlation coefficient? (Select only one)

   a When you want to find the association between two categorical variables

   b When you want to find the association between two continuous variables

   c When you want to find the association between one continuous variable and one categorical variable

   d When you want to see how efficient a researcher has been

15 Which of the following are non-parametric tests? (Select all that apply)

   a Wilcoxon signed-rank test

   b Student's t-test

   c Mann-Whitney U test

   d Spearman's rank correlation

16 Which of the following are parametric tests? (Select all that apply)

   a Chi-Squared test

   b Student's t-test

   c Pearson's correlation

   d One-Way Analysis of Variance

17 Confounding variables are associated with both the risk factor and outcome being studied. True or false?

18 On which of the following occasions is logistic regression used in contrast to linear regression? (Select all that apply)

   a When there is a non-linear relationship between two continuous variables

   b When there is a linear relationship between two continuous variables

   c When the outcome variable is binary

   d When the risk factors are not normally distributed

Chapter 11

How to critically appraise qualitative studies

This chapter will introduce you to three commonly-used qualitative methods – interviews, focus groups and observation – with relevant examples of each. It will also explore the contribution of ethnography to social work practice. Finally it will examine the key principles of qualitative research including sampling, data collection and analysis.

Rationale

A broad distinction between qualitative research and quantitative research is that the former explores the 'why?', 'what?' and 'how?' questions in contrast to the 'how many?' or 'how frequently?' of quantitative research. Whilst quantitative research examines connections between risk factors and outcomes, or evaluates the effectiveness of interventions, qualitative research principally explores the meaning of phenomena from a variety of perspectives. Qualitative research begins with the notion that each individual's experience is unique. It is frequently guided by the participants more than by the researchers, with data collection working as an iterative process.

Some questions that may be answered by qualitative research are, for example:

- How do people who use mental health services understand the role of social work within multi-disciplinary teams?

- What is the role of social support in the prevention of mental health crises?

- What is the experience of social workers within mental health home treatment teams?

Qualitative research is generally held in high regard within social work as its ethos seems to fit more easily with the social work value base than quantitative research. In mental health research, though, the primacy of the hierarchy of evidence (see Chapter 1) means that qualitative research is less well-respected than quantitative research. However, as discussed in Chapter 7, the Medical Research Council insists on the inclusion of qualitative research in the evaluation of complex interventions to help understand the processes at work within them (Medical Research Council, 2000). This underlines the importance of qualitative methods as complimentary to quantitative methods.

Interviews in qualitative research

Interviews in qualitative research are often in-depth and either semi-structured or unstructured. Unlike highly structured and standardised interviews in other research designs, qualitative researchers do not conduct identical interviews with every participant. They may start with a list of questions or themes to cover, known as a 'topic guide', but they would soon go beyond this to probe deeper into participants' understandings of the research topic. The topic guide itself develops as an iterative process throughout the life of the interviews.

The role of the researcher is not to simply gather data, but to expertly enable the participant to focus on areas of relevance to the research question and of most interest to them. It is important for the researcher to establish a good rapport with the participant. This is particularly crucial when repeated interviews are required or when sensitive issues are being discussed.

Interviews are useful for the construction of the meaning of phenomena from a variety of perspectives. Qualitative researchers encourage participants to talk about their experiences in order to create a narrative account in their own words. Participants are encouraged to discuss their unique perspective to enable them to construct their own meanings of phenomena under investigation.

A good example of how participants, in conjunction with the researcher, produce accounts of their lives is provided by Marcus Redley (2003). He conducted interviews with people who had self-harmed to explore how living in a deprived locality was associated with self-harming behaviour. He identified that the participants were not living the lives that they desired. For example:

> *Mr Medwin: '[. . .] because a had been doon tae the social security, cause it wis Jenny's [wife] birthday on Monday, an a, an a wis getting that piss, pissing me aboot wi money, right. Really fed up cause they never gave me anything, an a didnae any money to get her for her birthday, a jist got pissed off, an he's say's [man in a bar near to social security offices] 'ye want some vali's ye look awfae doon in the dumps', a say's fucking gie me them, and plus a has tha drink. So that's why, he's [the drug supplier] say's 'it'll calm am ye doon', calm me doon alright [laughs]' (unemployed builder and registered alcoholic living with his wife and three children). (Redley, 2003: 353)*

In this example, Mr Medwin's account can be read as constructing a 'gap' between the actual reality of being messed around by the social security office and the desire to buy his wife a birthday present.

Let us now take a look at a fuller example which demonstrates the usefulness of qualitative interviews in informing social work practice. The Scottish Recovery Network conducted a series of qualitative interviews in 2005 to develop narratives of individuals' recovery from severe mental health problems (Example 11.1).

EXAMPLE **11.1**

Recovery narratives (Brown and Kandirikirira, 2007)

Background

The recovery paradigm has recently come to the fore within mental health services, promoting the reality that people with severe and enduring mental health problems can lead independent lives even in the presence of symptoms. The definition and experience of

EXAMPLE **11.1** *(CONT.)*

recovery varies from individual to individual making it a unique experience. This research was conducted by the Scottish Recovery Network to produce narratives of recovery of people across Scotland.

Sample

64 people self-defined as recovered or recovering from long-term mental health problems in Scotland. Participants were purposively selected to achieve diversity in terms of geography, recovery stage, medical condition and demographics.

Method

Semi-structured face to face interviews which enabled participants to reflect on factors that had helped or hindered their recovery journey, factors that helped them to sustain their well-being and their subjective experiences of recovery. Interviews lasted between 40 and 90 minutes.

Analysis

Broad themes were developed by the researchers in liaison with the participants. The interview transcripts were independently analysed and coded thematically by two researchers.

Results

The results have been presented in a series of chapters based on recovering identity, re-engaging socially, re-building relationships, finding the right services and developing coping strategies. Each chapter is sub-divided into a series of inter-woven themes extracting key messages about the recovery experience for these 64 individuals. For example, in the relationships chapter one person found peer support invaluable, though didn't want to become sucked into the mental health system:

> *I've got a new social network which is mainly people with the same problems. I get a lot of support from them . . . they keep you away from the more chronic services because in a way, If you are going to get better then it is not a good idea to get sucked into mental health and spend all your time with unwell people . . . It would be better for me if I could branch out on my own and not rely so heavily on the user group.*

Another participant found her social worker useful in helping her GP to listen to her.

> *My doctor didn't seem to listen to me . . . I couldn't speak so I asked [social worker] to come with me to my GP. And he did . . . He made the appointment, took me in and my doctor was quite annoyed that 'oh why are you bringing your social worker in?' And I said . . . 'I really can't speak to you very well, I don't really feel you are listening . . . I am sorry I can't speak anymore I am too distressed'. And uhm [social worker] took over explaining everything. From that day on my GP, there has been a whole change of attitude, he now looks at me and he listens.*

Implications for practice

There are many useful ideas about good practice within these narratives and deserve to be read in full to do them justice.

Focus group interviews

Focus group interviews are in-depth group discussions of, usually, between eight and 12 people. The group is led by a skilled facilitator to discuss a topic of interest to them. The facilitator steers the group to discuss the key themes to be covered, but the content emerges from the dynamics and interaction of each group. Focus groups are used when it is likely that additional data will emerge from the group dynamics, which may determine the particular focus on the issues under discussion, a key distinction from individual interviews.

The participants must share some socio-demographic characteristics to ease the flow of discussion. However, the group would need to be sufficiently heterogeneous to ensure that a full discussion of the topic is undertaken. The facilitator must empower all group members to contribute and prevent any individuals from dominating the discussion, as this may diminish the full variety of views being expressed. The facilitator needs to be skilled in generating a wide-ranging discussion from the group to ensure that as many perspectives on the topic are covered as possible.

The focus group interview is tape-recorded and a second researcher is often present to take notes on non-verbal interactions and the flow of the discussion. These are linked to the transcripts to help identify participants on the tape-recording and ensure accuracy in the transcription.

Focus groups are useful for understanding shared experiences on generally non-sensitive topics. They can also be used for generating hypotheses for further research, or testing

---

*EXAMPLE **11.2***

User perspectives on day and accommodation services (Bryant et al., 2005)

Background

The National Service Framework for Mental Health (Department of Health, 1999c) and the Social Exclusion Unit's report (Social Exclusion Unit, 2004) have brought considerable changes to day services and housing provided for people with enduring mental health problems in recent years. In particular, they have become less institutionally-based and oriented towards goals of social inclusion. This study was conducted in the London Borough of Hillingdon to evaluate the day and accommodation services on the cusp of change.

Sample

A total of 72 people contributed to seven focus groups on day services, comprising people who used these services, their carers and staff. A smaller number (n = 23) contributed to five focus groups on accommodation services who again were either people who used these services, their carers or staff. Participants were self-selected and the mean age of the people who used the services were 51 years (day services) and 55 years (accommodation services).

Method

This study was comprised solely of focus groups with people who used services, their carers and staff contributing to separate groups. Two researchers independent of the

---

EXAMPLE 11.2 (CONT.)

service providers facilitated the groups. The focus groups were tape recorded and tran-scribed for analysis.

Analysis

The data were 'subjected to constant comparative analysis to identify recurrent and con-trasting aspects' (Bryant et al., 2005: 113). The researchers developed these into categories and then a range of relevant themes. Each group was analysed separately and then brought together for comparison.

Results

Four themes were common to both the day and accommodation services and were presented in this paper: defining services, supporting service users effectively, improving services and meaningful occupation. Here are two examples of the points raised in the groups.

Firstly, service users valued the role of support workers visiting regularly, resolving practi-cal difficulties and helping to prevent relapse:

> *. . . you are not very well she will see you a couple of times a week or take you to the shops . . . or give you a meal. (service user) (Bryant et al., 2005: 115)*

Secondly, day services staff were frustrated with a lack of medical support in managing and preventing crises, and they felt undervalued by doctors:

> *Because you work in a day programme so you are nothing, you don't know what you are talking about. They don't realize that you are the one dealing with the actual client. (day services staff) (Bryant et al., 2005: 116)*

Limitations

There are a number of limitations with this study that are worth mentioning. Firstly, as the sample was self-selected, it is possible that the study was unduly influenced by dominant voices. However, as there were a large number of participants, one hopes that some of the less dominant voices were heard. Individual interviews with people who did not feel comfortable in groups would have usefully supplemented the data collection. Secondly, this is a local study specific to the local services. Although the broad themes may be appli-cable elsewhere, without a full understanding of the local services this is difficult to deduce. Finally, the average age of the service users in this sample suggested that the groups were composed predominantly of people in their middle-age. It would be interest-ing to hear the views of younger service users, if there are any.

Implications for practice

Day and accommodation services provide a low key, but vital role in relapse prevention, facilitating long-term stability and independence. The people who used these services valued the informal mutual support that was available. Social workers can promote the value of these important social services to health colleagues in their multi-disciplinary teams, and help to ensure that the most highly valued and effective components remain in the modernisation of the mental health services.

concepts and questions in questionnaires or interview schedules (e.g. Evans *et al.*, 2006; Webber and Huxley, 2007).

An example of a focus group study that is of direct use for mental health social workers is a study on the views of mental health service users on day and accommodation services in the London Borough of Hillingdon conducted by Wendy Bryant and colleagues (2005 (Example 11.2).

Observational research

Probably the most influential piece of covert observational research in the field of mental health was conducted by Erving Goffman (1961). He worked as an Assistant Athletic Director in an asylum and conducted covert observation to discover the unofficial reality in a total institution. Amongst many other observations, he noted that patients were closely observed and had little privacy, they were highly disciplined and regimented by staff and were treated like children.

A decade later, David Rosenhan (1973) took the science of covert observation to the next level. He gained admission to a psychiatric hospital as a patient simultaneous with seven other 'pseudopatients' in a number of different hospitals across America. They each complained of hearing voices on admission, but subsequently behaved 'normally' with no further apparent symptoms. The lengths of hospitalisation varied from 7 to 52 days, with an average of 19 days. Rosenhan remarked on the inability of the doctors and nurses to identify that the pseudopatients were 'sane', although several other patients realised that they were.

Such covert observation today would not gain ethical approval from a research ethics committee and the method is only used by journalists, who arguably do not have such a strong moral code. However, in overt observational studies researchers observe study participants after gaining their consent to do so. The researcher may be either a passive observer or a participant observer. A passive observer does not interact with the study participants and simply observes their activities. In contrast a participant observer engages in the activities alongside the study participant.

Observational studies are a valuable way of discovering how social systems work. It is a particularly useful method for understanding mental health services which, although now mostly community-based, are frequently a series of permeable micro-institutions such as hospital wards, day services or residential homes.

The researcher may use diaries and checklists to record the activities of participants. They may also record conversations and interviews, or conduct focus groups to supplement the data gathered through observation. Observational methods are particularly suitable for non-verbal people or those with cognitive impairments who may not be able to participate in interviews.

There is some potential for bias in observational research. Firstly, the process of observation may alter that which is being observed. If participants know that they are being observed this is likely to affect their behaviour. The effect of the researcher could be minimised by observing a large number of people at the same time or observing the same people on numerous occasions.

Secondly, the process of a researcher participating in an activity may change its nature. This can be difficult to overcome in observational research and would ideally be ascertained by combining both passive and participant observation of the same activities.

The value of observational research can best be seen through an example. Christabel Owens (2004) conducted participant observation as part of a pilot evaluation of a housing project in south Devon (Example 11.3). This supplemented interviews and provided data on the day-to-day experience of living in one of the organisation's houses.

EXAMPLE **11.3**

The glass-walled asylum (Owens, 2004)

Background

Mental health services struggle to provide safe and secure services for people with complex and high levels of need, the so-called 'new long-stay population'. A gulf has grown between notions of 'asylum' and 'community' within services. This paper describes a unique housing project run by lay people on the basis of genuine acceptance of all humankind.

Sample

The sample comprised residents and staff of six community homes in south Devon managed by The Community of St Antony and St Elias.

Method

The researcher spent twelve days in participant observation interspersed with semi-structured interviews with staff and residents.

Analysis

Analysis was conducted as an iterative process alongside data collection to inform later interviews and observations.

Results

The participant observation method gained numerous insights into the life of these communities which interviews would not be able to, as the following quotes from Owen's (2004) paper illustrates:

> *Entering a house for the first time as an observer, it was never easy to distinguish staff members from residents. They would often be sitting round casually drinking coffee, chatting and listening to music. (Owens, 2004: 325–6)*

> *So simple, so natural and full of common sense did the Community's approach appear that during my time there I toyed with the question of whether there was anything to research at all. It did indeed seem that what I was observing was a group of people living ordinary lives. (Owens, 2004: 326)*

> *There is an appearance of autonomy and self-determination. Residents are constantly encouraged to make choices, to decide how they will spend their day and to take*

171

EXAMPLE *11.3* *(CONT.)*

responsibility for regular household activities, but in practice they rarely do. My field notes reveal that it was invariably a staff member who organized the shopping trip, started the meal preparations, filled and switched on the washing machine, ensured that dental appointments were kept, and so on. Although in interviews and discussions, staff members expressed dissatisfaction with the parental model of care, in practice they were repeatedly seen to adopt a parental role, simply because it was the only way to get things done. They would say things like: 'Put your shoes on please, Joe. We're going to the shops,' or 'Lunch is ready. Can you come and sit down please?' (Owens, 2004: 327)

Implications for practice

This study offers a first-hand account of life within the homes of this organisation and provides an invaluable insight into what a prospective resident may expect when coming to live there.

Ethnography and social work practice

Ethnographers describe human social behaviour to assist our understanding of communities, cultures or population sub-groups. They use a range of qualitative methods to investigate the meaning of social interactions within the particular community of interest. Ethnographers immerse themselves within the community using participant observation to record the minutiae of everyday life. However, their observations are supplemented by individual and group interviews when necessary. Drawing upon both sociological and anthropological methods, ethnography has much to offer social work practice as it gives a real insight into the hidden processes that underpin life within groups.

As with other researchers, ethnographers begin with a research question which gives their enquiry a clear focus. For example, in their ethnographic study of three in-patient wards in London, Alan Quirk and colleagues (2006) set out to answer a number of research questions including whether Goffman's (1961) idea of a 'total institution' still applied to psychiatric in-patient facilities.

In addition to spending three to four months in each in-patient ward, Alan Quirk also conducted in-depth interviews with key informants that were identified by progressively focusing on selected themes and issues. In the presentation of their results, they drew upon field notes and insights gained from their observations. For example, here is an illustration of the contact that inpatients have with the outside world:

Feeding the dog (summary of field-note entry for ward B)

A patient on the inner-London ward was concerned about his dog, which had been placed in an animal shelter by the man's social worker. Unknown to staff on the ward, he retrieved his dog the first chance he got, took it back to his flat, and continued to feed it every afternoon during his daily leave from hospital. (Quirk et al., 2006: 2110)

Ethnography can compliment epidemiology, producing a true combination of qualitative and quantitative methods. A good example of this is an ethnographic study of Gospel Oak (Whitley and Prince, 2005), a community in the London Borough of Camden.

In previous cross-sectional research it was noted that Gospel Oak had a particularly high prevalence of depression (Prince *et al.*, 1997a). Loneliness and social isolation were associated with both the incidence (Prince *et al.*, 1998) and prevalence (Prince *et al.*, 1997b) of depression in Gospel Oak. Martin Prince hypothesised that these results were caused by contextual characteristics of the neighbourhood and cited low social capital as a potential explanation. Adopting Robert Putnam's (2000) conceptualisation of social capital, he hypothesised that poor facilities and a lack of opportunities for community interaction contributed to individual social isolation and depression.

Rob Whitley spent a year in the community to investigate if it was starved of associational opportunities, but found quite the opposite. This view was typical of the majority of residents:

> *Yeah the facilities are quite good, there is quite a lot of community spirit, with the caretaker and all that. There are flower shows and all that and I get quite involved in that . . . the people in the flats we get on well, the flats are nice here, that's good, I like them. I think the council does quite a lot, I think Camden Council does quite a lot for the community and that . . . if I was offered another flat I wouldn't take it. I quite like it here. It is nice, yeah . . . I mean we have got the caretaker, who is a great help, the housing office down the road, yeah. (Whitley and Prince, 2005: 244)*

Using similar methods, Vicky Cattell (2001) also found that although poor neighbourhoods may be economically deprived, they can be rich in associational activity. Ethnographic studies of deprived communities are invaluable to social workers as they offer a vital insight into the context of the lives of many recipients of social work services.

Other qualitative methods

There are many other qualitative methods that may be used in research of relevance to mental health social workers. For example, it may be simply the use of open-ended questions in questionnaires that were otherwise gathering data for quantitative analysis (e.g. Huxley *et al.*, 2005a). Another method is content analysis of textual, visual or audio-visual sources. Diana Rose's (1998b) content analysis of the media's portrayal of mental illness is an excellent example of this. Finally, expert panels providing an authoritative view are a further method of gathering data about a particular issue. They are frequently used in the generation of consensus about an idea, such as the inclusion or exclusion of items in a questionnaire (e.g. Webber and Huxley, 2007).

Key principles of good qualitative research

Let us now turn to some of the key principles that underpin good qualitative research that are worth bearing in mind when critically appraising such studies.

Sampling

Firstly, it is important to examine the sampling strategy that is employed in the research. This will obviously vary from study to study because of the different approaches required by different research questions. However, the key element of the sampling strategy must be an attempt to capture the full breadth of opinion about the topic being investigated. This may require participants from diverse backgrounds or those who may have divergent perspectives on the topic.

This can be difficult to achieve in reality. For example, our small focus group study, which helped us to evaluate the content validity of a research instrument (the Resource Generator-UK), involved only 22 participants (Webber and Huxley, 2007). Although all age groups, broad social class groups and both genders were represented, and a fifth of the participants were not of white British origin, it was difficult to know whether a full diversity of opinion was achieved.

Data collection

Data collection in qualitative research is an iterative process. Researchers pause data collection to begin analysis after a few interviews or observations. The analysis informs the next phase of data collection as it highlights important themes or areas that need further exploration. In particular, immersion in the data allows the researcher to understand which key informants they need to interview or social phenomena they need to observe to gain a full understanding of the research topic. Both Alan Quirk (2006) and Rob Whitley's (2005) ethnographic studies provide good examples of this.

It is important to ascertain exactly how the data was collected and recorded. For example, if interviews were not tape-recorded and transcribed verbatim there is some potential for researcher bias. A researcher making notes whilst interviewing will only record a fraction of the interview and is likely to be influenced by his or her perspective in what he or she records. Interview summaries can be problematic as the researcher may impose his or her own bias on it.

When researchers make and use field notes as data in observation studies it is difficult to ascertain the extent to which these reflect the researcher's background or own interests. In such circumstances it is important for the researcher to declare their perspective or theoretical orientation to enable the reader to judge the extent to which these notes or perspectives may be biased or show only part of the full picture.

A key issue in the process of data collection is knowing the appropriate point at which to stop. Qualitative researchers use the principle of 'theoretical saturation' to determine the end-point of data collection. This refers to the situation when:

> *. . . no additional data are being found whereby the (researcher) can develop properties of the category. As he sees similar instances over and over again, the researcher becomes empirically confident that a category is saturated . . . when one category is saturated, nothing remains but to go on to new groups for data on other categories, and attempt to saturate these categories also. (Glaser and Strauss, 1967: 65)*

Analysis

Data analysis in qualitative research is frequently conducted as an iterative process throughout data collection. To minimise bias, this process needs to be conducted systematically and, if possible, by more than one person.

The data gathered is first transcribed verbatim. This is to ensure that all the material, irrespective of how it may appear at first sight to the researcher, is available for analysis. The analysis itself begins through a process of coding, which is a grouping together of ideas, themes and concepts which arise from the data. This process is structured through the use of a coding frame which, in its simplest form, is a list of the themes the researcher is exploring. The coding frame may be pre-determined by researchers on the basis of interview themes or an a priori theoretical position. However, it may also be developed on the basis of grounded theory.

Grounded theory was developed by Barney Glaser and Anselm Strauss in the 1960s (Glaser and Strauss, 1967). It refers to the process of generating theory from data in a systematic fashion and is often cited in papers as the process used in analysis. Although grounded theory is frequently invoked by qualitative researchers, it is often cited as an overriding principle rather than a specific methodology. Barney Glaser's Institute of Grounded Theory and journal (*The Grounded Theory Review*) are no doubt appreciative of the international recognition of the phenomena, but are likely to be critical of its many misapplications.

The process of coding qualitative data can be an onerous task, particularly in large ethnographic studies. Computer software assists this task and helps the researcher to organise the data into recurring themes. NVivo is the most popular piece of software for this task, but unlike statistical software it is only a tool and does not do the analysis for you!

Rigorous data analysis requires two researchers to independently code the transcripts. This ensures that the opinions of one researcher do not dominate the presentation of the results. Inter-rater reliability is checked by examining the different emerging coding structures to see if alternative explanations for the phenomena being studied emerge.

Researchers may also undertake a process of data triangulation. This involves comparing their results with those of other qualitative or quantitative studies. It may also be invoked in the data collection phase when an alternative method may be used to confirm patterns, themes or ideas that are emerging from the data.

Reporting qualitative research

As qualitative data analysis is prone to bias if the researcher does not take a systematic approach to it, the writing-up process must ensure that the phenomenon being studied is accurately and fairly portrayed. Occasionally, preliminary findings are shown to study participants to ascertain whether or not it represents what they actually said. This helps to improve the accuracy of the results and informs researchers whether or not they have correctly interpreted the social phenomena they were studying.

The findings need to be placed in the context in which the study took place to enable the reader to judge their reliability. The context includes a full description of the setting, target population, participants' characteristics and a detailed account of the methods used.

Finally, it is rare to find evidence in qualitative studies all pointing in the same direction. There are frequently dissenting voices who disagree with the consensus opinion. Although these are minority voices, it is important for them to be heard to ensure that a full and balanced account of the phenomenon being described is given.

FURTHER READING

This has been only a brief introduction to qualitative research and there are numerous text books to extend your understanding. The following are regarded as classic texts and are a good place to start:

Glaser, B. G. and Strauss, A. L. (1967) *The discovery of grounded theory: strategies for qualitative research.* New York, Aldine.

Strauss, A. (1987) *Qualitative analysis for social scientists.* Cambridge: Cambridge University Press.

BOX 11.4

Critical appraisal questions

The following questions will help you to appraise the quality of qualitative research. Use them when reading a paper reporting the results of a qualitative study.

1 Was the research design appropriate to address the research aims?

2 Was the recruitment strategy appropriate?

3 Were the data collected in a way that addressed the research issue?

4 Has the relationship between researcher and participants been adequately considered?

5 Was the data analysis sufficiently rigorous?

6 Is there a clear statement of findings?

7 How valuable is the study?

BOX 11.5

Multiple choice self-test

Test your understanding of the ideas contained within this chapter with this self-test. The answers can be found in Appendix 1.

1 Which of the following are forms of qualitative research? (Select all that apply)

a Cross-sectional surveys

b In-depth unstructured interviews

BOX **11.5** *(CONT.)*

c Focus groups

d Participant observation

2 Sampling is not an important consideration in qualitative research. True or false.

3 Which one of the following sampling strategies is usually the most appropriate method of obtaining a sample for a focus group study?

a Simple random sampling

b Purposive sampling

c Cluster random sampling

d Stratified random sampling

4 Interview schedules in qualitative research can be changed in between interviews. True or false?

5 Qualitative researchers must wait until they have collected all their data before beginning their analysis. True or false?

6 What are the advantages of participant observation in contrast to non-participant observation? (Select all that apply)

a Researchers can get 'closer' to participants by engaging in the same activity

b The researcher is likely to be less obtrusive if they engage in the activity with the participant

c The participation of the researcher may make participants behave differently

d The non-participation of the researcher may make participants behave differently

7 What is the potential for reporting bias when using quotations from research partici pants in the presentation of the results of qualitative research? (Select all that apply)

a They give a truly representative picture of the views of all participants – there is no potential for bias

b The researcher may only present quotes that lend support their ideas

c The quotations used may be atypical of the sample as a whole

d The quotations used may represent those who are most vocal rather than a broad cross-section of opinions

8 Is qualitative research always more important than quantitative research to social workers? (Select one response only)

a Yes, it is always more relevant to social work practice than qualitative research

b No, because quantitative research enables us to demonstrate that interventions work

c Qualitative and quantitative methods are complimentary and each make a unique contribution to social work practice

d Don't know

Chapter 12

Professional leadership in mental health social work: bringing research into practice

Introduction

In Chapter 5 we outlined four steps to becoming an evidence-based practitioner. In this final chapter we will discuss the fourth step: implementing research in practice. Using the concept of 'advanced practitioner' (Nathan, 2002) as a framework for our discussion, we will demonstrate how integrating empirical research into frontline mental health social work practice can improve outcomes for service users. We will make some practical suggestions and present two case studies to highlight how advanced practitioners can provide professional leadership within their teams and agencies. Finally, we will suggest that empirical research can be a powerful tool to effect change and help mental health social workers to regain control of their practice at a time of professional uncertainty.

Advanced practitioners in mental health social work

The importance of high quality practice in social work is a recurrent theme within contemporary social policy. However, discussions about how to achieve this rarely refer to the role of experienced and highly trained social work practitioners. These advanced practitioners can lead the profession in driving up the quality of social work interventions. They have the experience, skills and training to offer practice leadership, contribute to the development of high quality practice within agencies and undertake work-based research projects.

In common with *Options for excellence* (Department of Health and Department for Education and Skills, 2006), *Every child matters* (Her Majesty's Government, 2003) and *Our health, our Care, our say* (Department of Health, 2006) both highlight the importance of high quality social work interventions in meeting the needs of vulnerable children and adults. People with long-term and complex needs deserve the same high-quality service as those who are less demanding on a social worker's time. Advanced practitioners have the training and skills to reflect on their practice, perhaps using their counter-transference to examine the meaning of their responses to service users, to help ensure that they are able to deliver high quality social work in demanding situations. In particular, advanced practitioners need to be at the forefront of these developments providing leadership and role models in the development of the excellence that is required in social work.

At the Institute of Psychiatry we have many years' experience of training advanced practitioners on our advanced post-qualifying masters programme. We define an advanced practitioner as someone 'who has an explicit and articulated knowledge base that is theory-driven and research-based and who can create new forms of social work knowledge that inform and shape policies and practice' (Nathan, 2002: 78).

There are three essential components to our definition of an advanced practitioner. Firstly, developing Schon's (1987) notion of 'reflective practitioners', we suggest that advanced practitioners have the capacity to reflect on their reflections. What constitutes the reflective practitioner is their capacity to reflect on their work with a service user, including the ability to appreciate the role of self in such encounters. At the next level, the advanced practitioner is able to reflect on these reflections. This involves the capacity to be both research literate and to develop new forms of social work knowledge through original research.

In some social work settings practitioners operate as brokers and have limited opportunities for emotionally engaging with service users and their needs. However, one of the enduring strengths of social work is the ability to engage in complex cases where the inter-personal dynamics are fraught with difficulties and many different professionals maybe involved. In particular, child protection work or meeting the needs of adults with enduring mental health problems requires confident and experienced practitioners developing effective working relationships which promote change.

In these settings, advanced practitioners draw on a range of therapeutic modalities – humanistic and psychodynamic psychotherapy, cognitive-behavioural therapy and systemic therapy, for example – to inform their practice. They act as practice consultants to colleagues bringing knowledge of the best practice in the field. They offer professional leadership and can promote the strengths of the profession in multi-disciplinary environments where social workers are often viewed as junior colleagues of health professionals such as psychologists or psychiatrists.

Secondly, advanced practitioners are able to draw on the best available research evidence to inform their work with service users or develop effective services. In mental health settings, for example, this involves an ability to understand and critique evidence produced in medical or psychological paradigms as well as having a mastery of the social work evidence base. Our focus on quantitative research methods and statistics in Chapters 6 to 10 helps to equip practitioners to undertake this.

Informing their practice with a critical appreciation of relevant research does not necessarily mean that their professional autonomy will be restricted, as some critics of evidence-based practice claim (e.g. Webb, 2001). Although research literacy assists practitioners to determine which intervention is likely to have the greatest benefits in any particular situation, the social worker needs to apply their professional judgement in liaison with the service user's wishes to decide whether or not a particular intervention should be pursued.

Furthermore, research literacy enables advanced practitioners to critique existing service models from a social work perspective. For example, mental health assertive outreach teams are now established throughout the country, although the UK evidence for their effectiveness over standard community mental health services is not convincing as discussed in Chapter 4. It is essential for social workers to be at the forefront of such developments armed with up-to-date research evidence. Service developments are increasingly driven by research evidence and it is important for social workers to be aware of potential limitations in order to be able to appropriately critique service models.

Thirdly, advanced practitioners create new forms of knowledge that inform social work practice and social policy through original research. Practitioner research is particularly important as it assists social workers to reclaim their professional identity and develop ownership of their knowledge base. This is crucial in settings such as multi-disciplinary mental health teams where service models are increasingly determined by national frameworks or evidence-based guidelines dominated by medical or psychological research. The challenge for mental health social workers is to produce high quality research that can be respected and valued in equal measure to professions with higher academic standing.

Advanced practitioners are essential to the future of the social work profession. They provide professional leadership, demonstrate advanced practice competence and contribute to the social work evidence base. Unfortunately, there are few opportunities for advanced practitioners to remain in front-line practice as most social work career structures are orientated towards management rather than advanced practice. However, some mental health trusts have created Consultant Social Worker positions to retain experienced and highly-skilled practitioners in front-line practice to supervise junior colleagues and counterbalance equivalent positions that can be found in the health professions. The introduction of Agenda for Change in the NHS in 2004 provided a model of consultant practitioners as now operates for nurses, psychologists and adult psychotherapists.

Consultant Social Workers in mental health teams are ideally placed to take on the role of Approved Clinician in the Mental Health Act 2007. They will also be able to promote social models with some authority and help to ensure that Approved Mental Health Professionals (AMHP) retain an essential check against the professional dominance of psychiatry. Although there have been justified anxieties about this new role, paradoxically the introduction of the AMHP provides an opportunity for mental health social workers to take *the* lead role in advancing psychosocial perspectives. Although re-branded as the 'recovery model', it is something that social workers have always championed for their service users and now have an opportunity to take a lead on this within mental health services.

Using research to inform practice: advanced practitioners in action

There are a number of ways in which mental health social workers can use research to inform their practice. For example, decision making in complex cases can be facilitated by a critical appreciation of relevant empirical literature and service models can be reviewed by reflecting on evidence of 'what works'. Advanced practitioners can use research findings as the catalyst to service development and professional leadership, as the following two case studies demonstrate.

Women's social group in early intervention service

Sarah (not her real name) is a social worker in an early intervention in psychosis team. She works with young people experiencing their first episode of psychosis, helping them to learn about it and cope with it. She finds it helpful for the young people to meet others who have had similar experiences so that they can learn from, and support, one another. Therefore she encourages them to attend the groups that the team facilitates.

Sarah reviewed the evidence about the effectiveness of group participation in first episode psychosis and found that it helps to prevent relapse, and improve both treatment compliance and satisfaction with services (Penn et al., 2005). Further, she was concerned that women with psychosis were amongst the most stigmatised and marginalised in society. A study exploring the perspectives of women living with schizophrenia found that they felt that mental health services focused on their illness and they had become invisible as women (Chernomas et al., 2000). Further evidence suggests that in mental health care women's unique needs have been neglected and many issues such as trauma, domestic violence, vulnerability, motherhood, stigma and victimisation have not received adequate attention (Kohen, 2001).

Sarah had several young vulnerable women on her caseload who expressed an interest in meeting others. As evidence suggested that the majority of women with psychosis function better than men, and respond better to psychosocial interventions (Seeman and Cohen, 1998), it seemed appropriate to consider a specific intervention for this group. Further, a service user survey of her team's provision of groups highlighted the need for a women's group. This prompted Sarah to set up a women's social group.

Sarah developed a 12 week programme for the group that included themes such as confidence building, motivation, stress management, relationships, healthy living and life skills. Fifteen young women supported by the team were identified as suitable for the group and were invited to attend. Ten expressed an interest and between seven and nine attended weekly sessions, which were co-facilitated with a colleague.

She used both informal and formal methods to evaluate the group. At the end of each session she asked for feedback and reflection on the group. This was very positive and the women said that they found its gender-specificity helped them to relax and feel less anxious. One commented that she would not have come if there were men present as she finds them intimidating and she feels self-conscious in their presence. Another woman felt inspired by a group member speaking openly about her illness. Formal evaluation comprised standardised questionnaires which measured self-esteem, social functioning and anxiety and depression which were administered before and after the twelve sessions.

Sarah found that the group improved the engagement of the young women in their process of recovery. Some of the group members made plans to see each other socially outside the group and they were generally more open to discuss their experiences. She anticipates running the group again.

CASE STUDY 2

Mental health awareness training for police officers

Simon (not his real name) is an approved social worker (ASW) in a London borough. He became interested in the relationship between the police and people with mental health problems through observations from his practice. On the one hand, he experienced diffi- culties in working with the police who occasionally were reluctant to attend Mental Health Act assessments. This appeared to be a problem which was also prevalent in other London boroughs (Mental Health Act Commission, 2005). On the other hand, he found from an audit of the use of section 136 of the Mental Health Act 1983 (the police deten- tion powers) that over half of those detained by officers in his borough were subsequently discharged on assessment. Although the data on use of section 136 was inconsistent (Wall et al., 1999) this percentage seemed quite high and more in keeping with a rural rather than an urban authority (Greenberg and Haines, 2003; Greenberg et al., 2002; Simmons and Hoar, 2001). This was likely to indicate inappropriate use of the police powers under the Mental Health Act 1983.

Simon reflected on his experience, the available research evidence and the London Development Centre for Mental Health's framework for joint working on mental health act assessments, which recommended local mental health awareness training involving both ASWs and police officers (London Development Centre for Mental Health, 2005), and decided to arrange mental health awareness training for local police officers.

Simon developed a training programme with an ASW colleague, the police mental health liaison Inspector and the borough police training department. A mental health service user was also involved in the planning but was unable to participate in the training itself. He delivered a four-hour training package to eight groups of 20–25 police officers. Although he identified some limitations with the training, such as the lack of service user involvement or interactivity within sessions, he received favourable feedback from the police training department.

Simon evaluated the training by undertaking a further audit of the s.136 detentions after the training. He found that the number of people discharged following assessment fell to around 30 per cent, which was more in line with the London average (Mental Health Act Commission, 2005), and the absolute number of admissions under this section also declined quite steeply. He felt that the whole process had fostered greater mutual under- standing between police officers and ASWs.

Challenges and opportunities for mental health social work

Mental health social work is at a crossroads. Morale in the profession in England and Wales has suffered a blow following the lengthy review of the Mental Health Act 1983, which resulted in the opening up of the ASW role to other mental health professionals.

Some social workers feel that their unique contribution to mental health services has been eroded and that they may become expendable. For others, integration of social services and health has been an uncomfortable experience. Practitioners will now appreciate a period of time to consolidate their professional position within mental health services, but there is no guarantee that this will be provided.

Evidence-based practice is a paradigm borrowed from health professionals. Some may claim that it has been foisted upon social work and does not correspond with its value base. Others may feel it is irrelevant for day-to-day practice. However, if it has done nothing else, this book has demonstrated its potential utility to mental health social workers.

Becoming research literate and being mindful of the evidential foundations of mental health policy will help social workers to attain a more equal footing in multi-disciplinary teams alongside higher status professionals such as psychologists or psychiatrists. Maintaining a focus on outcomes for mental health service users and their carers – which evidence-based practice encourages – will help social workers to intervene as effectively as possible. Finally, an ability to use research to demonstrate the effectiveness of social work within contemporary mental health services may provide the profession with a means to secure its own future.

Appendix 1
Multiple choice self-test answers

Chapter 6

1   c

2   a and c

3   b

4   a, b, c and d

5   b, c and d

6   a and c

7   true

8   c

9   a, b and c

10 false

Chapter 7

1   a, b and d

2   b

3   c

4   a, c and d

5   b

6   true

7   a, b and d

8   false

9   a, b, c and d

Chapter 8

1 c

2 true

3 a and c

4 a, c and d

5 b

6 c

7 a, b and c

8 a, b and c

9 false

10 true

Chapter 9

1 outcome

2 b

3 a, c and d

4 incident

5 false

6 a, c and d

7 selection bias, recall bias, investigator bias

8 b, c and d

9 a, b, c and d

Chapter 10

1 b

2 b

3 true

4 a

5 b and c

6   true

7   c

8   true

9   false

10   true

11   a, b, c and d

12   true

13   a, b and c

14   b

15   a, c and d

16   b, c and d

17   true

18   a, c and d

Chapter 11

1   b, c and d

2   false

3   b

4   true

5   false

6   a, b and d

7   b, c and d

8   c

Appendix 2

Useful web resources for evidence-based practice

Bibliographic databases

Social Care Online: www.scie-socialcareonline.org.uk
PubMed: www.ncbi.nlm.nih.gov/sites/entrez
Cochrane Collaboration: www.cochrane.org
Campbell Collaboration: www.campbellcollaboration.org
Index to theses: www.theses.com

Search engines

Scirus: www.scirus.com
Google scholar: www.scholar.google.co.uk
Google: www.google.co.uk
Ask: www.ask.com
Yahoo: www.yahoo.co.uk

Social care research dissemination organisations

Social Care Institute for Excellence: www.scie.org.uk
Research in Practice: www.rip.org.uk
Research in Practice for Adults: www.ripfa.org.uk
Making Research Count: www.uea.ac.uk/swk/MRC_web/public_html/
Care knowledge: www.careknowledge.com
Community Care Inform: www.ccinform.co.uk

Information gateways

Intute: Social Sciences: www.intute.ac.uk/socialsciences

Online tutorials

Internet Social Worker: www.vts.intute.ac.uk/he/tutorial/social-worker

Miscellaneous

Research Mindedness in Social Work and Social Care: www.resmind.swap.ac.uk (no longer updated, but a good place to start nonetheless)

NHS Public Health Resource Unit – Critical appraisal skills programme: www.phru.nhs.uk/Pages/PHD/CASP.htm (useful for critical appraisal tips and training

ESRC UK Centre for Evidence Based Policy and Practice: www.evidencenetowrk.org (good for non-medical critiques of evidence based practice)

References

Abel, K. M., Webb, R. T., Salmon, M. P., Wan, M. W. and Appleby, L. (2005) Prevalence and predictors of parenting outcomes in a cohort of mothers with schizophrenia admitted for joint mother and baby psychiatric care in England. *Journal of Clinical Psychiatry*, 66, 781–9.

Al-Uzri, M. M., Reveley, M. A., Owen, L., Bruce, J., Frost, S., Mackintosh, D. and Moran, P. M. (2006) Measuring memory impairment in community-based patients with schizophrenia: Case-control study. *British Journal of Psychiatry*, 189, 132–6.

Alikasifoglu, M., Erginoz, E., Ercan, O., Albayrak-Kaymak, D., Uysal, O. and Ilter, O. (2006) Sexual abuse among female high school students in Istanbul, Turkey. *Child Abuse and Neglect*, 30, 247–55.

American Psychiatric Association (1994) *Diagnostic and statistical manual of mental disorders, 4th edition (DSM-IV)*. Washington, DC, American Psychiatric Association.

Andreasen, N. (1989) Scale for the assessment of negative symptoms (SANS). *British Journal of Psychiatry*, 7, 53–8.

Andrews, F. and Withey, S. B. (1976) *Social indicators of well-being: Americans' perceptions of quality of life*. New York, Plenum Press.

Appleby, L. (1999) *Safer services. National confidential inquiry into suicide and homicide by people with mental illness*. London, Department of Health.

Appleby, L. (2004) *The national service framework for mental health – five years on*. London, Department of Health.

Appleby, L. (2007a) *Breaking down barriers. The clinical case for change*. London, Department of Health.

Appleby, L. (2007b) *Mental health ten years on: progress on mental health care reform*. London, Department of Health.

Asberg, M., Montgomery, S. A., Perris, C., Schalling, D. and Sedvall, G. (1978) A comprehensive psychopathological rating scale. *Acta Psychiatrica Scandinavica*, 271 Suppl, 5–27.

Asher, R. (1956) Arrangements for the mentally ill (letter). *The Lancet*, 268, 1265–1266.

Audini, B. and Lelliott, P. (2002) Age, gender and ethnicity of those detained under Part II of the Mental Health Act 1983. *British Journal of Psychiatry*, 180, 222–6.

Barnes, M., Bowl, R. and Fisher, M. (1990) *Sectioned. Social services and the 1983 Mental Health Act*. London, Routledge.

Bateman, A. and Fonagy, P. (1999) Effectiveness of partial hospitalization in the treatment of borderline personality disorder: A randomized controlled trial. *American Journal of Psychiatry*, 156, 1563–9.

Bateman, A. W. and Fonagy, P. (2003) Health service utilization costs for borderline personality disorder patients treated with psychoanalytically oriented partial hospitalization versus general psychiatric care. *American Journal of Psychiatry*, 160, 169–71.

Bateman, A. W. and Fonagy, P. (2006) *Mentalization based treatment for borderline personality disorder: A practical guide.* Oxford, Oxford University Press.

Bates, P. (2007) Safe and sound. *Mental Health Today*, February, 32–4.

Beck, A. T. and Steer, R. A. (1984) Internal consistencies of the original and revised Beck Depression Inventory. *Journal of Clinical Psychology*, 40, 1365–7.

Bhui, K., Stansfeld, S., Hull, S., Priebe, S., Mole, F. and Feder, G. (2003) Ethnic variations in pathways to and use of specialist mental health services in the UK: Systematic review. *British Journal of Psychiatry*, 182, 105–16.

Bindman, J., Tighe, J., Thornicroft, G. and Leese, M. (2002) Poverty, poor services, and compulsory psychiatric admission in England. *Social Psychiatry and Psychiatric Epidemiology*, 37, 341–5.

Birchwood, M., McGorry, P. and Jackson, H. (1997) Early intervention in schizophrenia. *British Journal of Psychiatry*, 170, 2–5.

Bland, J. M. and Altman, D. G. (2000) Statistics Notes: The odds ratio. *British Medical Journal*, 320, 1468.

Bland, R. and Renouf, N. (2001) Social work and the mental health team. *Australasian Psychiatry*, 9, 238–41.

Blom-Cooper, L., Hally, H. and Murphy, E. (1995) *The falling shadow: one patient's mental health care 1978–1993.* London, Duckworth.

Bolton, D. (2002) Knowledge in the human sciences. In Priebe, S. and Slade, M. (eds) *Evidence in mental health care.* Hove, Brunner-Routledge, pp. 1–10.

Booth, S. H., Booth, A. and Falzon, L. J. (2003) The need for information and research skills training to support evidence-based social care: a literature review and survey. *Learning in Health and Social Care*, 2, 191–201.

Boydell, J., Van Os, J., Lambri, M., Castle, D., Allardyce, J., McCreadie, R. G. and Murray, R. M. (2003) Incidence of schizophrenia in south-east London between 1965 and 1997. *British Journal of Psychiatry*, 182, 45–9.

Brock, A., Baker, A., Griffiths, C., Jackson, G., Fegan, G. and Marshall, D. (2006) Suicide trends and geographical variations in the United Kingdom, 1991–2004. *Health Statistics Quarterly*, 31, 6–22.

Brown, P. (1985) *Mental health care and social policy.* London, Routledge and Kegan Paul.

Brown, R. (2006) *The approved social worker's guide to mental health law.* Exeter, Learning Matters.

Brown, R. and Barber, P. (2008) *The social worker's guide to the Mental Capacity Act 2005.* Exeter, Learning Matters.

Brown, W. and Kandirikirira, N. (2007) *Recovering mental health in Scotland. Report on narrative investigation of mental health recovery.* Glasgow, Scottish Recovery Network.

Brugha, T. S., Wheatley, S., Taub, N. A., Culverwell, A., Friedman, T., Kirwan, P., Jones, D. R. and Shapiro, D. A. (2000) Pragmatic randomized trial of antenatal intervention to prevent post-natal depression by reducing psychosocial risk factors. *Psychological Medicine*, 30, 1273–81.

Brunt, D. and Hansson, L. (2004) The quality of life of persons with severe mental illness across housing settings. *Nordic Journal of Psychiatry*, 58, 293–8.

Bryant, W., Craik, C. and McKay, E. (2005) Perspectives of day and accommodation services for people with enduring mental illness. *Journal of Mental Health*, 14, 109–20.

Burns, T., Catty, J., Dash, M., Roberts, C., Lockwood, A. and Marshall, M. (2007) Use of intensive case management to reduce time in hospital in people with severe mental illness: systematic review and meta-regression. *British Medical Journal*, 335, 336–40.

Burns, T., Creed, F., Fahy, T., Thompson, S., Tyrer, P. and White, I. (1999) Intensive versus standard case management for severe psychotic illness: a randomised trial. *The Lancet*, 353, 2185–9.

Burns, T., Knapp, M., Catty, J., Healey, A., Henderson, A. S., Watt, H. and Wright, C. (2001) Home treatment for mental health problems: a systematic review. *Health Technology Assessment*, 5.

Busfield, J. (1986) *Managing mental illness*. London, Hutchinson.

Byford, S., Harrington, R., Torgerson, D., Kerfoot, M., Dyer, E., Harrington, V., Woodham, A., Gill, J. and McNiven, F. (1999) Cost-effectiveness analysis of a home-based social work intervention for children and adolescents who have deliberately poisoned themselves. Results of a randomised controlled trial. *The British Journal of Psychiatry*, 174, 56–62.

Cambridge Dictionaries (2007) *Cambridge advanced learner's dictionary*. Cambridge, Cambridge University Press.

Campbell, J., Brophy, L., Healy, B. and O'Brien, A. M. (2006) International perspectives on the use of community treatment orders: implications for mental health social workers. *British Journal of Social Work*, 36, 1101–18.

Canvin, K., Bartlett, A. and Pinfold, V. (2005) Acceptability of compulsory powers in the community: the ethical considerations of mental health service users on Supervised Discharge and Guardianship. *Journal of Medical Ethics*, 31, 457–62.

Carroll, A., Pickworth, J. and Protheroe, D. (2001) Service innovations: an Australian approach to community care – the Northern Crisis Assessment and Treatment Team. *Psychiatric Bulletin*, 25, 439–41.

Carter, G., Reith, D. M., Whyte, I. M. and McPherson, M. (2005) Repeated self-poisoning: increasing severity of self-harm as a predictor of subsequent suicide. *British Journal of Psychiatry*, 186, 253–7.

Cattell, V. (2001) Poor people, poor places, and poor health: the mediating role of social networks and social capital. *Social Science and Medicine*, 52, 1501–16.

Catty, J., Goddard, K., White, S. and Burns, T. (2005) Social networks among users of mental health day care. *Social Psychiatry and Psychiatric Epidemiology*, 40, 467–474.

Chernomas, W., Clarke, D. and Chisholm, F. (2000) Perspectives of women living with schizophrenia. *Psychiatric Services*, 51, 1517–21.

Chilvers, R., Macdonald, G. M. and Hayes, A. A. (2006) Supported housing for people with severe mental disorders. *Cochrane Database of Systematic Reviews 2006*. Issue 4. Art. No.: CD000453. DOI: 10.1002/14651858. CD000453.pub2.

Chitsabesan, P., Kroll, L. E. O., Bailey, S. U. E., Kenning, C., Sneider, S., MacDonald, W. and Theodosiou, L. (2006) Mental health needs of young offenders in custody and in the community. *British Journal of Psychiatry*, 188, 534–40.

Churchill, R. (2007) *International experiences of using community treatment orders*. London, Institute of Psychiatry, King's College London.

Clegg, F. (1990) *Simple Statistics. A course book for the social sciences*. Cambridge, Cambridge University Press.

Cohen, J. (1990) Introduction – social work and the principle of the 'least restrictive alternative' In Cohen, J. and Ramon, S. (eds) *Social work and the Mental Health Act 1983*. Birmingham, BASW, pp. 1–6.

Coleman, M. and DeLeire, T. (2003) An economic model of locus of control and the human capital investment decision. *Journal of Human Resources*, 38, 701–21.

Commander, M., Sashidharan, S., Rana, T. and Ratnayake, T. (2005) North Birmingham assertive out-reach evaluation. Patient characteristics and clinical outcomes. *Social Psychiatry and Psychiatric Epidemiology*, 40, 988–93.

Commission for Healthcare Audit and Inspection (2007) *No voice, no choice. A joint review of adult community mental health services in England*. London, Commission for Healthcare Audit and Inspection.

Corney, R. H. and Clare, A. W. (1983) The effectiveness of attached social workers in the management of depressed women in general practice. *British Journal of Social Work*, 13, 57–74.

Cox, J. L., Holden, J. M. and Sagovsky, R. (1987) Detection of postnatal depression. Development of the 10 item Edinburgh Postnatal Depression Scale. *British Journal of Psychiatry*, 150, 782–6.

Craig, T. K. J., Garety, P., Power, P., Rahaman, N., Colbert, S., Fornells-Ambrojo, M. and Dunn, G. (2004) The Lambeth Early Onset (LEO) Team: randomised controlled trial of the effectiveness of specialised care for early psychosis. *British Medical Journal*, 329, 1067–70.

Crichton, J. and Darjee, R. (2007) New mental health legislation. *British Medical Journal*, 334, 596–7.

Cronbach, L. J. (1951) Coefficient alpha and the internal structure of tests. *Psychometrika*, 16, 297–334.

Crowther, R. E., Marshall, M., Bond, G. R. and Huxley, P. (2001) Helping people with severe mental illness to obtain work: systematic review. *British Medical Journal*, 322, 204–8.

Daley, A. (1949) Mental health social work. *Public Health*, 62, 148–50.

Department of Health (1998a) *Modernising mental health services. Safe, sound and supportive*. London, Department of Health.

Department of Health (1998b) *Modernising social services. Promoting independence, improving protection, raising standards*. London, Department of Health.

Department of Health (1999a) *Caring about carers: a national strategy for carers*. London, Stationery Office.

Department of Health (1999b) *Effective care co-ordination in mental health services. Modernising the care Programme approach – a policy booklet*. London, Department of Health.

Department of Health (1999c) *National service framework for mental health. Modern standards and service models.* London, Department of Health.

Department of Health (1999d) *Saving lives: our healthier nation.* London, Department of Health.

Department of Health (2000a) *Framework for the assessment of children in Need and their Families.* London, The Stationery Office.

Department of Health (2000b) *The NHS plan. A plan for investment. A plan for reform.* London, Department of Health.

Department of Health (2000c) *Reform of the Mental Health Act 1983. Summary of consultation responses.* London, Department of Health.

Department of Health (2001a) *The mental health policy implementation guide.* London, Department of Health.

Department of Health (2001b) *National service framework for older people.* London, Department of Health.

Department of Health (2002) *Draft Mental Health Bill.* Cm 5538–I.

Department of Health (2004a) *Draft Mental Health Bill.* Cm 6305.

Department of Health (2004b) National service framework for children, young people and maternity services. London, Department of Health.

Department of Health (2005) *Delivering race equality in mental health care: An action plan for reform inside and outside services and the Government's response to the Independent inquiry into the death of David Bennett.* London, Department of Health.

Department of Health (2006) *Our health, our care, our say: a new direction for community services.* London, The Stationery Office.

Department of Health and Department for Education and Skills (2006) *Options for excellence. Building the social care workforce of the future.* London, Department of Health.

Department of Health and Home Office (1999) *Reform of the Mental Health Act 1983. Proposals for consultation.* London, The Stationery Office.

Department of Health and Home Office (2000) *Reforming the Mental Health Act.* London, The Stationery Office.

Department of Health and Welsh Office (1999) *Mental Health Act 1983 Code of Practice.* London, Stationery Office.

Desai, S. and Kinton, M. (2006) *Who's been sleeping in my bed? The incidence and impact of bed overoccupancy in the mental health acute sector. Findings of the Mental Health Act Commission's Bed Occupancy Survey.* London, Mental Health Act Commission.

Drucker, P. (1954) *The practice of management.* New York, HarperCollins.

Dunn, L. (2001) Mental health act assessments: does a community treatment team make a difference? *International Journal of Social Psychiatry,* 47, 1–19.

Eagles, J. M., Carson, D. P., Begg, A. and Naji, S. A. (2003) Suicide prevention: a study of patients' views. *British Journal of Psychiatry*, 182, 261–5.

Evans, S., Huxley, P., Gately, C., Webber, M., Mears, A., Pajak, S., Medina, J., Kendall, T. I. M. and Katona, C. (2006) Mental health, burnout and job satisfaction among mental health social workers in England and Wales. *British Journal of Psychiatry*, 188, 75–80.

Evans, S., Huxley, P., Webber, M., Katona, C., Gately, C., Mears, A., Medina, J., Pajak, S. and Kendall, T. (2005) The impact of 'statutory duties' on mental health social workers in the UK. *Health and Social Care in the Community*, 13, 145–54.

Fairplay and Co (1902) The certifying of lunatics (letter). Lancet, 160, 960.

Fonagy, P. and Bateman, A. W. (2007) Mentalizing and borderline personality disorder. *Journal of Mental Health*, 16, 83–101.

Fook, J., Ryan, M. and Hawkins, L. (2000) *Professional expertise: practice, theory and education for working in uncertainty.* London, Whiting and Birch.

Fuller, T. L. (2005) Child safety at reunification: a case-control study of maltreatment recurrence following return home from substitute care. *Children and Youth Services Review*, 27, 1293–1306.

Furminger, E. and Webber, M. (in press) The effect of crisis resolution and home treatment on assessments under the Mental Health Act 1983. An increased workload for Approved Social Workers? *British Journal of Social Work.*

Garety, P. A., Craig, T. K. J., Dunn, G., Fornells-Ambrojo, M., Colbert, S., Rahaman, N., Read, J. and Power, P. (2006) Specialised care for early psychosis: symptoms, social functioning and patient satisfaction: Randomised controlled trial. *The British Journal of Psychiatry*, 188, 37–45.

Geddes, J. R. and Kendell, R. E. (1995) Schizophrenic subjects with no history of admission to hospital. *Psychological Medicine*, 25, 859–68.

Gibbons, J. S., Butler, J., Urwin, P. and Gibbons, J. L. (1978) Evaluation of a social work service for self-poisoning patients. *British Journal of Psychiatry*, 133, 111–18.

Gilbert, P. (2003) *The value of everything: social work and its importance in the field of mental health.* Lyme Regis, Russell House Publishing.

Glaser, B. G. and Strauss, A. L. (1967) *The discovery of grounded theory: strategies for qualitative research.* New York, Aldine.

Glover, G., Arts, G. and Babu, K. S. (2006) Crisis resolution/home treatment teams and psychiatric admission rates in England. *British Journal of Psychiatry*, 189, 441–5.

Goffman, E. (1961) *Asylums. Essays on the social situation and other inmates.* New York, Anchor Books.

Goldberg, D. (1981) Estimating the prevalence of a psychiatric disorder from the results of a screening test. In Wing, J. K., Bebbington, P. and Robins, L. N. (eds) *What is a Case?* London, Grant McIntyre, pp. 129–36.

Goldberg, D. and Williams, P. (1988) *A user's guide to the general health questionnaire.* Windsor, NFER-Nelson.

Goodwin, S. (1997) *Comparative mental health policy. From institutional to community care.* London, Sage Publications.

Gould, N. (2006) An inclusive approach to knowledge for mental health social work practice and policy. *British Journal of Social Work*, 36, 109–25.

Greatley, A. and Ford, R. (2002) *Out of the maze. Reaching and supporting Londoners with severe mental health problems.* London, The Sainsbury Centre for Mental Health.

Greenberg, N. and Haines, N. (2003) The use of Section 136 of the Mental Health Act 1983 in a family of rural English police forces. *Medicine, Science and the Law*, 43, 75–9.

Greenberg, N., Lloyd, K., O'Brien, C., McIver, S., Hessford, A. and Donovan, M. (2002) A prospective survey of section 136 in rural England (Devon and Cornwall). *Medicine, Science and the Law*, 42, 129–34.

Gunderson, J. G., Kolb, J. E. and Austin, V. (1981) The diagnostic interview for borderline patients. *American Journal of Psychiatry*, 138, 896–903.

Gunnell, D. and Frankel, S. (1994) Prevention of suicide: aspirations and evidence. British Medical Journal, 308, 1227–33.

Guy, W. (1996) *ECDEU assessment manual for psychopharmacology.* Washington, DC, Department of Health Education and Welfare.

Harrington, R., Kerfoot, M., Dyer, E., McNiven, F., Gill, J., Harrington, V., Woodham, A. and Byford, S. (1998) Randomized trial of a home-based family intervention for children who have deliberately poisoned themselves. *Journal of the American Acadamy of Child and Adolescent Psychiatry*, 37, 512–18.

Harris, T. (2001) Recent developments in understanding the psychosocial aspects of depression. *British Medical Bulletin*, 57, 17–32.

Harris, T., Brown, G. W. and Robinson, R. (1999) Befriending as an intervention for chronic depression among women in an inner city. 1: Randomised controlled trial. *British Journal of Psychiatry*, 174, 219–24.

Harrison, G. (2002) Ethnic minority and the Mental Health Act. *British Journal of Psychiatry*, 180, 198–9.

Harwood, D., Hawton, K., Hope, T. and Jacoby, R. (2001) Psychiatric disorder and personality factors associated with suicide in older people: a descriptive and case-control study. I*nternational Journal of Geriatric Psychiatry*, 16, 155–65.

Hatfield, B. (in press) Powers to detain under mental health legislation in England and the role of the approved social worker: an analysis of patterns and trends under the 1983 Mental Health Act in six local authorities. *British Journal of Social Work.*

Hatfield, B., Bindman, J. and Pinfold, V. (2004) Evaluating the use of supervised discharge and guardianship in cases of severe mental illness: a follow-up study. *Journal of Mental Health*, 13, 197–209.

Hatfield, B., Mohamad, H. and Huxley, P. (1992) The 1983 Mental Health Act in five local authorities: A study of the practice of Approved Social Workers. *International Journal of Social Psychiatry*, 38, 189–207.

Hatfield, B., Shaw, J., Pinfold, V., Bindman, J., Evans, S., Huxley, P. and Thornicroft, G. (2001) Managing severe mental illness in the community using the Mental Health Act 1983: a comparison of supervised discharge and guardianship in England. *Social Psychiatry and Psychiatric Epidemiology*, 36, 508–15.

Hayes, D. P. (1992) The growing inaccessibility of science. *Nature*, 356, 739–40.

Henderson, C., Flood, C., Leese, M., Thornicroft, G., Sutherby, K. and Szmukler, G. (2004) Effect of joint crisis plans on use of compulsory treatment in psychiatry: single blind randomised controlled trial. *British Medical Journal*, 329, 136.

Henderson, M. and Page, L. (2007) Appraising the evidence: what is selection bias? *Evidence Based Mental Health*, 10, 67–8.

Her Majesty's Government (2003) *Every child matters: change for children*. London, Department for Education and Skills.

Hopkins, C. and Niemiec, S. (2007) Mental health crisis at home: service user perspectives on what helps and what hinders. *Journal of Psychiatric and Mental Health Nursing*, 14, 310–18.

Hotopf, M., Wall, S., Buchanan, A., Wessely, S. and Churchill, R. (2000) Changing patterns in the use of the Mental Health Act 1983, 1984–1996. *British Journal of Psychiatry*, 176, 479–84.

Howard, L. and Thornicroft, G. (2006) Patient preference randomised controlled trials in mental health research. British Journal of Psychiatry, 188, 303–4.

Howkins, A. (1985) *Poor labouring men. Rural radicalism in Norfolk, 1870–1923*. London, Routledge and Kegan Paul.

Huxley, P. (2001) The contribution of social science to mental health services research and development: A SWOT analysis. *Journal of Mental Health*, 10, 117–20.

Huxley, P. (2002) Evidence in social care: the policy context. In Priebe, S. and Slade, M. (eds) *Evidence in mental health care*. Hove, Brunner-Routledge, pp. 193–203.

Huxley, P., Evans, S., Burns, T., Fahy, T. and Green, J. (2001) Quality of life outcome in a randomized controlled trial of case management. *Social Psychiatry and Psychiatric Epidemiology*, 36, 249–55.

Huxley, P., Evans, S., Gately, C., Webber, M., Mears, A., Pajak, S., Kendall, T., Medina, J. and Katona, C. (2005a) Stress and pressures in Mental Health Social Work: The worker speaks. *British Journal of Social Work*, 35, 1063–79.

Huxley, P., Evans, S., Munroe, M. and Cestari, L. (2008) Mental health policy reforms and case complexity in CMHTs in England: replication study. *Psychiatric Bulletin*, 32, 49–52.

Huxley, P., Evans, S., Webber, M. and Gately, C. (2005b) Staff shortages in the mental health workforce: the case of the disappearing approved social worker. *Health and Social Care in the Community*, 13, 504–13.

Huxley, P. and Kerfoot, M. (1993) Variation in requests to social services departments for assessment for compulsory psychiatric admission. *Social Psychiatry and Psychiatric Epidemiology*, 28, 71–6.

Ipsos MORI (2007) Ten years of Blair. (http://www.ipsos-mori.com/political/ten-years-of-blair.pdf).

Itzen, C. (2006) *Tackling the health and mental health effects of domestic and sexual violence and abuse*. London, Department of Health.

Jablensky, A., Schwartz, R. and Tomov, T. (1980) WHO collaborative study of impairments and disabilities associated with schizophrenic disorders: a preliminary communication-objectives and methods. *Acta Psychiatrica Scandinavica*, 62, 152–63.

Jackson, P. and Warr, P. (1984) Unemployment and psychological ill health: the moderating role of duration and age. *Psychological Medicine*, 14, 605–14.

Jenkins, R. and Meltzer, H. (1995) The national survey of psychiatric morbidity in Great Britain. *Social Psychiatry and Psychiatric Epidemiology*, 30, 1–4.

Johnson, S. (2007) Crisis resolution and intensive home treatment teams. *Psychiatry*, 6, 339–42.

Johnson, S., Nolan, F., Hoult, J., White, I. R., Bebbington, P., Sandor, A., McKenzie, N., Patel, S. N. and Pilling, S. (2005a) Outcomes of crises before and after introduction of a crisis resolution team. *British Journal of Psychiatry*, 187, 68–75.

Johnson, S., Nolan, F., Pilling, S., Sandor, A., Hoult, J., McKenzie, N., White, I. R., Thompson, M. and Bebbington, P. (2005b) Randomised controlled trial of acute mental health care by a crisis resolution team: the north Islington crisis study. *British Medical Journal*, 331, 599–603.

Jones, K. (1999) *Taming the troublesome child. American families, child guidance and limits of psychiatric authority*. Cambridge, MA, Harvard University Press.

Joy, C. B., Adams, C. E. and Rice, K. (1998) Crisis intervention for people with severe mental illnesses. The Cochrane Library, Issue 4. Oxford, Update Software.

Karasek, R. (1979) Job demands, job decision latitude and mental strain. Implications for job redesign. *Administrative Quarterly*, 24, 285–308.

Keller, M. B., Ryan, N. D., Strober, M. P., Klein, R. G., Kutcher, S. P., Birmaher, B. M., Hagino, O. R., Koplewicz, H. M., Carlson, G. A., Clarke, G. N., Emslie, G. J., Feinberg, D. M., Geller, B. M., Kusumakar, V. M., Papatheodorou, G. M., Sack, W. H., Sweeney, M. P., Wagner, K. D. M., Weller, E. B., Winters, N. C., Oakes, R. M. and McCafferty, J. P. (2001) Efficacy of paroxetine in the treatment of adolescent major depression: A randomized, controlled trial. *Journal of the American Academy of Child and Adolescent Psychiatry*, 40, 762–72.

Kendler, H. (1991) Ethics and science: a psychological perspective. In Kurtines, W. M., Azmitia, M. and Gerwirtz, J. L. (eds) *The role of values in psychology and human development*. New York, Wiley, pp. 131–60.

Killaspy, H., Bebbington, P., Blizard, R., Johnson, S., Nolan, F., Pilling, S. and King, M. (2006) The REACT study: randomised evaluation of assertive community treatment in north London. *British Medical Journal*, 332, 815–19.

Kohen, D. (2001) Psychiatric services for women. Advances in Psychiatric Treatment, 7, 328–334.

Kuipers, E., Garety, P., Fowler, D., Dunn, G., Bebbington, P., Freeman, D. and Hadley, C. (1997) London-East Anglia randomised controlled trial of cognitive-behavioural therapy for psychosis. I: effects of the treatment phase. *British Journal of Psychiatry*, 171, 319–27.

Kuipers, E., Holloway, F., Rabe-Hesketh, S. and Tennakoon, L. (2004) An RCT of early intervention in psychosis: Croydon Outreach and Assertive Support Team (COAST). *Social Psychiatry and Psychiatric Epidemiology*, 39, 358–363.

Kunz, R. and Oxman, A. D. (1998) The unpredictability paradox: review of empirical comparisons of randomised and non-randomised clinical trials. *British Medical Journal*, 317, 1185–90.

Larsen, J. A. (2007) Understanding a complex intervention: person-centred ethnography in early psychosis. *Journal of Mental Health*, 16, 333–45.

Last, J. (ed.) (2000) *A Dictionary of Epidemiology*, Oxford, Oxford University Press.

Leff, J. and Warner, R. (2006) *Social inclusion of people with mental illness*. Cambridge, Cambridge University Press.

Lelliott, P. and Audini, B. (2003) Trends in the use of Part II of the Mental Health Act 1983 in seven English local authority areas. *British Journal of Psychiatry*, 182, 68–70.

Lester, H., Freemantle, N., Wilson, S., Sorohan, H., England, E., Griffin, C. and Shankar, A. (2007) Cluster randomised controlled trial of the effectiveness of primary care mental health workers. *British Journal of General Practice*, 57, 196–203.

Lewis, G. and Sloggett, A. (1998) Suicide, deprivation, and unemployment: record linkage study. *British Medical Journal*, 317, 1283–6.

Lilford, R. J. and Jackson, J. (1995) Equipoise and the ethics of randomization. *Journal of the Royal Society of Medicine*, 88, 552–9.

London Development Centre for Mental Health (2005) *Review of assessments on private premises. Report and recommendations*. London, London Development Centre for Mental Health.

Lyons-Ruth, K., Yellin, C., Melnick, S. and Atwood, G. (2005) Expanding the concept of unresolved mental states: Hostile/helpless states of mind on the Adult Attachment Interview are associated with disrupted mother-infant communication and infant disorganization. *Developmental Psychopathology*, 17, 1–23.

Macdonald, G., Sheldon, B. and Gillespie, J. (1992) Contemporary Studies of the Effectiveness of Social Work. *British Journal of Social Work*, 22, 615–43.

Malone, D., Marriott, S., Newton-Howes, G., Simmonds, S. and Tyrer, P. (2007) Community mental health teams (CMHTs) for people with severe mental illnesses and disordered personality. *Cochrane Database of Systematic Reviews Issue 3*. Chichester, John Wiley and Sons.

Manktelow, R., Hughes, P., Britton, F., Campbell, J., Hamilton, B. and Wilson, G. (2002) The experience and practice of approved social workers in Northern Ireland. *British Journal of Social Work*, 32, 443–61.

Marriott, S., Audini, B., Lelliott, P., Webb, Y. and Duffett, R. (2001) Research into the Mental Health Act: A qualitative study of the views of those using or affected by it. *Journal of Mental Health*, 10, 33–9.

Marshall, M., Gray, A., Lockwood, A. and Green, R. (1998) Case management for people with severe mental disorders. Cochrane Database of Systematic Reviews , Issue 2. Art. No.: CD000050. DOI: 10.1002/14651858.CD000050.

Marshall, M., Lewis, S., Lockwood, A., Drake, R., Jones, P. and Croudace, T. (2005) Association between duration of untreated psychosis and outcome in cohorts of first-episode patients: a systematic review. *Archives of General Psychiatry*, 62, 975–83.

Marshall, M. and Lockwood, A. (1998) Assertive community treatment for people with severe mental disorders. *The Cochrane Library, Issue 2*. Oxford, Update Software.

Marshall, M., Lockwood, A., Lewis, S. and Fiander, M. (2004) Essential elements of an early intervention service for psychosis: the opinions of expert clinicians. *BMC Psychiatry*, 4, 17.

Marshall, M. and Rathbone, J. (2004) Early intervention for psychosis. *Cochrane Database of Systematic Reviews, Issue 2*. Art. No.: CD004718. DOI: 10.1002/14651858.CD004718.pub2.

Maslach, C. and Jackson, S. E. (1986) *Manual of the Maslach Burnout Inventory*. 2nd ed. Palo Alto, CA, Consulting Psychologists Press.

McCrae, N., Murray, J., Huxley, P. and Evans, S. (2004) Prospects for mental health social work: A qualitative study of attitudes of service managers and academic staff. *Journal of Mental Health*, 13, 305–17.

McCrae, N., Murray, J., Huxley, P. and Evans, S. (2005) The research potential of mental health social workers: a qualitative study of the views of senior mental health service managers. *British Journal of Social Work*, 35, 55–71.

McCrae, N., Murray, J., Huxley, P., Thornicroft, G. and Evans, S. (2003) *The social care contribution to mental health research*. London, Health Services Research Department, Institute of Psychiatry, Kings' College London.

McKenzie, K. and Harpham, T. (eds) (2006) *Social capital and mental health*. London, Jessica Kingsley.

McPherson, A. and Jones, R. G. (2003) The use of sections 2 and 3 of the Mental Health Act (1983) with older people: a prospective study. *Aging and Mental Health*, 7, 153–7.

Mears, A., Pajak, S., Kendall, T., Katona, C., Medina, J., Huxley, P., Evans, S. and Gately, C. (2007) Consultant psychiatrists' working patterns. *Psychiatric Bulletin*, 31, 252–5.

Medical Research Council (2000) *A framework for development and evaluation of RCTs for complex interventions to improve health*. London, Medical Research Council.

Mental Health Act Commission (2005) *In place of fear*. London, Mental Health Act Commission.

Miles, H. L., Loudon, J. B. and Rawnsley, K. (1961) Attitudes and practice of mental welfare officers. *Public Health*, 76, 32–47.

Miller, P. J. and Jones-Harris, A. R. (2005) The evidence-based hierarchy: is it time for change? A suggested alternative. *Journal of Manipulative and Physiological Therapeutics*, 28, 453–7.

Mitchell, F. and Patience, D. A. (2002) Conjoint multi-disciplinary assessment in a community mental health team: the impact on the social work role. *Social Work in Health Care*, 35, 605–13.

Mokken, R. J. (1997) Nonparametric Models for Dichotomous Responses. In Van Der Linden, W. J. and Hambleton, R. K. (eds) *Handbook of modern item Response Theory*. New York, Springer, pp. 351–68.

Morgan, C., Dazzan, P., Morgan, K., Jones, P., Harrison, G., Leff, J., Murray, R. and Fearon, P., on behalf of the AeSOP Study Group, (2006) First episode psychosis and ethnicity: initial findings from the AESOP study. *World Psychiatry*, 5, 40–6.

Morgan, C., Mallett, R., Hutchinson, G., Bagalkote, H., Morgan, K., Fearon, P., Dazzan, P., Boydell, J., McKenzie, K., Harrison, G., Murray, R., Jones, P., Craig, T., Leff, J. and on behalf of the AeSOP Study Group (2005) Pathways to care and ethnicity. 1: Sample characteristics and compulsory admission: Report from the AeSOP study. *British Journal of Psychiatry*, 186, 281–9.

Morrison, K., Bradley, R. and Westen, D. (2003) The external validity of controlled clinical trials of psychotherapy for depression and anxiety: a naturalistic study. *Psychology and Psychotherapy: Theory, Research and Practice*, 76, 109–32.

Moscovici, S. and Hewstone, M. (1983) Social representations and social explanations: from the 'naive' to the 'amateur' scientist. In Hewstone, M. (ed.) *Attribution theory*. Oxford, Blackwell.

Moses, T. and Kirk, S. A. (2006) Social workers' attitudes about psychotropic drug treatment with youths. *Social Work*, 51, 211–22.

Mujica Mota, R., Lorgelly, P. K., Mugford, M., Toroyan, T., Oakley, A., Laing, G. and Roberts, I. (2006) Out-of-home day care for families living in a disadvantaged area of London: economic evaluation alongside a RCT. *Child: Care, Health and Development*, 32, 287–302.

Mullen, E. J. and Bacon, W. (2004) A survey of practitioner adoption and implementation of practice guidelines and evidence based treatments. In Roberts, A. R. and Yeager, K. (eds) *Evidence based practice manual: Research and outcome measures in health and human services*. New York, Oxford University Press, pp. 210–18.

Munro, E. (2002) The role of theory in social work research: a further contribution to the debate. *Journal of Social Work Education*, 38, 461–70.

Nathan, J. (2002) The advanced practitioner: beyond reflective practice. *Journal of Practice Teaching*, 4, 59–84.

National Collaborating Centre for Mental Health (2004) Depression: Management of depression in primary and secondary care. National Clinical Practice Guideline Number 23. London, National Institute for Health and Clinical Excellence.

National Research Ethics Service (2007) Medicines for human use (Clinical Trials Regulations) 2004. London, National Patient Safety Agency.

Nelson, G., Sylvestre, J., Aubry, T., George, L. and Trainor, J. (2007) Housing choice and control, housing quality, and control over professional support as contributors to the subjective quality of life and community adaptation of people with severe mental illness. *Administration and Policy in Mental Health and Mental Health Services Research*, 34, 89–100.

Newman, T., Moseley, A., Tierney, S. and Ellis, A. (2005) *Evidence-based social work. A guide for the perplexed*. Lyme Regis, Russell House Publishing.

NHS Confederation (2003) *The draft Mental Health Bill: an assessment of the implications for mental health service organisations*. London, NHS Confederation.

Noble, M., Wright, G., Dibben, C., Smith, G. A. N., McLennan, D., Anttila, C., Barnes, H., Mokhtar, C., Noble, S., Avenell, D., Gardner, J., Covizzi, I. and Lloyd, M. (2004) *The English indices of deprivation (revised)*. London, Office of the Deputy Prime Minister.

Oakley, A., Rajan, L., Roberts, I. and Turner, H. (2002) *A feasibility study for a randomised controlled trial of day-care for pre-school children*. London, Institute of Education, University of London.

Office of the Deputy Prime Minister (2004) *Action on mental health. A guide to promoting social inclusion*. London, Office of the Deputy Prime Minister.

Oliver, J. P., Huxley, P. J., Priebe, S. and Kaiser, W. (1997) Measuring the quality of life of severely mentally ill people using the Lancashire quality of life profile. *Social Psychiatry and Psychiatric Epidemiology*, 32, 76–83.

Osmo, R. and Rosen, A. (2002) Social workers' strategies for treatment hypothesis testing. *Social Work Research*, 26, 9–18.

Owens, C. (2004) The glass-walled asylum: a description of a lay residential community for the severely mentally ill. *Journal of Mental Health*, 13, 319– 32.

Papageorgiou, A., King, M., Janmohamed, A., Davidson, O. and Dawson, J. (2002) Advance directives for patients compulsorily admitted to hospital with serious mental illness. Randomised controlled trial. *British Journal of Psychiatry*, 181, 513–9.

Pargiter, R. and Hodgson, T. D. (1959) The mental welfare officer and the psychiatrist. *The Lancet*, 274, 727–8.

Parton, N. (1996) Social work, risk and 'the blaming system'. In Parton, N. (ed.) *Social Theory, Social Change and Social Work.* London, Routledge.

Pawson, R., Boaz, A., Grayson, L., Long, A. and Barnes, C. (2003) *Knowledge review 3:Types and quality of knowledge in social care.* London, Social Care Institute for Excellence / Policy Press.

Pelosi, A. J. and Jackson, G. A. (2000) Home treatment-enigmas and fantasies. *British Medical Journal,* 320, 308–9.

Penn, D., Waldheter, E., Perkins, D., Mueser, K. and Lieberman, J. (2005) Psychosocial treatment for first-episode psychosis. a research update. *American Journal of Psychiatry*, 162, 2220–32.

Perkins, D. O., Gu, H., Boteva, K. and Lieberman, J. A. (2005) Relationship between duration of untreated psychosis and outcome in first-episode schizophrenia: a critical review and meta-analysis. *American Journal of Psychiatry*, 162, 1785–1804.

Petersen, L., Jeppesen, P., Thorup, A., Abel, M.-B., Ohlenschlaeger, J., Christensen, T. O., Krarup, G., Jorgensen, P. and Nordentoft, M. (2005) A randomised multicentre trial of integrated versus standard treatment for patients with a first episode of psychotic illness. *British Medical Journal*, 331, 602–5.

Pharoah, F. M., Mari, J. J. and Streiner, D. (2003) Family intervention for schizophrenia. *The Cochrane Library*, Issue 1. Oxford, Update Software.

Phelan, M., Slade, M., Thornicroft, G., Dunn, G., Holloway, F., Wykes, T., Strathdee, G., Loftus, L., McCrone, P. and Hayward, P. (1995) The Camberwell Assessment of Need: the validity and reliability of an instrument to assess the needs of people with severe mental illness. *British Journal of Psychiatry*, 167, 589–95.

Pilgrim, D. and Rogers, A. (2005) *A sociology of mental health and illness.* 3rd ed. Maidenhead, Open University Press.

Pinfold, V., Bindman, J., Thornicroft, G., Franklin, D. and Hatfield, B. (2001) Persuading the persuadable: evaluating compulsory treatment in England using Supervised Discharge Orders. *Social Psychiatry and Psychiatric Epidemiology*, 36, 260–6.

Pinfold, V., Rowe, A., Hatfield, B., Bindman, J., Huxley, P., Thornicroft, G. and Shaw, J. (2002) Lines of resistance: Exploring professionals' views of compulsory community supervision. *Journal of Mental Health*, 11, 177–90.

Pinfold, V., Smith, J. and Shiers, D. (2007) Audit of early intervention in psychosis service development in England in 2005. *Psychiatric Bulletin*, 31, 7–10.

Polanyi, M. (1967) The growth of science in society. *Minerva*, 5, 533–45.

Popper, K. (1959) *The logic of scientific discovery*. London, Hutchison.

Préville, M., Hébert, R., Boyer, R., Bravo, G. and Seguin, M. (2005) Physical health and mental disorder in elderly suicide: A case-control study. *Aging and Mental Health*, 9, 576–84.

Priebe, S., Badesconyi, A., Fioritti, A., Hansson, L., Kilian, R., Torres-Gonzales, F., Turner, T. and Wiersma, D. (2005) Reinstitutionalisation in mental health care: comparison of data on service provision from six European countries. *British Medical Journal*, 330, 123–6.

Priebe, S., Huxley, P., Knight, S. and Evans, S. (1999) Application and results of the Manchester Short Assessment of Quality of Life (MANSA). *International Journal of Social Psychiatry*, 45, 7–12.

Prince, M., Harwood, R. H., Blizard, R. A., Thomas, A. and Mann, A. H. (1997a) Impairment, disability and handicap as risk factors for depression in old age. The Gospel Oak Project V. *Psychological Medicine*, 27, 311–21.

Prince, M. J., Harwood, R. H., Blizard, R. A., Thomas, A. and Mann, A. H. (1997b) Social support deficits, loneliness and life events as risk factors for depression in old age. The Gospel Oak Project VI. *Psychological Medicine*, 27, 323–32.

Prince, M. J., Harwood, R. H., Thomas, A. and Mann, A. H. (1998) A Prospective population based cohort study of the effects of disablement and social milieu on the onset and maintenance of late-life depression. *Psychological Medicine*, 28, 337–50.

Prince, M., Stewart, R., Ford, T. and Hotopf, M. (eds) (2003) *Practical Psychiatric Epidemiology*, Oxford, Oxford University Press.

Putnam, R. (2000) *Bowling alone: the collapse and revival of American community*. New York, Simon and Schuster.

Qin, P. and Nordentoft, M. (2005) Suicide risk in relation to psychiatric hospitalization: evidence based on longitudinal registers. *Archives of General Psychiatry*, 62, 427–32.

Quirk, A., Lelliott, P., Audini, B. and Buston, K. (2000) Performing the act: a qualitative study of the process of mental health act assessments. Final report to the Department of Health. London, Royal College of Psychiatrists' Research Unit.

Quirk, A., Lelliott, P., Audini, B. and Buston, K. (2003) Non-clinical and extra-legal influences on decisions about compulsory admission to psychiatric hospital. *Journal of Mental Health*, 12, 119–30.

Quirk, A., Lelliott, P. and Seale, C. (2006) The permeable institution: An ethnographic study of three acute psychiatric wards in London. *Social Science and Medicine*, 63, 2105–17.

Rapaport, J. and Manthorpe, J. (in press) Family matters: developments concerning the role of the nearest relative and social worker under mental health law in England and Wales. *British Journal of Social Work*.

Ray, L. J. (1981) Models of madness in Victorian asylum practice. *European Journal of Sociology*, 22, 229–64.

Redley, M. (2003) Towards a new perspective on deliberate self-harm in an area of multiple deprivation. *Sociology of Health and Illness*, 25, 348–72.

Reid, W. and Hanrahan, P. (1980) The effectiveness of social work: recent evidence. In Goldberg, E. M. and Connelly, N. (eds) *The effectiveness of social care for the elderly*. London, Heinemann.

Richardson, G. (1999) *Report of the expert committee. Review of the Mental Health Act 1983*. London, Department of Health.

Rickwood, D., Cavanagh, S., Curtis, L. and Sakrouge, R. (2004) Educating young people about mental health and mental illness: evaluating a school-based programme. *International Journal of Mental Health Promotion*, 6, 23–32.

Rimmer, M. A., O'Connor, S. and Anderson, D. (2002) Appeal against detention under the Mental Health Act 1983: Relationship to age and incapacity. *International Journal of Geriatric Psychiatry*, 17, 884–5.

Ritchie, J. H., Dick, D. and Lingham, R. (1994) *The report of the inquiry into the care and treatment of Christopher Clunis*. London, HMSO.

Rogers, A. and Pilgrim, D. (1996) *Mental health policy in Britain*. London, Macmillan.

Rogers, A. and Pilgrim, D. (2003) *Mental health and inequality*. Basingstoke, Palgrave Macmillan.

Rolph, S., Adams, J. and Atkinson, D. (2003a) Taking account of history. In Henderson, J. and Atkinson, D. (eds) *Managing care in context*. London, Routledge, pp. 283–308.

Rolph, S., Atkinson, D. and Walmsley, J. (2003b) 'A pair of stout shoes and an umbrella': the role of the Mental Welfare Officer in delivering community care in East Anglia: 1946–1970. *British Journal of Social Work*, 33, 339–59.

Rolph, S., Walmsley, J. and Atkinson, D. (2002) 'A man's job'?: Gender issues and the role of mental health welfare officers, 1948–1970. *Oral History*, 30, 28–41.

Rose, D. (1998a) *In our experience*. London, Sainsbury Centre for Mental Health.

Rose, D. (1998b) Television, madness and community care. *Journal of Community and Applied Social Psychology*, 8, 213–28.

Rosenhan, D. L. (1973) On being sane in insane places. *Science*, 179, 250–8.

Rotter, J. B. (1972) Generalized expectancies for internal versus external control of reinforcement. In Rotter, J. B., Chance, J. E. and Phares, E. J. (eds) *Applications of a social learning theory of personality*. New York, Holt, Rinehart and Winston, Inc, pp. 260–95.

Rummel, R. J. (1976) Understanding Correlation. (http://www.mega.nu/ampp/rummel/uc.htm).

Ryan, M., Dowden, C., Healy, B. and Renouf, N. (2005) Watching the experts: findings from an Australian study of expertise in mental health social work. *Journal of Social Work*, 5, 279–98.

Ryan, L., Leavey, G., Golden, A., Blizard, R. and King, M. (2006) Depression in Irish migrants living in London: case-control study. *British Journal of Psychiatry*, 188, 560–6.

Ryan, M., Merighi, J. R., Healy, B. and Renouf, N. (2004) Belief, optimism and caring: findings from a cross-national study of expertise in mental health social work. *Qualitative Social Work*, 3, 411–29.

Sackett, D. L., Rosenberg, W. M. C., Gray, J. A. M., Haynes, R. B. and Richardson, W. S. (1996) Evidence based medicine: what it is and what it isn't. *British Medical Journal*, 312, 71–2.

Schardt, C., Adams, M., Owens, T., Keitz, S. and Fontelo, P. (2007) Utilization of the PICO framework to improve searching PubMed for clinical questions. *BMC Medical Informatics and Decision Making*, 7, 16.

Schon, D. (1987) *Educating the reflective practitioner.* San Francisco, Jossey Bass.

Schultz, K. F., Chalmers, I., Hayes, R. J. and Altman, D. G. (1995) Empirical evidence of bias.Dimensions of methodological quality associated with estimates of treatment effects in controlled trials. *Journal of the American Medical Association*, 273, 408–12.

Scott, A. and Freeman, C. (1992) Edinburgh primary care depression study: treatment outcome, patient satisfaction, and cost after 16 weeks. *British Medical Journal*, 304, 883–7.

Scull, A. (1977) *Decarceration: community treatment and the deviant – a radical view.* Englewood Cliffs, NJ, Prentice-Hall.

Seebohm, F. (1968) *Report of the committee on local authority and allied personal social services.* London, HMSO.

Seeman, M. and Cohen, R. (1998) Focus on women: a service for women with schizophrenia. *Psychiatric Services*, 49, 674–7.

Shaw, P., Hotopf, M. and Davies, A. (2003) In relative danger?: the outcome of patients discharged by their nearest relative from sections 2 and 3 of the Mental Health Act. *Psychiatric Bulletin*, 27, 50–4.

Sheldon, B. (2001) The validity of evidence-based practice in social work: a reply to Stephen Webb. *British Journal of Social Work*, 31, 801–9.

Sheldon, B. and Chilvers, R. (2000) *Evidence-based social care. a study of prospects and problems.* Lyme Regis, Russell House Publishing.

Sheldon, B. and Macdonald, G. (1999) *Research and practice in social care: mind the gap.* Exeter University, Centre for Evidence-Based Social Services.

Sheppard, M. (1991a) *Mental health work in the community: theory and practice in social work and community psychiatric nursing.* London, Falmer Press.

Sheppard, M. (1991b) Referral source and process of assessment: a comparative analysis of assessments for compulsory admission under the Mental Health Act 1983. *Practice*, 5, 294–8.

Siegel, C. E., Samuels, J., Tang, D.-I., Berg, I., Jones, K. and Hopper, K. (2006) Tenant outcomes in supported housing and community residences in New York City. *Psychiatric Services*, 57, 982–91.

Simmons, P. and Hoar, A. (2001) Section 136 use in the London borough of Haringey. *Medicine, Science and the Law*, 41, 342–8.

Singh, S. P. and Fisher, H. L. (2007) Early intervention services. *Psychiatry*, 6, 333–8.

Singh, S. P. and Grange, T. (2006) Measuring pathways to care in first-episode psychosis: a systematic review. *Schizophrenia Research*, 81, 75–82.

Slade, M., Pinfold, V., Rapaport, J., Bellringer, S., Banerjee, S., Kuipers, E. and Huxley, P. (2007) Best practice when service users do not consent to sharing information with carers: National multimethod study. *British Journal of Psychiatry*, 190, 148–55.

Slade, M. and Priebe, S. (2001) Are randomised controlled trials the only gold that glitters? *British Journal of Psychiatry*, 179, 286–7.

Smith, C. (2006) Family, community and the Victorian asylum: a case study of the Northampton General Lunatic Asylum and its pauper lunatics. *Family and Community History*, 9, 109–24.

Smith, G. C. S. and Pell, J. P. (2003) Parachute use to prevent death and major trauma related to gravitational challenge: systematic review of randomised controlled trials. *British Medical Journal*, 327, 1459–61.

Social Exclusion Unit (2004) *Social exclusion and mental health. Social exclusion unit report*. London, Office of Deputy Prime Minister.

Spencer, L. and Pahl, R. (2006) *Rethinking friendship. hidden solidarities today*. Princeton, Princeton University Press.

Spitzer, R. L., Williams, J. B. W., Gibbon, M. and First, M. B. (1990) *User's guide for the structured clinical interview for DSM-III-R (SCID)*. Washington, DC, American Psychiatric Press.

Sproston, K. and Nazroo, J. (2002) *Empiric: ethnicity and psychiatric morbidity in the community*. London, The Stationery Office.

Sroufe, L. A., Egeland, B., Carlson, E. and Collins, W. A. (2005) *The development of the person: the Minnesota study of risk and adaptation from birth to adulthood*. New York, Guilford.

Staff reporter (1851) The police courts – Thames. *Daily News*, 8 May, 7.

Stanley, N. and Manthorpe, J. (2001) Reading mental health inquiries. Messages for social work. *Journal of Social Work*, 1, 77–99.

Stansfeld, S. A., Fuhrer, R. and Shipley, M. J. (1998) Types of social support as predictors of psychiatric morbidity in a cohort of British Civil Servants (Whitehall II Study). *Psychological Medicine*, 28, 881–92.

Stansfeld, S. and Marmot, M. (1992) Deriving a survey measure of social support: the reliability and validity of the close persons questionnaire. *Social Science and Medicine*, 35, 1027–35.

Student (1908) The probable error of a mean. *Biometrika*, 6, 1–25.

Sundquist, K., Frank, G. and Sundquist, J. A. N. (2004) Urbanisation and incidence of psychosis and depression: follow-up study of 4.4 million women and men in Sweden. *British Journal of Psychiatry*, 184, 293–8.

Sundquist, K. and Yang, M. (2007) Linking social capital and self-rated health: a multilevel analysis of 11,175 men and women in Sweden. *Health and Place*, 13, 324–34.

Surtees, P. G. and Miller, P. M. (1990) The interval general health questionnaire. *British Journal of Psychiatry*, 157, 686–93.

Sutton, A. J., Duval, S. J., Tweedie, R. L., Abrams, K. R. and Jones, D. R. (2000) Empirical assessment of effect of publication bias on meta-analyses. *British Medical Journal*, 320, 1574–77.

Taylor, P. J. and Gunn, J. (1999) Homicides by people with mental illness: myth and reality. *British Journal of Psychiatry*, 174, 9–14.

Test, M. A. (1998) The origins of PACT. *The Journal of NAMI California*, 9, 5–6.

Thornicroft, G. (2000) National Service Framework for Mental Health. *Psychiatric Bulletin*, 24, 203–6.

Thornicroft, G., Bindman, J., Goldberg, D., Gournay, K. and Huxley, P. (2002) Researchable questions to support evidence-based mental health policy concerning adult mental illness. *Psychiatric Bulletin*, 26, 364–7.

Thornicroft, G., Strathdee, G., Phelan, M., Holloway, F., Wykes, T., Dunn, G., McCrone, P., Leese, M., Johnson, S. and Szmukler, G. (1998) Rationale and design. PRiSM psychosis study I. *British Journal of Psychiatry*, 173, 363–70.

Thornicroft, G. and Szmukler, G. (2005) The Draft Mental Health Bill in England: without principles. *Psychiatric Bulletin*, 29, 244–7.

Tidemalm, D., Elofsson, S., Stefansson, C.-G., Waern, M. and Runeson, B. (2005) Predictors of suicide in a community-based cohort of individuals with severe mental disorder. *Social Psychiatry and Psychiatric Epidemiology*, 40, 595–600.

Toroyan, T., Roberts, I., Oakley, A., Laing, G., Mugford, M. and Frost, C. (2003) Effectiveness of out-of-home day care for disadvantaged families: randomised controlled trial. *British Medical Journal*, 327, 906–9.

Trieman, N., Leff, J. and Glover, G. (1999) Outcome of long stay psychiatric patients resettled in the community: prospective cohort study. *British Medical Journal*, 319, 13–16.

Trinder, L. (1996) Social work research: the state of the art (or science). *Child and Family Social Work*, 1, 233–42.

Tyrer, P. J. and Remington, M. (1979) Controlled comparison of day-hospital and outpatient treatment for neurotic disorders. The *Lancet*, i, 1014–16.

Unwin, C., Blatchley, N., Coker, W., Ferry, S., Hotopf, M., Hull, L., Ismail, K., Palmer, I., David, A. and Wessely, S. (1999) Health of UK servicemen who served in Persian Gulf War. *The Lancet*, 353, 169–78.

Van der Gaag, M. and Snijders, T. A. B. (2005) The Resource Generator: social capital quantification with concrete items. *Social Networks*, 27, 1–29.

Wall, S., Churchill, R., Hotopf, M., Buchanan, A. and Wessely, S. (1999) *A systematic review of research relating to the Mental Health Act (1983)*. London, Department of Health.

Ward, E., King, M., Lloyd, M., Bower, P., Sibbald, B., Farrelly, S., Gabbay, M., Tarrier, N. and Addington-Hall, J. (2000) Randomised controlled trial of non-directive counselling, cognitive-behaviour therapy, and usual general practitioner care for patients with depression. I: Clinical effectiveness. *British Medical Journal*, 321, 1383–8.

Warner, R. (2000) *The environment of schizophrenia: innovations in practice, policy and communications*. London, Routledge.

Warr, P. and Jackson, P. (1985) Factors influencing the psychological impact of prolonged unemployment and of re-employment. *Psychological Medicine*, 15, 795–807.

Webb, S. (2001) Some considerations on the validity of evidence-based practice in social work. *British Journal of Social Work*, 31, 57–79.

Webber, M. (2005) Social capital and mental health. In Tew, J. (ed.) *Social perspectives in mental health. Developing social models to understand and work with mental distress.* London, Jessica Kingsley Publishers, pp. 90–111.

Webber, M. and Huxley, P. (2004) Social exclusion and risk of emergency compulsory admission. A case-control study. *Social Psychiatry and Psychiatric Epidemiology*, 39, 1000–9.

Webber, M. and Huxley, P. (2007) Measuring access to social capital: the validity and reliability of the Resource Generator-UK and its association with common mental disorder. *Social Science and Medicine*, 65, 481–92.

Weich, S. and Lewis, G. (1998) Poverty, unemployment, and common mental disorders: population based cohort study. *British Medical Journal*, 317, 115–19.

Weich, S. and Prince, M. (2003) Cohort studies. In Prince, M., Stewart, R., Ford, T. and Hotopf, M. (eds) *Practical Psychiatric Epidemiology.* Oxford, Oxford University Press, pp. 155–75.

Westen, D. and Morrison, K. (2001) A multidimensional meta-analysis of treatments for depression, panic, and generalized anxiety disorder: an empirical examination of the status of empirically supported therapies. *Journal of Consulting and Clinical Psychology*, 69, 875–99.

Westmoreland, J. (1964) The Mental Welfare Officer. *Mental Welfare Officer,* Spring, 29–35.

Whitley, R. and Prince, M. (2005) Is there a link between rates of common mental disorder and deficits in social capital in Gospel Oak, London?: Results from a qualitative study. *Health and Place*, 11, 237–48.

Wing, J. K., Babor, T., Brugha, T., Burke, J., Cooper, J. E., Giel, R., Jablenski, A., Regier, D. and Sartorius, N. (1990) SCAN. Schedules for clinical assessment in neuropsychiatry. *Archives of General Psychiatry*, 47, 589–93.

Winterton, R. (2007) Mental health services: hospital beds. *House of Commons written answers,* Hansard, 6 Feb 2007 Column 805W.

Wood, A., Harrington, R. and Moore, A. (1996) Controlled trial of a brief cognitive-behavioural intervention in adolescent patients with depressive disorders. *Journal of Child Psychology and Psychiatry*, 37, 737–46.

Woodbury-Smith, M. R., Clare, I. C. H., Holland, A. J., Kearns, A., Staufenberg, E. and Watson, P. (2005) A case-control study of offenders with high functioning autistic spectrum disorders. *Journal of Forensic Psychiatry and Psychology*, 16, 747–63.

Wright, C., Burns, T. O. M., James, P., Billings, J., Johnson, S., Muijen, M., Priebe, S., Ryrie, I., Watts, J. and White, I. A. N. (2003) Assertive outreach teams in London: models of operation: Pan-London Assertive Outreach Study, Part 1. *British Journal of Psychiatry*, 183, 132–8.

Wright, D. (1999) The discharge of pauper lunatics from county asylums in mid-Victorian England. The case of Buckinghamshire, 1853 –1872. In Melling, J. and Forsythe, B. (eds) I*nsanity, institutions and society, 1800–1914. A social history of madness in comparative perspective.* London, Routledge.

Zammit, S., Allebeck, P., Andreasson, S., Lundberg, I. and Lewis, G. (2002) Self reported cannabis use as a risk factor for schizophrenia in Swedish conscripts of 1969: historical cohort study. *British Medical Journal*, 325, 1199–1201.

Zigmond, A. S. and Snaith, R. P. (1983) The hospital anxiety and depression scale. *Acta Psychiatrica Scandinavica*, 67, 361–70.

Zoritch, B., Roberts, I. and Oakley, A. (2000) Day care for pre-school children. *Cochrane Database of Systematic Reviews*, 3, CD000564.

Index